THE EARLIEST GOSPEL

OTHER BOOKS BY THE SAME AUTHOR

THE EARLIEST GOSPEL

*Studies of the evangelic tradition at its
point of crystallization in writing*

By

FREDERICK C. GRANT

The Cole Lectures for 1943

ABINGDON-COKESBURY PRESS

New York • Nashville

G

THE EARLIEST GOSPEL
COPYRIGHT, MCMXLIII
BY WHITMORE & STONE

SET UP, PRINTED, AND BOUND BY THE
PARTHENON PRESS AT NASHVILLE, TEN-
NESSEE, UNITED STATES OF AMERICA

To Jean

Many daughters have done worthily,
But thou excellest them all.

CONTENTS

PREFACE

How is it possible at a time like the present, when
the whole world is at war, to sit down calmly and consider
such a subject as the Earliest Gospel, to study the evangelic tradition at the stage in which it first took literary
form, to discuss such fine points as the emergence of a particular theology in early Christianity or the transition from
primitive Christian messianism to the normative doctrine
of later creeds, confessions, hymns, and prayers? Would
it not be better to consider the more fundamental question of the relevance of Christian faith in general to the
world we live in, and the practicability of the Christian
ethic in a society which has never wholeheartedly accepted Christianity and now threatens to renounce even
its moderate and partial adherence to Christian principles?
The answer to these questions involves an examination of
the whole problem of the relation of the Gospels to modern civilization, and I beg leave to refer the reader to an
article on this subject recently published in *Religion in
Life*.[1] It is not a final statement, but it attempts to open
up the subject and to suggest some of the considerations
which are relevant to the final answer.

All Christians ought to be concerned over this question,

[1] "The Gospels and Civilization," 12:231-37.

for the whole Christian church is involved in the solution of the problem it presents. And if, as I believe, a major factor is our answer to the further question, "What essentially *is* the gospel?" then the subject of this book is also relevant.

Most of us would no doubt say that the gospel is, first of all, Jesus' own proclamation of the Kingdom of God, the terms of admission into it and the conditions of its coming; and then that it is, in the second place, the apostolic proclamation of this message of salvation, with the added emphasis and fresh meaning given to it by the resurrection of Jesus and the continuing work of the holy Spirit in the church. But if we are Christians who take scripture seriously we will recognize that right at this point we have a task of understanding and interpretation. How was the new apostolic formulation of the message of salvation related to the message of Jesus? If, as some persons maintain, Christianity was a total transformation of the message of Jesus—a doctrine *about* Jesus rather than Jesus' own teaching—then it is of paramount importance to see how and why this transformation took place, or rather, first of all, whether the theory of transformation is true. If, moreover, as Professor Dodd and others affirm, Jesus taught that the Kingdom had already come ("realized eschatology"), then the steps taken by the apostolic church were short and few: the apostles proclaimed only the further signs and proofs of the arrival of the Kingdom, and warned men to prepare for the final judgment and resurrection that was to usher in the full, universal manifestation of the Reign of God.[2] But if, on the other hand, Jesus thought of the Kingdom as still future, and the apostles continued to hold this view, then their proclamation of the Resurrection and of the approaching Parousia had a somewhat different orientation.

The truth lies, I believe, between the two extremes. The coming of the Kingdom was viewed, not as a sudden, momentary incident in world history, but as a process. I do not mean that the New Testament represents it as a *long* historical process, spread over the length and breadth of future ages; prophecy always "foreshortens the future." But it was a process, not a single event; and the process had *already begun*—its full realization was inevitable and only a matter of time, however long or short the interval before the full consummation. Men were already living in the "last days"; the end of the ages had come upon their generation. This central outlook of all New Testament theology is, I believe, characteristic of both the teaching of Jesus and that of the apostolic church. And it is in the light of this central conviction that the whole development of primitive Christology— the basic, unique doctrine of Christianity as distinct from earlier Judaism—must be studied.

It is not enough to say that Jesus, or the apostles, took over the whole framework of apocalyptic eschatology, and that Jesus thought of himself as the "Son of Man" described in the Book of Enoch, or that he claimed in so

[2] I have attempted to examine this view in an earlier article, " 'Realized' Eschatology," *Christendom*, 6:82-95. See also C. T. Craig, *Journal of Biblical Literature*, 56:17-26; K. W. Clark, *ibid.*, 59:367-83.

many words to be the Jewish Messiah but gave the concept a different meaning or content than any current Jewish interpretation gave to it. For it is all too clear that at least some phases of the Christian interpretation reflect later Christian experience and speculation rather than the teaching of Jesus himself. What needs to be shown is not a mere filiation of concepts or the use of words, but the *religious value* men found in the concepts, the *religious meaning* they undertook to set forth in the words. For the religious and ethical significance of the Christian faith—and that is its relevance today, as it was in apostolic days—is something more than even the highest categories of apocalyptic speculation could set forth. Men used these terms in describing Jesus only because they were the highest categories then available, though in the end they proved inadequate and the church eventually either left them behind or totally transformed them; what is everlastingly important is not the fact that these terms were once used, but the *motive* that led to their use—for that motive is still alive at the heart of all Christian faith and endeavor.

Moreover, the problem of primitive Christianity is not to account for early Christian messianism—for there was enough of that element in ancient Judaism, after the second century before Christ—but to explain why Christianity survived when other messianic movements came to nothing and disappeared. What was different and distinctive about it? Was it its social emphasis? Its religious quality? Its ethics? It is not the apocalyptic messianism of the early church that needs to be explained; it is some-

thing deeper, what we may call the *motivation* in the use
of this scheme of thought, something that not only out-
lasted messianism but helps to explain its use in the
first place.

It is thoroughly relevant, then, to discuss the questions
that are asked about the early Christian tradition: How
did it originate? What was its earliest form? Was the
gospel tradition influenced by a theological view later
than Jesus? Were the Gospels—even the earliest of them,
the Gospel of Mark—originally Aramaic writings, later
translated into Greek? Can the gospel tradition be lo-
calized, as originating in Galilee or in Jerusalem? If so,
did this affect the form of its transmission, with more
emphasis upon some interests in one place, and upon
others elsewhere? Was the Earliest Gospel influenced by
Paul? Was it anti-Semitic in outlook? Was there anything about it that might be described as "social" in outlook, or was it purely individual? And does this affect
our view of Jesus' own teaching? All these questions are
relevant, today as at other times, and some of them are
more relevant today than ever before.

The present volume is really a collection of studies,
and it might easily have grown to twice its size if other
topics had been included: for example the miracle stories
—I should have liked to examine Alan Richardson's new
book on *The Miracle-Stories of the Gospels* (1942)—or a
fuller study of the so-called messianic consciousness of
Jesus, the theory of interim ethics, the relation of eschatology and ethics in Jesus' teachings—see Professor Amos
N. Wilder's book on the subject, *Eschatology and Ethics*

in the Teaching of Jesus (1939)—the influence of the
Old Testament upon the earliest interpretation of the life
of Jesus—see Professor David E. Adams' new book, *Man
of God* (1941), and Professor E. W. K. Mould's *The
World-View of Jesus* (1941)—or some of the topics treated
in the new volume of essays presented to Professor Wil-
liam Jackson Lowstuter, *New Testament Studies* (1942),
edited by Professor Edwin Prince Booth. But no one book
can cover everything, and perhaps the writer will readily
be excused if he, a single author, does not try to say
everything that is to be said on any one subject, or even
everything that is in his own mind!

In general, the point of view of this volume is the
same as that taken in my book *The Growth of the Gospels* (1933). A certain amount of repetition is unavoid-
able in discussing a variety of themes, especially in view
of the limited data contained in the New Testament and
the necessity of using the same data, and the inferences
we may draw from them, in different combinations for
different purposes. Moreover, as all teachers know, it is
sometimes necessary to repeat, and often to underscore
the obvious, if only to make clear the steps really involved in an argument. Assumptions of agreement upon
unstated or undefined factors are often fatal; the risk of
repetition is a less serious danger—only the author will be
blamed, while the argument, let us hope, will receive a
more adequate consideration!

I

THE ORAL GOSPEL

THE EARLIEST GOSPEL WAS ORAL. IT WAS THE PROCLAMA-
tion, by the apostolic church, of the message of salvation.
This salvation had already been proclaimed by Jesus of
Nazareth, and the proclamation had been ratified and
authenticated by the "mighty works" which God wrought
through him—chiefly now by the mightiest work of all,
when God had raised him from the dead and installed
him in glory as the Messiah-who-is-to-come. The resurrection of Jesus was the great act of God which had closed
the old era and inaugurated the new. For the New Age
had already dawned—the time was short—the judgment
was now near at hand—therefore, "Repent . . . . Save
yourselves from this crooked generation." [1]

It is clear, both from the speeches in Acts 1–12 and
from what is presupposed in the New Testament, especially in the letters of Paul, that the primitive gospel was
essentially an eschatological proclamation. The salvation
it announced was future—but in the near future. Like
the Old Testament prophets, the church fixed its gaze
upon coming events. Only, these events were not, as with
the prophets, partly political and partly spiritual, partly
mundane and partly supernatural—though the cause of

[1] Acts 2:38, 40.

15

the coming change was always supernatural. In the case of the primitive Christian community, the coming events were viewed as entirely supernatural. They were non-political, not in the sense of segregation from political life and interests, as the signs of a purely "spiritual" change in the world, say in human hearts, but in the sense of total supernaturalism: the whole present world order, with its politics and its oppression, its hunger and its hatred, was to be completely done away. The Judgment was to usher in the full and final establishment of the divine reign. A pure theocracy, such as the prophets had envisioned and foretold, a state of affairs contemplated by Jesus himself and described in his prayer: "Thy Kingdom come, thy will be done on earth as it is in heaven"—this was to take the place of "the present evil age."

In the meantime, the followers of Jesus were to live in close fellowship with their exalted Master, now the heavenly Messiah, and with one another; their fellowship, as a later writer put it, was truly "in him." They were to observe the rules set forth in his interpretation of the Law, his *Halakah,* and submit themselves to the guidance of the Spirit, which he had sent upon them from his place at God's right hand. Admission into the community of his followers was by the same rite that John and his followers—and perhaps Jesus himself [2] and his disciples—had observed, namely baptism. It was the normal rite of admission to Judaism, in addition to circumcision—perhaps even as early as the beginnings of the Christian

[2] Though see John 4:2.

movement;[3] and even for born Jews baptism was indispensable for admission into the circle of John's followers, and of Jesus' after his death and resurrection. Even
when the gift of the Spirit came first, baptism was added.[4]
The fellowship was not only symbolized but also effected
by the common meal, some kind or *kiddush* or "sanctifi-
cation," not now of the Sabbath but of the first day of the
week,[5] which Hellenists were soon to call, appropriately,
"the Lord's day."

The earliest Christian society was thus a band of hope,
a group who "waited for the redemption of Israel," confident that the events which had already transpired were
the complete guarantee of the certainty of eventual salvation. From the very first this salvation was believed to lie,
not in a perfect observance of the Jewish law, whether
as expounded by scribes and wise men or even by Jesus
himself, but in attachment to the heavenly Messiah, Jesus
raised and glorified, who would on the last day acknowledge those who had fearlessly confessed him in spite of
persecution and ostracism.[6] A "Christology" lay at the very
heart of Christianity—not only of its theology but of its
worship, its teaching, its practice—from the very outset.

[3] See Louis Finkelstein, "The Institution of Baptism for Proselytes,"
Journal of Biblical Literature, 52:203-11.

[4] Acts 10:44-48.

[5] Prof. E. F. Scott has advanced the view, in his recent work on *The
Nature of the Early Church* (1941), that the Christian observance of Sunday
resulted from the celebration of the common meal after the Jewish Sabbath
observances were over. This came in the evening—but on Jewish reckoning
it was the beginning of the next day, which was Sunday. See pp. 72 ff.; also
S. V. McCasland, "The Origin of the Lord's Day," *Journal of Biblical Literature,* 49:65-82, and *The Resurrection of Jesus* (1932), chap. vi.

[6] Luke 12:8.

It is no use, then, trying to show that theology was introduced at some later stage, for example by Paul; a theology was implicit in Christian faith, practice, and worship from the beginning. As Dodd finely puts it,[7] fact and interpretation were present from the beginning: the facts about the life of Christ were remembered and handed down solely because of the meaning they possessed for those who cherished and handed down the record.

The facts were, chiefly, these: Jesus of Nazareth, a man anointed by the Spirit and divinely accredited by mighty works, who went about doing good, and healing all those who were oppressed by the devil (for God was with him), who was put to death by the blind and misguided authorities, religious and civil, at Jerusalem, where he was crucified—all this is preliminary and descriptive, as identifying him, like the central clauses in the Apostles' Creed. Then comes the statement: God raised him up, and manifested him to certain chosen witnesses, his disciples, who were now commissioned to preach to the people and to testify that he was the one "appointed by God to be the judge of the living and the dead; to him all the prophets bear witness, that through his name everyone who believes on him [trusts in him] shall receive remission of sins" and so be saved in the last great Day, now close at hand.[8] Whether or not the passage from which this abstract is taken was once a written source used by Luke, and therefore a very "early" document, it certainly rings true; and it represents the central conviction uni-

---

[7] See his *History and the Gospel* (1938), pp. 26 ff.
[8] Acts 10:38-43.

formly presupposed by the earliest Christianity of which
we have any record. Even if it is only a reconstruction by
the author of Luke-Acts, it is still a reconstruction by our
earliest, and before Eusebius our only surviving, historian
of the rise of Christianity—one who was in a position to
know the conviction which inspired the earliest apostolic
preaching.

This emphasis upon the *fact,* Jesus' resurrection, and
upon the *message,* (*a*) the expectation of the coming judgment, with Christ as judge, and (*b*) the promise of salvation of those who repented and trusted in him, taken
along with (*c*) the purely subsidiary and qualifying or evi-
dential reference to Jesus' earthly life and ministry—this
very relation between hope, proof, and historic fact is the
relation which prevailed in the period of the oral tradition
of the sayings and deeds of Jesus, and eventually fashioned
the structure of the Synoptic Gospels. Jesus of Nazareth,
who went about Galilee, "*him* God raised up"; the Greek
is as emphatic as is our English version—even more so:
"*this one* God raised," τοῦτον ὁ θεὸς ἤγειρεν. So it is in
the Gospels: the story of Jesus' life and teaching, his ministry among the people, his cures and other wonders, is
no biography, and was never meant to be. The heart of
the story is the passion narrative, and the heart of that
is—not the Cross but—the Resurrection to which it looks
forward. It was because the Resurrection followed it that
the Passion had significance. What the witnesses[9] told of
his earlier life, his call, his ministry, "what he did both
in the country of the Jews [the Jewish-populated terri-

[9] Vs. 39.

tory in Palestine] and in Jerusalem," and even how he died—all that is viewed as subsidiary and preparatory to the great fact and act of his resurrection, exaltation, and future coming. It was the fact and act of God himself, God's intervention in history. Once again now, and finally, "the arm of the Lord" had been "laid bare," as of old. In the resurrection and exaltation of Jesus, God was already "taking his great power" and was about to reign, finally and forever, over that part of his universal Kingdom which had rebelled against his wise and just rule. Human sin and disobedience, with all their long train of evils not only for mankind but also for God's world generally, were about to be put down forever.

The "earthly ministry" of Jesus, then, is really incidental and preparatory to his exaltation and the coming salvation and judgment. There lies the center of the long perspective; there lies the focus—in the heavenly places, and in the future—like a dramatic scene whose center is off-stage, as in the *Agamemnon* of Aeschylus; like a symphony whose climax is still to come;[10] like a building whose interior orientation is incomplete, for example a cathedral in process of building, where all its converging lines point steadily forward to some point in the sanctuary which is still hid by the scaffolding and the mason's tarpaulins. If this is true of the Gospels—where, if anywhere, the inclination toward a biographical treatment of the life of Jesus would have been present—it must certainly have been true in the oral period, and probably

[10] A view which I have tried to set forth in an article, "Eschatology and Reunion," *Religion in Life*, 10:83-91.

even more emphatically so. The anecdotes, sayings, parables, controversies coming down from the period of Jesus'
public ministry are told and retold *because* they are anecdotes about and teaching given by the one who is to be
"the judge of the living and the dead." Their "theological"
orientation is obvious—and it has affected their transmission from the very beginning.

Now this is not to say that there prevailed in the primitive church one uniform theology—let alone any "system"
of theology!—to which all items in the oral tradition
were carefully squared; nor is it to say that during Jesus'
own lifetime, and before the Resurrection, nothing was
reported about him, or learned from him, which did not
fit a theological scheme. On the contrary, as there are
several varieties of theology in the New Testament as a
whole, so there is theological variety in the sources underlying the Gospels.[11] What we have said applies only generally, and explains (*a*) the *preservation* of the tradition
as a whole and (*b*) the particular *form* given to most of
its separate items. This is the whole point of form criticism—or tradition criticism, as it ought to be called: the
units in the evangelic tradition were handed down orally,
in separation, and in the form given them by the earliest
preachers and teachers of the gospel, the "gospel" being,
not the total story of the life of Jesus, but the proclamation of the message of salvation through him, a salvation
fully to be effected in the future, though it could be

[11] See "The Significance of Divergence and Growth in the New Testament," *Christendom*, 4:575-87; also B. H. Streeter, "The Rise of Christianity," *The Cambridge Ancient History*, XI (1936), chap. vii.

realized in anticipation even now, before the final Parousia.[12]

As for the reports of the "witnesses" during Jesus' lifetime, the stories told about him, the reports of his teaching, his sayings, parables, interpretations of the Law, controversies with the scribes, and the application of Old Testament laws and prophecies—all this was undoubtedly orientated and controlled by the eschatological outlook of his teaching and ministry as a whole, but also undoubtedly it lacked the sharpness of focus which the Resurrection was later to give it. To his contemporaries he was certainly a man anointed by God with the Spirit and with power; a man who went about doing good; a *chasid* or Jewish saint; perhaps a prophet, "like one of the prophets of old," or even "more than a prophet," perhaps *the* prophet, "like unto Moses";[13] possibly even the Messiah, the Son of David, or even the heavenly Son of Man of Daniel's vision, walking the earth incognito and eventually "to come on the clouds." Different persons thought of him in different terms, even within the little band of his intimate disciples. How much more variety must have characterized the views of those outside this circle! Naturally, then, the reports that circulated about him were couched in different terms, and were given a diverse interpretation and orientation.

[12] See my articles: "Form Criticism: A New Method of Research," *Religion in Life*, 3:351-66; "Further Thoughts on Form Criticism," *ibid.*, 5:532-43.

[13] Prof. David E. Adams' *Man of God* (1941) is a study of the Old Testament pattern used repeatedly in biographies and presupposed in stories of holy men in the Old Testament and in related literature. This pattern undoubtedly had an influence upon the formation of the gospel tradition.

This oral tradition formed the basis or main body of the evangelic tradition up to but not including the passion narrative; it was the common knowledge of Jesus as it circulated in Palestine during, and soon after, the lifetime of Jesus—"the report ($\rho\hat{\eta}\mu\alpha$) that spread all over Jewish Palestine, as you yourselves know, beginning in Galilee after 'the baptism' which John preached" and continuing down to the present.[14] That is to say, the original circulation, transmission, and consequent preservation of the evangelic tradition, by separate items, were not controlled or determined by any one particular theological idea, let alone created by it; but it was nevertheless believed to have a significance which can be stated only theologically, though the controlling theological ideas no doubt varied from person to person, and from group to group.[15] That is why we have the amount of variety in theological outlook which is still recognizable in the Gospels. In spite of the major control set up by the fact of the Resurrection, the tradition continued to reflect the variety in point of view, in hope, in confidence and expectation that prevailed, even among his close followers, during Jesus' earthly ministry. Here Jesus is addressed—and it is reported with apparent approval—as "Son of David"; here he refers to himself as "the Son of Man"; here he is viewed as exercising an authority greater than Moses, not hesitating to criticize not only the scribes and their "human traditions" but even the sacred Law itself; here he is "a prophet," or "the Coming One," perhaps Elijah, or

---

[14] Acts 10:37.
[15] See my article "The Christ of the Gospels," *Religion in Life*, 10:430-41.

Jeremiah, or "one of the ancient prophets" come back to earth; here he is "the Christ," "God's Anointed One," "the Son," "the Beloved." Not all of these terms reflect a postresurrection theology; some of them are surely survivals, embedded deeply in the tradition.

Later "theologies," if we may call them such, were eventually to come on the scene—the theology of the Hellenists, in Jerusalem, and later in Antioch; the theology of the early Gentile church, before Paul, with its term "Lord" and its view of the gospel as a mystery; above all the theology of Paul himself, with his bold modernizations, his unhesitating combination of things new with things old, of tradition and interpretation in the light of personal religious experience; and then the theologies reflected in Mark, in the Epistle to Hebrews, in James, in the Pastorals, in the Apocalypse of John, in the M stratum of the Gospel of Matthew, in Luke-Acts, and finally in the Gospel and First Epistle of John. Early Christianity was a growing thing, alive, and therefore changing. Variety, or rather unity in variety, is clearly its hallmark and stamp of authenticity. It could not well be otherwise. For early Christianity was no product of a single school, the long shadow cast by a single figure; its New Testament was no product of one sole individual, say Peter, or Paul. Christianity was a widespreading social-religious movement, and possessed a consequent variety from the beginning. The Koran, by way of contrast, is the product of one single mind; not so the New Testament, which has all the variety of the Old, and is a "social" product, a "traditional" book—that is, a book enshrining traditions, letters, anecdotes, revelations, sayings, stories—and its unity is found only in its central affirmations, convictions, loyalties, and the general way of life which it reflects.

The gospel was first of all an oral gospel—let us never forget that. In this respect the New Testament was perfectly in accord with the canons of ancient Jewish tradition and literature. The Old Testament "histories" are only the writing down of oral tradition. The records of Jewish saints and teachers, and of their teaching, were likewise handed down orally, as tradition, for a long time before they were committed to writing—for a much longer period of time, in fact, than was true of the Gospels. When the rabbinic traditions were finally written down, they were far less varied, far less lifelike, far less adequate in sheer quantity than the traditions in the Gospels—take the traditions of Hillel, Akiba, or Jochanan ben Zakkai, for example, as collected by Bacher in the first volume of his *Agada der Tannaiten.*[16] And these traditions, be it observed, were the traditions of legal interpretation or of Bible hermeneutics, for the most part, handed down in schools of Jewish law. Apart from the scattered traditions in the Mishnah and Talmud and the early Midrashim, we should know almost nothing about these great saints and teachers.

Moreover, the oral tradition underlying the Gospels was first formulated in the Aramaic language of the Palestinian populace. When it was that these oral tradi-

[16] Second ed., Strassburg, 1903.

tions were first translated into Greek, whether early or
late, and where this took place, we do not know. There
is of course evidence that Greek was spoken in Jewish
Palestine[17]—more evidence for the second century than
for the first—and there is evidence that "Hellenists,"
Greek-speaking Jews, were found in the Christian group
at Jerusalem from a very early date.[18] Accordingly, it
seems not improbable that Aramaic traditions about Jesus
were reproduced in oral Greek fairly early, perhaps even
during the first decade—the years between A.D. 30 and 40.
But such translation was doubtless done piecemeal, one
story or saying at a time, and by different persons—"according as each was able," to quote what Papias said of
Matthew's collection of the oracles.[19] Hence the divergent
forms of many sayings, as found in the Synoptic parallels; hence also the closest kind of agreement in other
passages. These agreements and divergences are not to
be credited wholly to the "authors" of the Gospels, the
final editors of the tradition. Agreement and divergence
no doubt characterized the gospel tradition from the very
beginning, and its translation into Greek "in many parts

[17] Saul Lieberman, Greek in Jewish Palestine (New York: Jewish Theological Seminary of America, 1942). See also the review by A. D. Nock in
Anglican Theological Review, April, 1943.

[18] Acts 6:1. The point is justly emphasized by Prof. Burton S. Easton in
his book The Gospel Before the Gospels (1928), which contains an excellent
criticism of form criticism, and also in his Hale Lectures, Christ in the
Gospels (1930). The importance of the Hellenistic element in primitive
Christianity is steadily gaining in recognition, along with that of the
Jewish substratum. In other words, the earliest Christian community was
even more Jewish than we used to think, and at the same time the Hellenistic element in the primitive church went back farther than we once
supposed.

[19] Eusebius, Ecclesiastical History 3. 39. 16.

and after divers manners" must have accelerated a process
which was perfectly natural in any case. It may be
thought that the process would not have gone so far if
the tradition had remained in Aramaic. The divergence
between Luke's and Matthew's versions of the Beatitudes,
for example, is as wide as possible; on the other hand,
their accounts of John the Baptist's prediction of the
Coming One are almost identical. The translation of the
tradition into another language had something to do
with this, though we incline to think that Matthew's
Beatitudes have been translated out of Aramaic at a later
stage than Luke's. Their poetic structure and fuller form,
and the interpretative clauses which have been added in
Matthew's version seem to reflect a longer period of
teaching and devotion in the Aramaic-speaking north-
Palestinian or Syrian church.[20] At the same time, there
are passages in the Gospels that can hardly have received their present form in Aramaic; their language,
structure, ethos, theology, all seem to point to a purely
Greek-speaking community for their main line of transmission and final formulation.[21]

Several eminent scholars are convinced that the Gospels
themselves, and not merely their underlying units of tradition, were originally composed in Aramaic and later
translated into Greek. This theory we shall consider in
detail in a later chapter; but even this theory, complicated

---

[20] See C. F. Burney, *The Poetry of Our Lord* (1925), pp. 166 ff. It
should be noted, however, that the added verses 5 and 8 *may* be influenced
by the Septuagint.

[21] See Martin Dibelius, *The Message of Jesus Christ* (1939), esp. Part II,
pp. 166 ff.; K. Kundsin, chap. xi in my *Form Criticism* (1934).

and unnecessary as we may think it to be, presupposes a
period of oral transmission before the composition—or
compilation—of the written Gospels took place. The
process, as I have said, is thoroughly natural and precisely what we should antecedently expect in such an
area. It is flying in the face of the, alas, too little-known
canons of Semitic historiography[22] to assume that the
Gospels are personal memoirs, or biographies, or scientific histories—say of the ancient Greek kind—rather than
"traditional books." The only "memoirs" in the Old Testament are those of Nehemiah, and possibly those of
Ezra. The prophetic cycles in Samuel and Kings are traditional; so are the "court memoirs" of David's reign;
Jeremiah's "Confessions," to use Professor Skinner's term,
were compiled by another, or by others; First Maccabees
is not a memoir but a history, using sources; it is only
Nehemiah who uses the first person singular in the auto-
biographic sense. Outside the Old Testament, Josephus'
Autobiography, appended to his *Antiquities,* is modeled
on a Greco-Roman pattern and is addressed to Greco-
Roman readers; so are Philo's *Legation to Caius* and his
Flaccus. We have, accordingly, no right to expect the
Gospels to give us personal memoirs. Justin's phrase, "The
Memoirs of the Apostles," [23] was either a careless one or

[22] See Julius Bewer, *The Literature of the Old Testament* (1922; 3rd ed.
1940), chap. iv, "The Growth of Historical Literature," also chaps. xv,
xviii; C. F. Kent, *Israel's Historical and Biographical Narratives* (1905), esp.
the Introduction; Otto Eissfeldt, *Einleitung in das Alte Testament* (1934),
§§ 5, 16, 26-30, 35-38; Johannes Hempel, *Die Althebräische Literatur* (1930);
G. W. Wade, *New Testament History* (1922), chap. v, "Prevailing Ideas and
Methods of Jewish Historians."

[23] *Apology* 67. 3.

was meant only to suggest an analogy. Professor Turner, I believe, went much too far in proposing[24] to turn Mark's third person plural "they" into a first person, "we" or "I." "All the city was gathered at my door"; "We followed him, ... and he said to us"; "As I was beneath in the court." [25] One might play this game indefinitely: "As he sat on the Mount of Olives, ... we asked him privately." [26] The fact remains, neither Mark nor any other of the Gospels is written in the first person. And although, as Streeter[27] and others have insisted, the tradition must go back to persons, to individuals, and is no impersonal creation of some unknown social-religious energy, a kind of "group consciousness," working automatically in the Christian community, still the *transmission* of the tradition was certainly social, and to some degree, therefore, impersonal.

It is the purpose of this volume to present certain studies of the gospel at the point where the oral tradition was being crystallized in writing; and for this reason we shall pay chief attention to the Gospel of Mark, though the other early source or cycle—Q, the "Sayings Source"—will also engage our attention now and then. But we cannot deal with that source in detail at present; indeed, we shall not have the time to deal adequately with Mark, and can study only some of its leading features and the problems to which these give rise. The point of view has already

[24] "Commentary on the Gospel of Mark," p. 9b, in C. Gore, *A New Commentary on Holy Scripture* (1928), New Testament, p. 48.

[25] Mark 1:33, 36-38; 14:66.

[26] Mark 13:3.

[27] Especially in his unpublished lectures on "The Historical Evidence for the Life of Christ" at Colgate-Rochester Theological Seminary in 1934.

been sufficiently indicated. Such an attempt as that of the late Professor Turner mentioned above to view the Gospel as autobiographical, at least from 1:14 to 14:72, with the exception of the doublets in 7:24–8:10 (or 12), we cannot follow. Far more promising is the approach of Professor Branscomb in "The Moffatt New Testament Commentary" (1937), who views the Gospel as based upon "the common tradition of the Gentile churches," though the use of sources, even of written sources, is not only not denied but even presupposed in the discussion of more than one section of the Gospel. This commentary and the one by A. E. J. Rawlinson in the Westminster series (1925) are the best we have in English. The works of the late Professor Bacon on this Gospel are always rewarding—*The Beginnings of Gospel Story* (1909), *Was Mark a Roman Gospel?* (1919), *The Gospel of Mark* (1925)—as is the older commentary of Allan Menzies, *The Earliest Gospel* (1901).[28] So also is that by W. C. Allen (1915). Swete's commentary is still important, at least philologically. So is Johannes Weiss's *Das älteste Evangelium* (1903), especially for literary analysis and interpretation, and also his commentary in *Die Schriften des Neuen Testaments* (1906; third edition, posthumous, 1917). The useful commentary by Professor John N. Davies in *The Abingdon Bible Commentary* (1929) is widely known and influential. Wellhausen's *Einleitung* (second edition, 1911) and commentary (second edition, 1909) will never be out of date! The commentary by E. Klostermann, in

[28] It is surprising how Menzies' Introduction in this volume anticipates present-day form criticism.

Lietzmann's *Handbuch zum Neuen Testament* (third edition, 1936), is indispensable. Loisy's work in *Les évangiles synoptiques* (1907), summarized in his *L'évangile selon Marc* (1912), has been used by all scholars for a generation. Lohmeyer's commentary in the Meyer series (1937) is one of the most thorough and most stimulating commentaries ever written. The student should not, however, undertake to use it without carefully reading through the book as a whole. Otherwise, he will be likely to gain a wrong impression of some passages. He should also read the little volume which Professor Lohmeyer wrote as a prolegomenon to the commentary, entitled *Galiläa und Jerusalem,* in which he deals with the question of the Jerusalem or Galilean location of the resurrection appearances and comes to the conclusion that both Galilee and Jerusalem were centers of primitive Christianity. We shall deal with this hypothesis later in the present volume.[29] Among important commentaries is the one by Père M.-J. Lagrange; the fifth edition appeared in 1929. This is a really great work of exegesis, no less valuable to Protestants than to Catholics, although naturally on some points of theology we cannot follow the author all the way. The second edition, revised and enlarged, of the late C. G. Montefiore's *Synoptic Gospels* (1927) contains in Volume I a full-length commentary on the Gospel of Mark from a liberal Jewish point of view. This important work was supplemented by the volume *Rabbinic Literature and Gospel Teachings* (1930). The additional notes contained in this latter volume deal

[29] Chap. vi, pp. 125 ff.

naturally with Matthew and Luke rather than with Mark
—since Mark gives such a very brief account of Jesus'
teaching. The older supplement to Montefiore's commentary, the two volumes by Israel Abrahams entitled
Studies in Pharisaism and the Gospels (1917, 1924), is
still as valuable as when it was first published. The great
work by Strack and Billerbeck, *Kommentar zum Neuen
Testament aus Talmud und Midrasch,* Volume II (1924),
contains fifty-four pages on the Gospel of Mark. Naturally the great bulk of material on the Gospels—1055 pages—
is found in Volume I dealing with the Gospel of Matthew, and also in the two volumes of *excursi* (1928).
The commentary on Mark should of course be read in
connection with these other volumes in the set. More
recent work on the sources and composition of the Second Gospel may be seen in such a book as J. M. C. Crum's
St. Mark's Gospel: Two Stages of Its Making (1936);
also in A. T. Cadoux, *The Sources of the Second Gospel*
(n.d.), Rudolph Thiel, *Drei Markus-Evangelien* (1938),
and—as supplying criteria for these hypotheses—in M.
Zerwick, *Untersuchungen zum Markus-Stil* (1937). These
books are of special interest to source critics and represent
in our generation the sort of analysis which forty years
ago was associated with the name of Emil Wendling
(*Ur-Marcus,* 1905; *Die Entstehung des Marcus-Evan-
geliums,* 1908). The main difficulty with most par-
tition theories is, of course, the homogeneity of Mark's
style.

The works on form criticism, all of which naturally
deal with the Gospel of Mark, are quite well known.

M. Dibelius, *From Tradition to Gospel* (English translation, 1925), K. L. Schmidt, *Der Rahmen der Geschichte Jesu* (1919), Rudolf Bultmann, *Die Geschichte der synoptischen Tradition* (second edition, 1931)—these books are all known to .workers in the field and are of course in constant use. My own *Form Criticism: A New Method of New Testament Research* (1934) contains a translation of "The Study of the Synoptic Gospels" by Rudolf Bultmann and of "Primitive Christianity in the Light of Gospel Research" by Karl Kundsin, two excellent little works introductory to the subject.

As for the text of the Gospel, students now have the advantage of Erwin Nestle's new edition (the seventeenth, 1941) with its full apparatus of variant readings, handy size, and low price; S. C. E. Legg's full—if not always accurate—apparatus in the new "Oxford Tischendorf" (1935); and F. L. Cross's edition of Hans Lietzmann's edition of A. Huck, *A Synopsis of the First Three Gospels* (ninth edition, with Introduction in English, section headings in German and English, text and apparatus in Greek, 1936).

II

ORIGIN OF THE GOSPEL OF MARK

THE EARLIEST ECCLESIASTICAL TRADITION REGARDING THE origin of the Gospel of Mark is that given by Papias of Hierapolis, who lived in the first half of the second century. This tradition is preserved in Eusebius' *Ecclesiastical History* 3. 39. 15. According to Eusebius, Papias wrote as follows:

This also the presbyter used to say: "Mark, indeed, who became the interpreter of Peter, wrote accurately, as far as he remembered them, the things said or done by the Lord, but not however in order." For he [Mark] had neither heard the Lord nor been his personal follower, but at a later stage, as I said, he had followed Peter, who used to adapt the teachings to the needs of the moment, but not as though he were drawing up a connected account of the oracles of the Lord: so that Mark committed no error in writing certain matters just as he remembered them. For he had only one object in view, namely to leave out nothing of the things which he had heard, and to include no false statement among them.[1]

With this "testimony" of Papias—or of the elder whose words he is quoting and commenting upon—tallies the oft-quoted statement of Irenaeus, about A.D. 180:

[1] See my *The Growth of the Gospels* (1933), pp. 98 ff.; also the article by my son, Robert M. Grant, "The Oldest Gospel Prologues," *Anglican Theological Review*, 23:231-45.

34

After the deaths [of Peter and Paul], Mark, the disciple and interpreter of Peter, himself also handed down to us in writing the things which Peter had proclaimed.[2]

The other, later, church fathers do little more than repeat or echo Papias or Irenaeus—as perhaps Irenaeus himself echoes Papias. They may accordingly be ignored in this brief discussion.

It is clear that the words of Papias—and certainly those of the "presbyter"—are meant to defend the Gospel of Mark against the double charge of inaccuracy and lack of order. Perhaps the inaccuracy was an inference from the lack of order: at least its accuracy is affirmed, though its lack of order is conceded. Upon what basis Mark's lack of order was maintained we can only surmise. Most students assume that it was by comparison with the Gospel of John, or perhaps with that of Matthew—where everything is strictly "in order," for didactic purposes.[3] What the presbyter affirms is that Mark's lack of "order" does not militate against his accuracy; what Papias adds is that this lack of order is easily explained—he was the "interpreter" of Peter. And certainly Peter did not go about giving a historical lecture on the life and teaching of Jesus. He was a preacher, a missionary, a martyr, not a scholar; and perhaps he did not even speak Greek, if that is what the office of "interpreter" implies. This is the defense that Papias elaborates, upon the basis of the

[2] *Against Heresies* 3. 1. 1; cf. Eusebius *Eccl. Hist.* 5. 8. 3.

[3] In an article "Papias and the Gospels," *Anglican Theological Review*, April, 1943, Robert M. Grant argues that Papias was contrasting Mark with Luke.

presbyter's words, though he takes up the question of
Mark's order first, and then deals with his accuracy—
which Papias understands to involve complete recording
as well as true. "For he had only one object in view,
namely to leave out nothing of the things which he had
heard, and to include no false statement among them."

The question now arises, How accurate was—not Mark
but—the presbyter? Professor Lake, in his recent *Introduction to the New Testament* (1937), has set this query
before all the statements in the church fathers regarding
the origin of the New Testament books: How far are
these statements merely inferences from the books themselves? Some of them are undoubtedly inferences—or
rather guesses—some of them perhaps inspired, some certainly uninspired, for example Augustine's view of Mark
as an abridgement of Matthew, or the popular idea that
the Gospel of Matthew was originally written in Hebrew!
In the case of the words of the presbyter regarding the
origin of the Gospel of Mark, however, it is out of the
question to describe this as an inference from the contents of the book, for there is nothing in the Gospel to
suggest that Peter is responsible for its contents. It is true,
of course, that when the hypothesis is applied, some passages at once fit in with the Petrine theory, especially
in chapter 1; but others definitely do not, and surely no
one with only this Gospel before him would ever suspect
that it was a mélange of Peter's reminiscences he was
reading. Hence we conclude that the presbyter is re-
porting *a genuine tradition,* namely of "Mark's" association with Peter and his recollection and writing down of

certain things Peter had said in his preaching; and this
is all the more probable in that (*a*) the presbyter uses the
tradition to meet a current objection, and (*b*) he presses
it a little too far—though not so far as Papias does—in
meeting the objection.

The soundness of the underlying tradition has been
questioned by certain modern writers who object, quite
properly, to the weight it has been forced to bear, not only
by Papias in the second century but by many exegetes
and interpreters since. For example, "the fresh and vivid
style of Mark" has been explained as the result of Peter's
vivid personal recollections—forgetting that people did
not usually write that way in ancient times, but far more
prosaically, far less romantically; the exploitation of
literary personality is a very modern innovation. Again,
the otherwise unexplained features in the story, for example the flight of a young man from the garden, or the
proceedings in the high priest's house, have been explained as incidents in Peter's own biography—or even
in Mark's!—forgetting that ancient religious writers, unlike scholarly historians, did not as a rule feel it incum-
bent upon them to give, in a footnote or otherwise,
their source for every anecdote or event, or to anticipate
the modern reader's constant query, "How can we know
that what you say is true, in every detail?"[4] Again, the
very frank admissions of weakness or stupidity or lack of
faith or downright blindness and disloyalty on the part

---

[4] Of course Mark does give a suggestion of the source of the testimony
at the end: the women viewing the crucifixion, the centurion, and so on.
But the Gospel never hints that Peter is the authority for any of its narratives.

of the disciples are sometimes explained as due to Peter's lifelong penitent self-accusation: he could not recall incidents from the life of his Master without breaking into tears once more, as once he did outside the high priest's house in Jerusalem. But this explanation entirely overlooks two facts of great importance: (1) One of the themes of the Gospel of Mark, destined later to be elaborated quite differently by Matthew and by John, is the hiding of the divine revelation—it was "hid from the eyes" not only of the "Jews" but to some extent even of the apostles. Then (2) historically the disciples during Jesus' earthly ministry did not yet possess the fully formed faith which sprang from his resurrection; the judgment upon their prior faith, at first crude and but slowly developed, could be made only in the light of the fuller experience which came later.[5] Hence the pathetic, personal interpretation, so appealing to a number of modern writers, is really quite out of touch with historical probability, and often verges close upon the abyss of sentimentality.

On the other hand there is an interpretation which not only gives due weight to the old tradition underlying the presbyter's words, but also maintains full contact with historical probability: it is the interpretation made possible by what is called form criticism.[6] The basic assumption and starting point of this type of investigation is the fact

[5] Cf. John 2:22.

[6] Instead of an author in search of a book, the Gospel of Mark illustrates the opposite situation—a book in search of an author! The gospel material had to be written down, sooner or later, and one person almost as well as another might have written it.

that oral tradition circulates, not in long consecutive narratives, but in brief, rounded units, each more or less complete in itself. What form criticism undertakes is to get back behind the written Gospels and their sources to the oral tradition as it circulated prior to the writing down of any account of the "mighty works," the sayings, the parables, or the discourses of Jesus. Its first tool is the scientific one of classification. Upon examination, the gospel traditions appear to fall into five or six main groups: anecdotes, parables, sayings, miracle tales, legends.[7] And each of these types, it appears, is probably subject to certain "laws of form" governing its oral transmission—factors affecting the modification, expansion, elaboration, and even the simplification of tradition—though we are not prepared, as yet, to formulate these "laws" with precision. Moreover, each of these types had its place in the preaching, worship, and teaching of the early Christian communities.

A better name for this type of investigation would be "tradition criticism"; but the movement began, over twenty years ago, as the study of the "forms" in which the tradition was handed down; and although it has swept into its orbit other studies and evaluations of the early Christian tradition, some of them older than

[7] See Martin Dibelius, *From Tradition to Gospel* (1925); Rudolf Bultmann, *Die Geschichte der synoptischen Tradition* (2nd ed., 1931); and also Karl Ludwig Schmidt, *Der Rahmen der Geschichte Jesu* (1919); Burton Scott Easton, *The Gospel Before the Gospels* (1928); Kendrick Grobel, *Formgeschichte und synoptische Quellenanalyse* (1937); E. Basil Redlich, *Form Criticism: Its Value and Limitations* (1939); Thomas S. Kepler, "The Jesus of 'Formgeschichte,'" in *New Testament Studies*, ed. Edwin Prince Booth (1942).

itself, it has retained its original name. The chief pioneer
of the movement is Martin Dibelius of Heidelberg, several of whose books have been translatetd into English;
with him must also be named Rudolf Bultmann and
Karl Ludwig Schmidt, the one a remarkable combination
of acute skepticism and ardent Barthianism, the other
an almost rigidly orthodox Reformed theologian. Dibelius' position is more moderate and "central" than that
held by either of the others: warmer and richer in appreciation of the religious values and motives enshrined in
the tradition; firmer and surer, it seems to me, in its
contact with historical probability. Bultmann is more
inclined to attribute certain sayings to the creative activity of the primitive community—and therefore not to the
historical Jesus—while Schmidt is more interested in the
final theological interpretation of the whole process of
revelation and redemption reflected in the New Testament.

Form criticism is a method of historical research, that
is, of investigation of historical sources, namely traditions. It is compatible with complete orthodoxy—certainly with Barthian orthodoxy!—as we see from
Schmidt's theology; and it is not necessarily to be
identified with "skepticism" as we see from the
contrast between Bultmann on one hand and Schmidt
and Dibelius on the other. There are, it is true, con-
servative scholars who view the method with distrust, or
even openly oppose it. But this can be explained partly
by the extremity of the conclusions drawn by some advocates of form criticism, for example by Professor R. H.

Lightfoot in his Bampton Lectures;[8] and partly by the
ultraconservatism of men who are incapable of altering
their views in later life. In spite of such opposition, it is
probable that form criticism has come to stay. For it has
behind it the momentum of all modern historical research in the field of the biblical literature—Old Testament as well as New. (In truth, form criticism first made
its appearance in the Old Testament field; Gunkel and
Wellhausen had a good deal to do with its first appearance.) More and more zealously, during the past fifty
years, historical criticism has pressed on toward the investigation of the traditions underlying the sources. Source
criticism, the recovery or reconstruction of the sources of
the Gospels and of the Book of Acts, was a far advance
in this direction, but it did not go the whole way. Now
that the existence of sources underlying the Gospels
is fairly assured, and also their extent and contents—
whether as written documents or as cycles of tradition—
the next step is to investigate the quality and character
of the traditions they contain, and the value of these traditions for historical purposes. It was maintained by some
critics, a decade ago, that form criticism had nothing to
do with the historicity of events whose purported records
had been handed down orally, but only with the outward form of the tradition; but this was an impossible
view. All literary criticism of the New Testament is ultimately historical criticism: literary criticism, in the sense
of aesthetic appreciation and evaluation, finds much to

[8] *History and Interpretation in the Gospels* (1934).

engage its attention in the New Testament, but it is not the main interest of modern biblical study.

If the oral tradition of Jesus' life and teaching, prior to the writing of the Gospels or their sources, circulated in brief, detached, independent units—and this is not only the first assumption of form criticism; it is also assumed by almost all modern New Testament criticism of whatever school—then we must read the Gospels with this fact in mind. We must ignore, for the time being, the editorial introductions, transitions, conclusions, and inferences or interpretations which have been added to the separate units, as also the order in which they are given, and the presumed bearing of one upon another. The chronological sequence disappears, but this is not much of a loss. It has always been an insoluble problem for harmonists and writers of the life of Christ; and it is clear from the way Matthew—and perhaps John—and even Luke used the materials of the Gospel of Mark that they, who were its earliest editors and commentators, did not view the Marcan order as chronological or final and unalterable—save in one section, the passion narrative, though even here they did not hesitate to make some changes in order. But not only the chronological order— some of the interpretative comments or explanations added to the original pericopes must also be set aside: for example, the slaughter of the rebels in Luke's version of the parable of the talents,[9] and the moral, "Make to yourselves friends by means of the mammon of unright-

[9] Luke 19:27.

eousness," appended to the parable of the unjust steward.[10] Whether these interpretative "morals" were added by the authors—or editors—of the Gospels or represent accretions to the narratives in the oral period does not greatly matter; what we want is the original parable or saying as it came from the lips of Jesus.

Now some authors, like Principal H. D. A. Major in his recent joint work, *The Mission and Message of Jesus,* (1938), holds this analysis of the tradition to be more loss than gain. Dr. Major refers to it as "unstringing the beads," assuming, apparently, that once unstrung they can never be put together again. But it may be pointed out that (1) no one has ever "unstrung" the Marcan sequence more completely than the author of Matthew did in revising and reorganizing the Gospel of Mark for his special purposes: the book is taken apart and put together again in a new order, combined with the "Sayings Source" (Q) and with other materials, and arranged apparently for didactic use—as a manual, one might say, for the religious educators of the early Syrian church! And in the next place, (2) the circulation and transmission of separate units of tradition is precisely what the presbyter is describing in Eusebius' quotation from Papias: "Mark, ... who became the interpreter of Peter, wrote accurately, as far as he remembered them, the things said or done by the Lord, but not however in order." The presbyter *implies* that Mark's information was derived from Peter, but he does not say so explicitly; that is Papias' inference. The wording of the presbyter's

[10] Luke 16:9.

remark leaves open the question of Mark's use of other sources than Peter, whose "interpreter" he was: sources, or traditions, in circulation among the Christians in Rome no doubt from the first founding of the church in that community, long before Paul's arrival and perhaps some time before Peter's coming; and also, no doubt, traditions that were added to the common stock by every believer who came to Rome from Palestine. Papias' further inference from the presbyter's words is doubtless a correct one: Mark was not a disciple of Jesus, and had in fact never heard him—this rules out his identification with the young man in the garden!—but later on followed Peter and became his interpreter; and Peter "used to adapt the teachings to the needs of the moment, but not as though he were drawing up a connected account of the oracles of the Lord," so that Mark was perfectly justified in setting them down "just as he remembered them." In fact, his whole procedure was praiseworthy— he aimed only to omit nothing and to misrepresent nothing. Could we have a better account of what, according to form criticism, was the normal process of transmission of the gospel tradition in its oral period? The parables, sayings, and anecdotes from the life of Jesus were used as "paradigms," illustrations, *exempla* in the early Christian preaching and teaching, rather than as quotations from a finished and complete biography, based perhaps upon the memoir of an apostle. Finally, (3) this is precisely the kind of record we might antecedently expect. For early Christianity was in its origin a Jewish movement, and the records of the lives and teachings of Jewish

religious leaders in that period were invariably preserved
in the form of scattered sayings, parables, and anecdotes,
handed down by their disciples, quoted and requoted in
the schools, and not committed to writing until long
after. The materials that we possess for reconstructing the
life and teaching of even the greatest of them—Hillel, for
example, or Gamaliel II—fill less than a dozen pages, and
must be collected from the most varied sources.[11] The
Christian tradition is in a far better state of preservation:
Christianity early became a religious movement in the
Greek world, and became literary within a generation;
it was the possession of a church, not of a school of legal
study; and it was from the first a sacred tradition, in an
even higher sense than were the floating records of Hillel,
Gamaliel, Jochanan ben Zakkai, or Akiba. But it never
wholly escaped the limitations of its origin as a body of
Jewish tradition, circulated and handed down orally from
the first. Even in the second century, a hundred years
and more after the time of Jesus, there were doubtless still
in circulation oral accounts of incidents in his life and
quotations of his teachings which had not until then been
committed to writing. In the preface to his five books on
The Interpretation of the Oracles of the Lord, Papias referred to "the living and abiding voice" of tradition, which
he even preferred to written records.[12] He was referring,
I believe, to *interpretations* of the Lord's teachings; but
the existence of the agrapha—the "unwritten sayings" of
the Lord—and the composition of the older apocryphal

[11] See W. Bacher, *Agada der Tannaiten*, referred to above.
[12] Eusebius, *Eccl. Hist.* 3. 39. 4.

Gospels both testify to the continuance of the oral tradition at least beyond the time of Papias.

On the other hand, it will be urged, there must have been some record of the general outline of Jesus' life. Peter, for example, would not fail to give some kind of sequence to his recollections, some hint or other as to the location of the incidents he related within the general framework of at least the public career of the Master. The speeches in Acts, to go no further,[13] give at least an outline of Jesus' career "in the land of the Jews." In spite of Papias—or the presbyter—who appears to assume the contrary, there must have been some principle of order observed from the first in narrating the life of Jesus. It is antecedently probable that those who remembered the sayings and parables of Jesus would also remember the general course of his ministry; and what conceivable order is more probable than that which Mark gives us! This view has been advocated with great skill by Professor C. H. Dodd, first in an article entitled "The Framework of the Gospel Narrative," published in *The Expository Times* (June, 1932), and then in his books, *The Apostolic Preaching* (1936) and *History and the Gospel* (1938). He examines the speeches in Acts and also the editorial skeleton in Mark, and he finds that they follow a more or less common pattern: the ministry began with the "baptism" of John, that is, his message of repentance and work as a baptizer; following John's arrest, Jesus began his own ministry in Galilee, and there "went about doing good," and "healing all that were pos-

[13] E. g., Acts 10:37-43.

sessed by the devil"; then he came up to Jerusalem, where
the rulers put him to death by crucifixion; on the third
day he rose again, and appeared to his disciples, who were
now "witnesses" to the truth of these reported events, namely to his resurrection from the dead. It is obvious at once
that the "pattern" in the speeches is approximately that of
the Gospel of Mark. We have, therefore, more than the
outline of Mark to rely upon; it is supplemented and con-
firmed by the tradition recorded in the speeches of Acts—
themselves perhaps embedded in old Judean, Jerusalem,
or Caesarean sources, oral or written, which had come
down from the primitive community and were incorporated by the author of Acts in his volume.

But the great objection to the argument advanced by
Dr. Dodd is (1) the probability that Luke—that is, the
author of Acts—had seen and used the Gospel of Mark
before writing these early chapters of his "second volume";
if so, he would naturally have the pattern of Mark still in
mind. How important he thought it to be is clearly recognized by the Proto-Luke theory,[14] according to which his
first account of the teaching of Jesus was later expanded
to include the Gospel of Mark, when at last he came upon
it—incorporating that work within his own in seven great
"blocks" or sections, but keeping it, for the most part, in
its own order. In the next place, (2) it is still a question if
the speeches in the Book of Acts are really derived from
earlier sources, and not composed by the author—though

[14] See B. H. Streeter, *The Four Gospels* (1924; 4th ed. 1930), chap. viii;
Vincent Taylor, *Behind the Third Gospel* (1926); also, his *The First Draft of
St. Luke's Gospel* (1927), and my *The Growth of the Gospels* (1933), pp.
157 ff. and Note E, p. 174.

most of us may grant the source hypothesis. They *sound* primitive, but we had best not assume the hypothesis as proved and make it the basis of further argument or additional hypothesis. It was the custom of ancient historians to compose appropriate speeches for historic personages and occasions. From Thucydides down, they all try to write speeches that fit the character of the speaker and the situation; it gave life and color to their narratives, and no one questioned the practice. Sometimes they gave the "substance" of what was said; often they composed freely— but appropriately. In the absence of stenographic records of speeches, no other course was open; and, I repeat, no one questioned the practice—but no one was deceived by it, or took the speeches as verbatim records. Even Tacitus, who had access to an abundance of sources, including the speeches of the emperors and many other memoirs—of consuls, generals, and civil officials—does not hesitate to compose a speech "in character" when the occasion demands it; in fact, he often writes two or more speeches, setting forth the views and arguments of both sides in a given situation. Fortunately, the writing of history was still an art, not a science; as one ancient author observed,[15] it was closely allied to poetry—especially to dramatic

[15] "For history has a certain affinity to poetry and may be regarded as a kind of prose poem, while it is written for the purpose of narrative, not of proof, and designed from beginning to end not for immediate effect or the instant necessities of forensic strife, but to record events for the benefit of posterity and to win glory for its author"—Quintilian x. 1. 31 (tr. H. E. Butler). This does not, of course, sum up the classical ideal of historical writing; there were writers who viewed their task forensically, and many who looked to history either for *exempla* or for light on their own troubled times. But most ancient historians, from Herodotus and Thucydides down, recognized the literary nature of their craft.

poetry, which gives in six lines of a chorus or a speech more than ten pages of "scientific" prose can convey. And if Luke, as many modern scholars suppose, was writing a history—or an apology for Christianity in the form of an account of its origin and expansion—he had every reason to follow the finest precedents of ancient historiography in composing speeches "in character" and placing them upon the lips of the persons in his narrative.

And yet, although we cannot accept without hesitation the evidence thus adduced for this view, it may be that the view itself is sound. And I think that as a matter of fact it is sound. For not only (1) is it perfectly natural and consistent with all the data in the Gospels to assume the existence of some such general pattern; but also (2) if the pattern had been wrong on any major point, there must have been traditions still in circulation by which to correct or discredit it. For example, had Jesus been a Gentile—as certain fantastic modern theories assume[16]— let us say an Aryan, a Hindu, a Greek, or a member of the Roman proletariat, something would surely be found to betray this fact in the diversified gospel tradition we possess; or if, say, he had had no connection with John the Baptist, or had not criticized the scribes, or had been stoned to death rather than crucified. Instead, the later evangelists one and all use Mark, and take for granted the general outline—though not the detailed order—of his account of Jesus' ministry. The "Marcan hypothesis," as Bishop Rawlinson insists in his Commentary, is no longer

[16] See now *The Nazi Christ*, by Eugene S. Tanner of the University of Tulsa (1942), a detailed criticism of these views.

tenable—the hypothesis, namely, that Mark's order and point of view are infallible and must be adhered to in every case—and yet the general outline of the ministry, as given by Mark, is not only the earliest outline we have, but commends itself upon grounds of probability. Briefly stated, that outline or "pattern" is this:

1. Jesus' ministry began when he left the group of John's disciples and returned to Galilee.
2. His work consisted chiefly in teaching and healing; the healings were, for the most part, exorcisms of demons.
3. Both as teacher and as healer he roused the opposition of the scribes, the official and accredited teachers of the Law, and of their lay adherents and supporters, the Pharisees.
4. After a time he withdrew from his public ministry and went into retirement.
5. Meanwhile, like other teachers, he had gathered about him a band of close disciples, whom he sent out, occasionally, to teach and to heal.
6. As Passover drew near, he journeyed to Jerusalem to keep the festival, accompanied by his disciples and other followers.
7. The opposition of his enemies broke out here with renewed force, the temple priesthood joining with them to destroy him after his prophetic demonstration in the "cleansing" of the temple.
8. He was seized by the temple authorities and handed over to the Roman governor as a dangerous insurrectionist and disturber of public order.
9. After a brief and half-hearted effort to ascertain the truth of the charges against him, Pilate ordered him to be scourged and crucified—one more disturber of the peace of this rebellious people thus put out of the way.
10. After only the briefest interval—so Mark implies all along—his followers were convinced that he had risen from the dead

—not as one more resuscitated Israelite, like the daughter of
Jairus, nor as a saint who had entered glory, like Moses or
Elijah, but as no one less than the transcendent, heavenly
Messiah, the "Son of Man" who was to come on the clouds
of heaven and hold the last judgment upon all mankind.

This "pattern," I say, not only is our earliest outline of
the public career of Jesus, but has in it every feature of
probability.[17] So far as we know anything whatever about
the life of Jesus of Nazareth, it agrees with this general
outline; and the whole of the early Christian tradition, in
Epistles, Gospels, the Book of Acts, and such of it as
survives in the noncanonical writings, fits in with it—or
rather, contains almost nothing that disagrees with it.
Even the outline of the Gospel of John is in fundamental
agreement. The fact may be explained by saying that
everything goes back to, or rests upon, the Gospel of
Mark; but I think we cannot assume that this Gospel
would have been accepted if upon any major point its
general outline had been found to be faulty or inaccurate
by those who were in touch with the primitive tradition
handed down in the churches in Palestine.

Thus form criticism, and modern New Testament criticism in general, far from undermining the authority of
the earliest Gospel, really support it; at the same time
form criticism provides a more satisfactory approach to
its contents than was provided in the old-fashioned view
according to which Mark's Gospel was really the Gospel

[17] This outline appears in expanded form in chap. iv of my *The Gospel
of the Kingdom* (1940).

according to Peter, and Mark was only that apostle's amanuensis or secretary—a view only one step removed from that which made the apostles themselves the amanuenses or secretaries of the Holy Spirit.

But have we not lost something? What has become of the familiar figure we knew as the nephew of Barnabas, the son of Mary of Jerusalem, the companion of Paul and Barnabas on the first missionary journey, the young man who lost heart and returned home, and whom Paul refused to take along a second time, but who later proved useful to Peter? So far as I know, he has not disappeared! But he never was the unquestioned author of the earliest Gospel, save in the same sense that Hebrews was assigned to Paul, Revelation to John, the Johannine Epistles to the Elder John, and so on—that is, by inference, and by hypothesis.[18] It is to be noted that Papias does not even pause to consider the possibility that Mark, the author of the Gospel, was the "follower" of Paul and Barnabas, the young man whose story is reported in the Book of Acts. He moves at once from the fact that "Mark" had not been a follower or hearer of the Lord to the fact that he followed *Peter*. It is of course a question if Papias knew and used Luke-Acts. His "testimony" relates to the origins of Mark and Matthew. It is Matthew, perhaps, with which he contrasts the order of Mark. And it is perhaps Matthew whose collection of oracles in five "books" he

[18] See the chapter in H. J. Holtzmann, *Lehrbuch der Neutestamentlichen Theologie* (2nd ed., 1911), I, 491-97; also Johannes Weiss, *Das älteste Evangelium* (1903), Pt. III, esp. § 8.

commented upon. Was Luke-Acts either unknown or little known in Hierapolis in his time? [19]

The Gospel nowhere claims to be written by Mark! And even if it had made this claim, we should probably not be able to tell which "Mark" was meant. Everyone recognizes the way in which several "Marys" in the gospel story are combined into one composite figure—even including other figures, for example the sinful woman in Luke 7:37. Similarly the Johns have been identified, and the Jameses—James the Apostle (or Apostles) and James the Lord's brother. This is a commonplace of oral tradition; but tradition is no worse, probably not so bad, as later popular exegesis and romance. And in the early Christian community at Rome, Marcus was no doubt as common a name as Jochanan or Jacob or Miriam had been in Palestine.

Positive evidence have we none—or at most very little—but we may conclude with a fantasy, for once tossing free the reins of the historical imagination. Perhaps the author of the earliest Gospel is best thought of as a young clerk in one of the Roman mercantile establishments, located, in the sixties of the first century, in the old business district now known as the Trastevere, down near the Tiber and partly surrounded by the bend in the river. He belonged to the Christian church in that city—a church still meeting in the house of one of the great families,[20]

[19] But see the article by Robert M. Grant, already referred to, "Papias and the Gospels," *Anglican Theological Review*, April, 1943; also his article, "The Oldest Gospel Prologues," *Anglican Theological Review*, 23:231-45.

[20] See F. V. Filson, "The Significance of the Early House Churches," *Journal of Biblical Literature* 58:105-12.

and not yet possessing a building of its own; in fact, it would be several generations before this new eastern sect had any buildings for public worship. Day by day young Marcus went through his routine tasks at the office of the firm, posting accounts, checking the long bills of lading; for he certainly could read and write, and was thus in touch with the outside world of trade. Not all of his fellow believers enjoyed this advantage, for many of them were slaves in the great *familiae* or households of the neighborhood. Marcus could read and write—though he could not write well, and had no inclinations to authorship, even in that publishing center of the western Mediterranean in the days of Nero—and so, as one of the few in the local congregation of Christians who could both read and write, he was commissioned to put together in his free time—probably late evenings, after the assembly of the Christians had broken up—the fragmentary translations of narratives from the story of Jesus and his teaching which were in circulation in the Roman church.

What was wanted was a consecutive, accurate, inclusive account of the ministry and death of the Messiah Jesus, who had lived in Galilee, had died and risen again at Jerusalem, and was soon to come again, in glory, to judge the world and inaugurate the Kingdom of God. The old Aramaic traditions had already been translated into Greek; Marcus' task was not to translate, but to arrange and to edit. Of course he was no literary artist, but only a humble clerk, not very familiar with Judaism or with the Old Testament; perhaps he had never seen Palestine in his life, but he had a good memory, and he had heard a great deal about that land, or rather about the Master who had lived and taught there. His style was crude—but so were the translations from the oral Aramaic. His theological theories, as far as he had any, were somewhat rigid and even, on one or two points, perverse; and yet he was capable of dealing fairly, in the main, with his material.

This tradition was certainly easier to handle than the somewhat abstruse letter of Paul to the Romans, which for twenty years the church had treasured and pondered, and read now and then along with the Law and the Prophets which Paul had expounded—though his spoken words had been far simpler than his dictated letter! Some of Paul's ideas Marcus had grasped, though he was not sure he could state them clearly, or even that he understood them fully. One thing he did understand from Paul or from other teachers: the Jewish authorities had crucified Jesus out of ignorance and disobedience, in blind zeal for their own false interpretation of the sacred Law; but God had turned evil to good, and had triumphed over their sin by accepting Jesus' death as a sacrifice or a ransom for many, Gentiles as well as Jews. That was an idea a Roman could grasp, and it certainly threw light upon the mystery of the Messiah's death, otherwise the blindest act of fate in all human experience. But for the most part Marcus preferred the preaching of Peter—simple and straightforward, stories and anecdotes rather than theological theories. And Peter he not only had often heard, but had even helped with his Greek; for Marcus knew a little Aramaic, and Peter spoke considerable Greek, but not always in good form and sometimes without finding the right word for what he wanted to say.

Most important of all, Marcus had to write in haste, and in the midst of danger. For the church was threatened with martyrdom; it had, in fact, only recently experienced the blood purge which resulted in the deaths of Peter and Paul. A few patrons of Christianity might possibly be found in the court: the wife of a general who had returned a few years before from Britain was said to be interested in the Christians, though she now lived in retirement.[21] But little help could be expected from that quarter at best; for Nero was himself at last, brutal, vindictive, merciless, and the massacre of Christians had become his latest diabolical diversion. Antichrist sat upon the throne; the last days had arrived—and yet the end might not come for a long time. True, the persecution had now relaxed, and some thought that it was over; there could be no complete extermination of the Christians, not at present; and news had come from other churches, elsewhere, that they were at peace—though the news from Palestine was ominous. It was in Rome alone that the Emperor's fury had thus far expended itself. There were Jews in Rome; but their own position at the moment was not sufficiently secure to enable them to persecute the followers of Jesus, had they wished to do so (we are thinking of the point of view of Marcus and his readers). Earlier emperors, Tiberius and Claudius, had driven the Jews from Rome; perhaps Nero would some day do the same. Nor did it occur to Marcus to write his

[21] Pomponia Graecina, the wife of Plautius—Tacitus, *Annals* 13. 32.

book for Jewish readers anyway; what he put together
was a narrative of the mighty works and death of Jesus—
a book largely devoted to explaining why Jesus had died
—and he wrote it, not for Jews, but for Gentile converts
and "listeners to the word." The Jews might be blind,
and deaf to the message; but the Gentiles, as Paul had
said—"they will listen."

III

THE EVANGELIC TRADITION

THE SOURCE MATERIAL AVAILABLE FOR THE COMPOSITION OF Mark's Gospel was the evangelic tradition as it circulated in the church at Rome in the middle or late sixties of the first century.[1] Not all of this material was public property —some traditions would naturally be better known than others. Nor must we suppose that Mark would use all that was available to him for the purposes of his book— he was not writing a modern "definitive" biography! In fact, he was not even writing a "Gospel" in our sense of the term, for no such book existed as a model. It was only a little book about Jesus the Messiah, the Son of God, gathering up the current information about his life and death, endeavoring to prove that he had already been the Messiah or "Son of Man" while he lived on earth, and explaining why he had died on the cross. His teaching is taken for granted, but it is not quoted extensively nor expounded. (Later writers of Gospels were to supply this lack.)

1. To begin with, there was the narrative of Jesus' death—the longest continuous narrative in the traditions about him and the earliest to take fixed form, according

[1] Of course Mark did not set out to look for "source material"; the material was already at hand.

58

to modern form critics. This, the current Roman *passion narrative,* Mark expanded and edited. For one thing, he believed the Last Supper had been a Passover meal, and so he revised the narrative to make this clear. For another, he believed that Jesus meant his death to be a sacrifice "for many"; that also had to be made clear. The Jewish trial and condemnation of Jesus provided another feature that must be added. As a result, our fourteenth and fifteenth chapters of Mark can be analyzed into two, or even three, classes of material: (1) the old, traditional passion narrative of the Roman church, ultimately derived from Palestine; (2) the additional material inserted into it by Mark, some of it perhaps from Palestine, some not; and finally, (3) some verses which may be later still, inserted in the interest of the risen Jesus' appearance in Galilee rather than in Jerusalem. Two verses, Mark 14:28; 16:7, may be later even than the Gospel of Luke, though earlier than Matthew. The Appendix to John, chapter 21, as well as Matthew's resurrection narrative, shows the influence of this conception of the location of the appearances.[2]

2. Of first importance, as leading up to the passion narrative, and explaining the opposition that led to Jesus' death, are the *controversies,* thirteen—possibly fifteen—in all, and found in 2:1–3:6; 3:22-30; 7:5-13 (or 23); 8:11-12 (or 21); 9:11-13; 10:2-12 (or 9?); 11:27-33; 12:13-34 (or 40). The material they contain was doubtless Palestinian

[2] See chap. vi below, "Jerusalem or Galilee?" See also B. W. Bacon, "The Resurrection in Judean and Galilean Tradition," *Journal of Religion* 11:506-16.

in origin; and though the controversies were still "live" issues in the sixties, wherever church and synagogue were still in conflict, there is little reason to question that they go back to Jesus himself.[3] They appear in Mark chiefly in two blocks, each with an appropriate editorial conclusion. The first block concludes, "Then the Pharisees left the synagogue and immediately consulted with the Herodians about Jesus, with a view to putting him to death."[4] The second ends, "And after that no one dared to question him."[5]

These controversies are the following:

1. Healing—2:1-12
2. Eating with sinners—2:13-17
3. Fasting—2:18-22 (19b is a gloss; 20 is probably editorial)
4. Sabbath observance—2:23-3:6 (two traditions are combined here)
5. The source of Jesus' "power"—3:22-30
6. External requirements of the Law—7:5-13
7. "Signs"—8:11-12
8. Elijah's return—9:11-13
9. The permission of divorce—10:2-9
10. Jesus' authority—11:27-33
11. Civil obedience (the tribute money)—12:13-17
12. The resurrection (marriage)—12:18-25
13. The interpretation of the Law (the chief commandment)—12:28-34
14. The Messiah not Son of David—12:35-37
15. Warning against the scribes—12:38-40

[3] See *The Growth of the Gospels,* chap. v, esp. pp. 105 ff.
[4] Mark 3:6.
[5] Mark 12:34b.

It is a question if the last two really belong to the controversy series: they are more like attacks upon the scribes
than controversies with them, and the question of the
Davidic sonship seems more like a debate within the
church than a controversy with the scribes, though its
form reminds us of number 8:

> 9:11 "Why do the scribes say . . . ."
> 12:35 "How can the scribes say . . . ."

Perhaps both subjects, the Son of David Messiahship and
the return of Elijah before the end, were questions of
even greater moment within the Christian community
than in the unadjourned debate with the synagogue.
Both were related to the expectation of the earthly kingdom—an idea which survived for a long time in early
Christianity,[6] and had been gradually overcome only by
the time of Origen.[7]

The first four of these controversies are obviously Galilean; those numbered 9-13 are located by Mark in Judea
—or Perea—and Jerusalem, where clearly 10 and 11 belong. Of the others, 5 and 7 may be drawn from the Q
cycle, and also 15. Like 8 and 14, number 6, on the external requirements of the Law, may reflect discussion of
the question, and appeal to Jesus' authority, within the
church itself.[8]

3. Into this material were inserted *other small collections:*

---

[6] Cf. Rev. 20:1-6; Luke 22:28-30; the Montanists.
[7] See "The Eschatology of the Second Century," *American Journal of
Theology,* 21:193-211.
[8] Cf. Acts 10-11 and 15. See *The Growth of the Gospels,* pp. 104-10.

1. The day in Capernaum, perhaps originally from Peter's reminiscences—1:21-39
2. The chapter of parables—4:1-34
3. The call, appointment, and mission of the disciples—1:16-20; 3:13-19; 6:7-13, etc.
4. The two parallel accounts of journeys about Galilee and in the north—6:34-7:37 and 8:1-26
5. The great "central section" on "the Way of the Cross," as Bacon called it—8:27-10:45
6. The journey to Jerusalem—10:1, 46-52; 11:1-24
7. The "Little Apocalypse"—for which no more appropriate place could be found than just before the passion narrative

This last, an originally Jewish, or Jewish-Christian, apocalypse—13:6-8, 14-20, 24-27 (31?)—had perhaps already received additions, from Q or elsewhere, which thus expanded it into practically its present form in Mark 13. Whether this Little Apocalypse, either in its original form or as expanded, was identical with the "oracle" which Eusebius says the Jerusalem Christians received some time before the fall of that city—and so were warned to flee and went to Pella, east of the Jordan[9]—is not at all certain, but is an interesting possibility. The material is old: "the abomination of desolation" is thought by many to be a reference to Caligula's attempt to set up his own statue in the temple at Jerusalem in the year 41.[10] Jews, and likewise Christian Jews, saw in it a fulfillment of the dire prophecy of Daniel.[11]

[9] *Eccl. Hist.* 3. 5. 3. It is a question whether fleeing to Pella is the same thing as fleeing "to the hills." Also, Pella was a "city of the Gentiles," as modern archaeology proves.
[10] Mark 13:14. See Josephus, *War* 2. 10 = §§184 ff.
[11] Daniel 9:27; 12:11.

4. Much of this material, the old evangelic tradition, contained *sayings of Jesus*. (1) Indeed, the earliest stories of his life and deeds were probably told because of the sayings they enshrined and illustrated—they were the simple settings for priceless jewels.[12] (2) Some of the sayings, however, were detached; and if we find them used in other connections by Luke and Matthew, and conclude that these later evangelists derived them from their common source, Q, the possibility is still open that Mark also drew them from this source—which was either a written collection or, more probably, still an oral collection, quoted by Mark from memory and therefore not always in the form followed by Luke or Matthew. The fact that Matthew and Luke use these sayings in other connections, and then repeat them when following Mark, together with the fact of the sometimes divergent form of the sayings in Mark, seems best to be explained by the hypothesis that Mark also is drawing from the common stock—either the collection Q or its equivalent in some common cycle of "sayings of the Lord."[13] (3) In addition, there is a group of sayings, fourteen in number, that deserve to be studied by themselves—the so-called *Son of Man sayings*. These reflect a distinct theological point of view, a very primitive one, and pre-Marcan; that is, they probably reflect a stage somewhere between the original Palestinian tradition and the form in which it was used

[12] See esp. Vincent Taylor, *The Formation of the Gospel Tradition* (1933); also Dibelius, *The Message of Jesus Christ*, esp. Pt. II.
[13] Cf. *The Growth of the Gospels*, pp. 129-31.

by Mark.[14] Some of the sayings seem to distinguish clearly between Jesus and the celestial figure so named; one or two might almost be translated "man" in general, or "men"; some of them identify Jesus with a celestial apocalyptic figure of the end of days to such an extent that the term is little more than an equivalent for the first person singular; and others view the celestial figure almost without reference to Jesus. Seven of the sayings occur in the central section—"the Way of the Cross"—where they are combined with, or form an integral part of, the three passion announcements.[15] The great "paradox of the cross," for Mark as for Paul and many another, was the self-humiliation of the glorious, celestial "Son of Man" in accepting suffering and death for the sake of "many." [16]

These fourteen "Son of Man" sayings are as follows:

2:10   "The Son of Man has authority on earth to forgive sins."
        The saying is found in a controversy section, and many
        scholars incline to view either the whole of vs. 10 or per-
        haps even vss. 5b-10a as secondary.[17]

2:28   "Hence the Son of Man is lord even of the Sabbath." The
        very form of the saying—"hence," or "so that"—and its

[14] See "Form Criticism and the Christian Faith," *Journal of Bible and Religion*, 7:9-17; also the symposium, ibid., 7:172-83.

[15] See J. Wellhausen, *Das Evangelium Marci* (2nd ed., 1909); A. H. McNeile, *New Testament Teaching in the Light of St. Paul's* (1933), chap. i.; B. H. Branscomb, *Commentary on Mark*, pp. 146-49; my *The Gospel of the Kingdom*, esp. chap. iv and note on p. 197; also the important essay by Clarence Tucker Craig, "The Problem of the Messiahship of Jesus," *New Testament Studies*, ed. E. P. Booth (1942).

[16] Mark 10:45. Paul does not use the term, "Son of Man," but he repeatedly emphasizes the self-humiliation of the Son of God.

[17] Cf. Bousset, *Kyrios Christos*, p. 40; also Menzies' note, *ad loc.*

dependence upon vs. 27, which is complete without it, suggest that the addition is inferential and editorial. Its motive is clearly theological, and it probably reflects the theology of the later Christian community, not the teaching of Jesus. Some scholars hold that vss. 10 and 28 were originally spoken of "man" in general; but Mark certainly understood "the Son of Man" to mean Jesus, the future celestial Messiah already living upon earth.

The next seven sayings are from the central section on "the Way of the Cross."

8:31 The first passion announcement. It is worth noting that Matthew substitutes a pronoun, "he," for "the Son of Man."

8:38 "The Son of Man will be ashamed of him, when he comes in the glory of his Father, with the holy angels." This is probably a Q saying, more briefly and more originally reported in Luke 12:9, "He who denies me in the presence of men *will be denied* in the presence of the angels of God" (the Son of Man is named in vs. 8). Matt. 10:33 has, "Anyone who denies me in the presence of men, *I too will deny* him in the presence of my Father who is in heaven." Apparently "the presence of men" belongs to the Q form of the saying. It is extraordinary that Matthew again substitutes a personal pronoun for the title. Some have thought that Mark here preserves the oldest form of the saying, and that Jesus thought of the future celestial judge as distinct from himself, the rewarder and punisher of those who confess or disown Jesus as their Master.

9:9 The disciples are to keep secret the story of the Transfiguration until after "the Son of Man should rise from the dead." Again this is an editorial setting, and introduces the dialogue about Elijah's return.

9:12*b* "And how is it written of the Son of Man, that he should suffer many things and be set at naught?" It is note-worthy that Luke omits the whole pericope, also that the outlook of the pericope is the same as that of the passion announcements, and even agrees with them in style: the Son of Man is to "rise," not—as elsewhere in the primitive tradition—to "be raised"; but first he is to "suffer many things"—as in 8:31. Lohmeyer, it is to be observed, brackets vs. 12*b* as a gloss.[18]

9:31   The second passion announcement.

10:33   The third passion announcement. These are clearly secondary, and are now generally recognized as such.

10:45   "The Son of Man did not come in order to be ministered to, but to minister, and to give his life as a ransom for many." This great climax to the central section, "the Way of the Cross," is either completely rewritten by Luke or omitted in favor of another saying, and is located in a wholly different place—22:27, "I am like a servant among you." Once again the theological outlook of the verse is apparent, especially in its second half, the "ransom" saying. It cites Jesus' example, apparently in proof of the sound-ness of his teaching. If we take Luke's parallel into ac-count, it is probable that the saying, originally detached, circulated at first in the form which Luke retains. The parallelistic form of Luke 22:27 is completely convincing.

Thus far, with one exception, the sayings have all been clearly of a type for which "the Son of Man" and the first person singular, whether verb or pronoun, were inter-changeable. (Matthew's usage, for example in 16:13, is

[18] *Commentary*, p. 183, n. 1.

good evidence that this could still take place even at the late date of the composition of that Gospel.) We come now to a text that cannot be treated thus.

13:26 "Then they will see the Son of Man coming on the clouds." This is practically a quotation from Dan. 7:13, and it occurs in the heart of the final section attributed to the Little Apocalypse—forming in fact its climax. Here is the verse with which our study of the Son of Man sayings should begin if we were trying to rearrange them in chronological order and study them in their progressive adaptation to later church theology and devotion. The source and present location of the saying, as part of the Little Apocalypse, and the probability that the section once circulated without reference to the belief that Jesus was the Son of Man both point toward the probable origin of this type of Christology: it originated among those for whom the vision of Daniel was the authoritative statement of eschatological doctrine.

The three sayings that come next—

14:21a "The Son of Man goes as it is written of him" (cf. 9:12),

14:21b "Alas for the man by whom the Son of Man is betrayed" (some manuscripts omit "the Son of Man" here), and

14:41 "The Son of Man is delivered into the hands of sinners" (Luke again omits, and the Sinaitic Syriac manuscript of Matthew reads "I am delivered")—all three of these sayings are clearly secondary. The first two are supper sayings, and read like devotional comments on the passion narrative; the third is closely allied to the passion announcements, especially the second, 9:31. It should also be observed that the saying occurs in the account of

Gethsemane, which as a whole is generally viewed as secondary tradition. Finally, the only reason for the substitution of the title for the first person singular is the backward
reference it affords to the passion announcements—here is
an example of what J. Weiss called Mark's "pragmatism."

Finally we come to

14:62   "You will see the Son of Man seated at the right hand of
the Power and coming with the clouds of heaven." Like
13:26, this is based upon Dan. 7:13. It belongs in a section, vss. 55-65, which has frequently been pronounced
secondary—especially have vss. 61*b*-62 been thus criticized
—on the basis that no disciples were present at the Jewish
"trial" and that the account is so patently at variance
with all normal Jewish legal procedure, and also for other
reasons which we will consider later. Further, the saying
is in no sense germane to the question of the high priest,
save upon the *Christian* assumption that the Son of Man
is identical with "the Christ, the Son of the Blessed," a
view the high priest and his colleagues could not be expected to share. The quotation seems to be appended to
the simple and emphatic "I am," and to be added for the
purpose of explaining how Jesus could be "the Christ"
in spite of the nonfulfillment of the messianic expectation
either then or later, including the period up to the date
of Mark's writing. The theological outlook of the quotation is practically identical with that of 8:38 and 9:1. This
outlook, in all three places, is in turn identical with that
of 13:26—and not only its origin, in Dan. 7:13, but also
its point of entry into the early pre-Marcan tradition
seems clear. It reflects the theology of those who thought
of Jesus exclusively in apocalyptic terms, and were prepared not only to go through the tradition and substitute
"the Son of Man" for his simple "I," but also to insert

appropriate quotations or paraphrases of their favorite apocalyptic texts in order to give his life its appropriate setting—as they assumed—and his teaching its proper interpretation. *Where* this took place, we shall discuss in a later lecture.

5. Still other material was found and used by Mark, including some that is clearly *legendary*—that is, "popular" stories handed down orally in extended form, and not necessarily all of them really Christian in origin—for example the great legends of the Gerasene demoniac, 5:1-20; the death of John the Baptizer, 6:17-29; the walking on the sea, 6:45-52; and the cursing of the figtree, 11:12-14, 20-25. The use of the term "legend" in this connection is one that is strictly accurate and at the same time severely limited in the field of literary and historical criticism. The term had its origin in the study of historical sources, chiefly the lives of the saints; and instead of emphasizing the unreliable or questionable character of the stories, it really suggests that a kernel of substantial fact is contained in them. As Martin Dibelius says:

A widely popular usage sees in the term "legend" the designation for false history. But that is not the meaning of the term. "Legends" mean, in the language of the Christian middle ages, stories of the life or death of a saint which were customarily read on the saint's day (*legenda* means "what is to be read"). And this presupposes that legend has to do with a "saintly" life and a blessed death, by which the believer can be edified and inspired to emulation. For this reason the legend must be told in such a way that two things are apparent: how the saint was so holy that he controlled his surroundings; and how his life, from infancy, was under divine guidance and protection and hence was lifted out, by God Himself, from the mass of human misfortune.[19]

We may not be sure, in every case, what is the "kernel of substantial fact" in Mark's legends, but we are certain that they were not spun out of thin air.

Thus grew our earliest Gospel, not as a literary composition by one skilled in historical or biographical writing, but as the transcript and ordered arrangement of the traditions current in the church of his day. It is a Western writing, Hellenistic, probably Roman; obviously written in Greek, and not, I believe, the translation of a completed work in a Semitic tongue; and yet resting back upon traditions that were certainly far older than its own date, undoubtedly Palestinian in origin, and circulating originally in the Aramaic language spoken by the common people of Galilee and Judea in the days of our Lord. The Aramaic substratum juts out repeatedly—*Boanerges, talithá kumi, effathá, korban, Abba, Hosannáh,* for example. And so do certain Latin words: *grabbatus* (bed), *legion, quadrans, denarius, speculator, centurion*—words not proving, perhaps, the Roman origin of the work, but certainly reflecting the Greco-Roman medium through which its traditions had passed.

To sum up the hypothesis briefly, then, the order of the "development" of the Gospel *in its author's own mind* was perhaps as follows:

1. The *passion narrative*—its basis derived from the

---

[19] *The Message of Jesus Christ,* p. 174—see the whole passage.

common Christian tradition of Jesus' last days in Jerusalem.

2. To this were prefaced the *controversies* with the Jewish authorities, leading up to the passion narrative, and explaining how Jesus came to be rejected by his own people.

3. The *Petrine element* was introduced into this combination, chiefly at the beginning of the narrative—adding much of the "vividness" for which Mark is famous.

4. In order to give examples of Jesus' teaching, certain *passages from Q*—or from the common *oral* tradition of the collection of Jesus' sayings designated by that symbol —were added, apparently from memory rather than by citation of a document. These are chiefly sayings relating to discipleship, a subject of great importance in Q.

5. The *Little Apocalypse* was added for a similar reason: it satisfied in some degree the urgent demand for Jesus' own answer to the question of the date of the Parousia and the "signs of the end." It was of course assumed by Mark to contain authentic teaching of Jesus.

6. Finally, the mass of current *oral tradition*—not so extensive in Rome, probably, as in Palestine and Syria— was drawn upon for additional material upon numerous points as the narrative proceeded.

7. The whole took shape—a more or less predetermined form, considering that the passion narrative, the controversies, and the Little Apocalypse were probably already in fixed oral if not partly documentary form—it took shape in the author's own mind in something like the order just sketched; and in the actual writing of it the

author supplied the introductions, summaries, transitions, and moralizing applications so characteristic of his work —the last-named so unlike the style and method of our Lord!

Thus grew the Marcan Gospel, not, I think, by successive stages, but in its author's own conception before he sat down and wrote it out at length, laboriously and painstakingly: its growth is the growth of its materials and sources, not the repeated redaction either of the author himself or of a succession of later "hands." No writing in the New Testament bears more clearly the marks of unity of authorship, from its brief title and swiftly moving first sentences to its abrupt and perhaps fragmentary close.

Such is the light which a study of the form and structure of the Gospel of Mark throws upon its purposes, its method of composition, its materials, and its sources. If it no longer betrays "the freshness and vividness of original composition," at least it bears the marks of the hard age in which it arose, reflects the circumscribed outlook of its author and first readers, and reveals most clearly the paucity of the materials at the author's disposal—especially for a presentation of Jesus' teaching. We are a whole generation, and more, removed from the events described in its pages, and many leagues removed geographically. Its author lives in another world than the Palestine of Jesus' days—one can scarcely believe that he ever saw Palestine, or knew Judaism and its sacred Scriptures intimately and sympathetically. He may, of course,

have known John Mark, as well as Peter; he may, indeed, have been John Mark; but I should feel much more
certain in describing him as a Roman Christian—though
possibly not born in Rome—who reflected at an early day
the somewhat cold and unimaginative outlook characteristic of at least a major strain in the heritage of that
ancient church. Yet such as it is—and the more certainly
so, the more clearly we recognize just what the book is—
it remains an extremely valuable document of primitive
Western Christianity; though it by no means provides us
with all we wish to know about the life and teaching of
our Lord, or the life and teaching, activities, and beliefs,
of the early church.[20]

The view I have been expounding may seem to some
persons to be inadequate, and a poor substitute for the
old-fashioned one which made Mark the secretary and
amanuensis of an apostle, writing down Peter's fresh and
vivid recollections of the Master. On the contrary, if I
may hazard a personal testimony, this "Multiple Source
Hypothesis" of modern criticism, and especially of form
criticism, seems to me definitely superior to the older
view. In place of the testimony of one man, we have the
"social" tradition of a whole community, the widely
shared possession of a whole group—of two groups, in
fact, the Palestinian and the Roman. In place of one individual's interpretation of Christ we have a tradition
which shines like a shaft of light through the refracting,

[20] These paragraphs are taken from *The Growth of the Gospels*,
pp. 136-39. See also Weiss, *The History of Primitive Christianity* (1937),
chap. xxii, § 4 (II, 687 ff.).

expanding prism of a rich and varied religious experience, and by its many-splendored radiance begins to prove how much was contained in the apparently simple and single, but really complex and manifold, manifestation of the divine mystery—the revelation of the mystery hid from past ages, the message of God through Jesus Christ, his Son, our Lord.

The Gospel may be outlined, on the basis of this analysis of its contents and sources, as follows:

Introduction—1:1-13

I. Jesus in Galilee—1:14-9:50

    a) About the Sea of Galilee—1:14-5:43; including the controversies in 2:1-3:6 (plus 3:22-30), and the collection of parables in chap. 4.

    b) Wider journeyings—6:1-9:50. The section 7:24-8:26 might be called Mark's "Great Insertion," [21] following 7:1-23, in which Jesus rejects the external requirements of the Law and then turns to the Gentiles.[22] It also includes the controversy over signs, 8:11-12, and the two apparently parallel narratives of the journey in 6:34-7:37 and 8:1-26. This is followed by the section on "the Way of the Cross," 8:27-10:45, with a nucleus of discipleship sayings in 9:33-50. These various groups were probably pre-Marcan collections of material.

II. On the way to Jerusalem—chap. 10

III. In Jerusalem—chaps. 11-12; including the second collection of controversies, 11:27-12:40

IV. The apocalyptic discourse—chap. 13; including material from

---

[21] *The Growth of the Gospels*, p. 140.
[22] So Johannes Weiss.

the "Little Apocalypse," in vss. 6-8, 14-20, 24-27, and possibly 31. There was no other place for his material than here, unless the whole discourse was to be made postresurrection—as in some of the later apocrypha.

IV

THE APOSTOLIC PREACHING

THE VIEW OF THE DEVELOPMENT OF MARK'S GOSPEL SET
forth in these lectures takes it for granted that the Gospel
grew backwards, so to speak. The earliest nucleus of the
Gospel was the *passion narrative*. To this was prefaced
the account of the ministry of Jesus as a kind of bridge-
approach, leading up to the great crucial and transform-
ing week in human history. The *controversies* explained
the opposition to Jesus. The *sayings* illustrated his teaching—the "Son of Man sayings" in particular explaining
Jesus' own view of his death, and expressing the earliest
attitude of the church to the death of Jesus: his death was
no blind whim of fate but the voluntarily accepted will
of God, and it had resulted in the working out of God's
purpose for the salvation of many. Other materials which
Mark found in the tradition and made use of in his book
showed Jesus in his career of healing and teaching, accompanied by his disciples—the group whom he "made
apostles" [1] and "appointed" to be the founders of the
church. But Mark is not writing history or biography, nor
even giving an account of Jesus' teaching; he is writing
an apology, an explanation of the death of the Messiah,

[1] Mark 3:14, 16 ff.

76

and the passion narrative is in his mind from the beginning.[2]

Perhaps in this preoccupation of the author is to be discovered the significance of a clause—which no one understands!—found in the very first chapter: that during the temptation in the wilderness Jesus "was with the wild animals." [3] Just as his followers had lately, at Rome, been forced into the arena to face the wild beasts, so the Master himself had faced them—and in facing them, and flouting Satan, he had accepted his martyrdom from the start. It is not suggested that Jesus fought the beasts and overcame them, physically. Perhaps they were considered, as often in Jewish folklore, to be "materializations" of demons, or as possessed by them—the wild *djinn* of the waste, with Satan as their owner and prince. If so, no doubt Mark—or whoever first so described our Lord's sojourn in the wilderness—thought that Jesus overawed them, and was among them like Adam, the first earthly man, in the Garden, or like Daniel, unharmed in the den.[4] They would not dare attack the Son of Man, the divine "second Man who is from heaven," as Paul had called him.[5]

The late Professor Bacon held that the Gospel of Mark centers, like an ellipse, about two great focal ideas, symbolized by the "two sacraments of the gospel, Baptism

[2] Mark 2:20; 3:6; etc.

[3] Mark 1:13.

[4] Both this pericope and the saying, "I saw Satan fall as lightning from heaven," Luke 10:18, reflect the same point of view as that of the old section on the binding of the strong man, Mark 3:27.

[5] I Cor. 15:47.

and the Supper of the Lord": the first half is the preaching of repentance, the second half the preparation for
death, the *Via Dolorosa* of the Messiah, his crucifixion
and death. Professor Bacon's suggestion is illuminating,
but the Gospel scarcely divides that neatly. Both ideas are
there—but both are present throughout; one flows into
the other. The whole Gospel deals with the question, Why
did Jesus die? This was a question which had been asked
from the outset of the Christian movement. Paul calls it
the "stumbling block," "the scandal," of the cross.[6] If
Jesus was the Messiah, God's Son, why then had he died
the shameful death on the cross, the last penalty of a
criminal in expiation of his misdeeds? How, in the first
place, had it come about historically, and as the consequence of what series of dire, unfortunate events? And
further, how had it come to pass in the eternal counsels
of God? To both forms of the question Mark undertakes
to provide an answer: He died (1) because the Jewish
leaders rejected him, and out of envy[7] delivered him up
to Pilate. The reason for their envy is clear from the
series of controversies which Mark gives. For he had
worsted them in argument, and his following had continued in spite of all their efforts to oppose him. He died,
moreover, (2) because he willed to die, to lay down his
life a ransom for many.[8] He died, finally, (3) because it
was the will of God, and so it had been written of him
in the ancient, inspired scriptures.[9] It had to be so, for God

[6] Gal. 5:11.
[7] Mark 15:10.
[8] Mark 10:45; 14:24; cf. John 10:18.
[9] Mark 8:31; 9:12, 31; 10:33; 14:21, 36.

willed it: δεῖ . . . . παθεῖν. The basic and fundamental structure of the Gospel thus had a very clear and decisive motive. We may call it apologetic: but Mark simply *had* to answer the questions which were in the minds of all his readers, Jewish and Gentile, Christian and non-Christian.[10]

Thus it was no accident that the Gospel grew around— or grew up to—the old traditional passion narrative embedded now in chapters 14–15. The same place had been held by the passion narrative—that is, by some account or other of the death of Jesus—in the apostolic preaching from its very start. It is taken for granted everywhere in Paul, whose letters are the oldest Christian writings we possess; and Paul implies that it was his oral teaching and preaching as well—in his reproach of the Galatians, for example, "before whose very eyes Jesus had been crucified" in his preaching,[11] and in his confession to the Corinthians that he had determined to "know nothing among you save Jesus Christ and him crucified." [12] It is found in the speeches in the first part of Acts—as historic fact, as a strange mystery, not yet as the luminous and revealing declaration of divine grace which we find in Paul. It is found in that summary of the early preaching in Philippians 2:6-11, perhaps quoted from some creed-like hymn of the early Gentile churches.[18] So Professor

---

[10] The latter part of this paragraph is taken from *The Growth of the Gospels,* p. 108.

[11] Gal. 3:1.

[12] I Cor. 2:2. See also I Cor. 15:1-4.

[18] See F. C. Porter, *The Mind of Christ in Paul* (1930); also Ernst Lohmeyer's new commentary in the Meyer Series (1930) and his Heidelberg Academy paper, "Kyrios Jesus" (1928).

Dibelius views it, and so I have translated his rendering:

> He lived a divine existence,
>   but thought nothing of grandeur
>   nor of the glory of divine nature;
> he gave up glory and grandeur,
>   taking a poor existence in exchange—
>   became humanlike in form,
>   and humanlike in bearing.
> He chose renunciation,
>   obedient to death—
>   to the death upon the cross.
> Therefore God exalted him to highest glory
> and gave him the name above all names. . . . .[14]

To put it briefly, the message of the gospel was an "evangelical" message from the beginning. It was the message of the Kingdom—which had been Jesus' own message, of course, from the outset of his ministry[15]—but it was also the message of the crucified Messiah, the Messiah Jesus who had died and risen from death, and whose death and resurrection were—or rather *was,* as one continuous act—the great crucial step in the inauguration of God's Kingdom, on the part of God himself. Something had to be got out of the way, some obstacle that lay in God's very path; and the Cross was the instrument of its removal, the tool by which the stone was rolled away—"it was a very great one!" To put it

---

[14] *The Message of Jesus Christ,* p. 5; see also his commentary in Lietzmann's *Handbuch* (3rd ed., 1937), esp. the long notes on pp. 72-74 and 79-82. The late B. W. Bacon pointed out in his *The Gospel of the Hellenists* (1933) the frequency of ten- and twelve-line hymns in ancient religious literature; see Pt. IV, pp. 311 ff.

[15] Mark 1:14-15.

still another way, overstating the case but perhaps making it somewhat clearer: Jesus' gospel was the gospel of the Kingdom; the apostolic gospel was the gospel of the death and resurrection of Jesus the Messiah; and yet the latter was believed to be the continuation and proclamation of the former. In opening the Gospel of Mark with what perhaps became later its title, "Beginning of the Gospel [of Jesus Christ the Son of God]," its author certainly recognized no distinction between the gospel *of* Jesus and the gospel *about* Jesus. That is a modern distinction! [16] Mark assumed that the two were one—and so did everyone else in the apostolic age! If it had not been so, many a passage in the Gospels might have been worded differently; and we should have had not only less of interpretation in the record of Jesus' life and teaching but also, probably, even less of a record!

Let us turn back once more to the speech of Peter in the house of Cornelius at Caesarea, given in Acts 10:37-43.

You know what has been taking place in the land of the Jews, following "the Baptism" preached by John—how it all began in Galilee with Jesus of Nazareth. God anointed him with holy Spirit and with power, and he went about doing good and healing all who were oppressed by the devil, for God was with him. (We are witnesses to all he did both in the country of the Jews and in Jerusalem!) And they put him to death, hanging him on a tree. Then God raised him up, on the third day, and let him appear visibly—not to all the people but to witnesses chosen in ad-

[16] The warning set forth by Henry J. Cadbury in his book, *The Peril of Modernizing Jesus* (1937), applies also to the Gospels.

vance by God, that is to us. . . . . And he [God] charged us to preach to the people and to testify that he is the one who is appointed by God to be the judge of the living and dead. All the prophets bear witness to him, that through his name everyone who believes in him shall receive remission of sins.[17]

Most of the main features of the apostolic preaching are to be found here, in brief summary—and as some of them were still being stated in the middle of the second century when the old Roman baptismal formula, the basis of our so-called Apostles' Creed, came into use: John and "the Baptism" he preached, which was all along "the beginning of the gospel";[18] Jesus' anointing by the holy Spirit, and his consequent power over the demons, over diseases, and even over death; his ministry of compassion and help; his death at Jerusalem, through the "envy" and hatred of the "rulers," that is, the Jewish authorities who denounced him before Pilate and so procured his death by crucifixion as an insurrectionist and disturber; his resurrection on the third day, when he became Messiah or Son of God and entered into his glory;[19] the message of forgiveness of sins "in his name"; his future coming to judge the living and the dead; the divine choice and calling of the apostolic "witnesses" to these events, who are the bearers of the new message of salvation; and the divine attestation in the words of the prophets of old. These are the main features of the apostolic

[17] See Dibelius, *The Message of Jesus Christ*, p. 4; also my "Historical Origins of the Church," *Anglican Theological Review* 21:190 ff.
[18] Acts 1:22; Mark 1:1. See *The Gospel of the Kingdom*, chap. iii.
[19] Cf. Rom. 1:3; Luke 24:26.

message; they represent the earliest interpretation of the
prophetic mission, death, and resurrection of Jesus, and
the earliest proclamation of the message of salvation—
that is, forgiveness of sins, preservation through the approaching crisis of the "last things," and safety in the
judgment. One cannot call it a system of theology. It is
too simple for that. Instead it is a set of convictions growing out of (1) Jesus' gospel of the Kingdom; (2) the
apostles' testimony to Jesus' death, resurrection, and exaltation; and (3) their experience of the outpoured Spirit.
Call it "mystical" if you like—though that surely is not a
very good description of it—but whatever the true and
adequate word for this tremendous apostolic experience,
it is perfectly clear that the earliest Christianity we know
had a twofold basis, and stood upon two feet, history
and experience. The history was there, in the oral traditions of Jesus' life and death; and the experience was
equally real, and could now be shared anywhere and by
anyone, by Saul the persecutor, by Gentile centurions and
treasurers and simple men of Cyprus and Cyrene and
Antioch, by pagan Galatians, and by cosmopolitan Corinthians and Romans—Jews and Greeks, bond and free.
There were no limits to the range of this experience of
the risen, glorified Christ.

It is so to this day; for we greatly lessen the effective-
ness of the Christian message if we insist upon getting it
all inside the four walls of past history, ignoring the
present reality of the risen, glorified Christ who still has
words to say to his church and to the world through his

Spirit.[20] Moreover, we shall never catch the real ethos of
the New Testament until we abandon our exaggerated
"historicism" and recognize that some things were spoken
and done by Christ after the death on the cross had ended
his earthly career. The words of Christian prophets,
speaking in his name, were undoubtedly inspired by his
Spirit. The interpretations of his life and teachings set
forth by the "teachers" of the early church were legitimate interpretations, the expansion and reformulation of
his sayings were legitimate expansions and reformula-
tions,[21] not because they were logically valid, or because
they represented justifiable historical inferences as to what
Jesus must have thought and said, but because they were
inspired by his Spirit and sprang out of the living tradition, out of the vital stream of religious experience which
came historically, and still came spiritually, from him.
Unless we are prepared to grant the reality of the Spirit,
and the valid basis of this primitive Christian experience,[22] I fear we shall not bring much back with us from
our critical forays in the field of New Testament history,
literature, and religion. That principle—the primary and

[20] See my "The Spiritual Christ," *Journal of Biblical Literature* 54:1-15;
also the "Note on Christology" in my *Frontiers of Christian Thinking*
(1935), and my essay, "The Significance of Critical Study of the Gospels
for Religious Thought Today," in the volume presented to Professor Harris
Franklin Rall, *Theology and Modern Life*, ed. Paul A. Schilpp (1940).

[21] Esp., e.g., in the central section of Mark, "the Way of the Cross,"
8:27–10:45. On the importance of the *teacher* in the early church—distinct from the preacher—see B. S. Easton, "The First Evangelic Tradition,"
Journal of Biblical Literature, 50:148-55; F. V. Filson, "The Christian
Teacher in the First Century," *ibid.*, 60:317-28.

[22] See P. G. S. Hopwood, *The Religious Experience of the Primitive
Church* (1937).

indisputable reality of the Spirit, to be apprehended by faith, and genuinely to be known through direct human experience—is the vital spark of evangelicalism, today no less than it has always been.[23]

As we view our religion, Christianity is essentially and always a doctrine of grace and presupposes the reality of the divine Spirit, one with the risen, glorified Christ himself. It has sometimes been represented as primarily a doctrine of man, of his finiteness, his sin, his unworthiness in God's sight, his inability to please God, indeed of his actual incapacity to receive or benefit by divine grace. But in the view of evangelical Christians—and that also includes Methodists and Anglicans—our theology is not anthropocentric, or *hamarto*-centric, but theocentric, Christocentric, *gratia*-centric. And our religion is forever a saving *faith*. This, we believe, was true of the earliest gospel, as it was first proclaimed in Galilee and throughout the world in apostolic days. If the Christian message had been a series of intellectual claims or affirmations, supported by the miracles of Jesus, let us say, as the complete evidence of the truth of these affirmations, then assent to the truth of Christianity would have been simply an act of the rational intellect, satisfied with the evidence thus adduced and subscribing without reserve to the various formulae of affirmation. But faith is never mere intellectual assent; it was not so in "the first days of the gospel" any more than it is today. Faith means believing

---

[23] The principle is also recognized in Catholicism, though by no means to the same extent, and combined with certain other principles, institutional and theological, which counterbalance it.

beyond the range of evidence—not in spite of the evidence, but beyond it. Faith means the discovery of further evidence, higher in kind and of a subtler validity than mere outward proofs. As virtue is its own reward, so faith supplies, in a similar way, its own verification. This does not mean that it supplies outward and visible proofs; the evidence is still the spiritual things "which are spiritually apprehended." A faith which rests upon tangible demonstration is a contradiction in terms, and is really "unfaith, clamoring to be coined to faith by proof," as the poet said. Faith means trust, adventure, self-committal; and its evidences are still the "things not seen."

Hence we may hold that the earliest Gospel, like the latest, was an *interpretation*. Mark undertook to interpret Jesus as the "Son of Man" of apocalyptic hopes, and John later undertook to interpret him as the eternal Logos veiled in flesh, while Matthew and Luke interpreted him as the Jewish Messiah or the new Lawgiver of ransomed Israel. The one whom they thus interpreted, in various categories of first-century thought, is the one whom we also must interpret—but equally from the standpoint of faith, not proof. For the progress of discipleship is still that of growing faith—as Paul described it, "from faith to faith."

The Gospel of Mark, I have tried to show, is a community possession, a "church book," the transcript of a living body of tradition then in circulation, rather than a private literary composition. It was written for the church's use, and it rested back upon the church's tradition and faith. It was anonymous from the start, and made no claim to literary consideration or quality. I doubt if it was to be found in the bookstalls of the capital. None of the littérateurs of the time ever laid eyes on it. It was a *Volksbuch,* circulating in private among the oppressed, despised, and persecuted handful of Christians—though copies were made, after a time, and carried to other Christian communities.[24] It probably got to Asia Minor and to Syria about as soon as anywhere else. As a transcript of a living community tradition, the Gospel of Mark relies not only upon the early passion narrative and the oral records of Jesus' life and teachings, some of which may already have been gathered into little collections, sequences, groups of sayings; it relies also upon the apostolic experience which supplemented and interpreted those traditions. The church, like Paul, aimed to know Christ not merely "after the flesh" but as a risen, glorified spirit: "to know him— and the power of his resurrection." Hence the background against which we must study the Gospel of Mark is twofold: the evangelic tradition, which we considered in the preceding chapter, and the apostolic faith and its formulation in preaching, which we are considering in the present one.

I said a little while ago that Mark had the passion narrative in mind from the very beginning of his book; now we must add that the passion narrative meant to

[24] See K. L. Schmidt, *Eucharistérion für Gunkel* (1923). See also Donald W. Riddle, *Early Christian Life as Reflected in Its Literature* (1936) and "Early Christian Hospitality: a Factor in the Gospel Transmission," *Journal of Biblical Literature*, 57:141-154.

him, as to every other early Christian, the events leading
up immediately to Jesus' resurrection and exaltation. And
that meant exaltation *as Messiah*—not a mere reanima-
tion of his body; not one more resuscitation of a dead
person, doomed to die again, like Lazarus or the youth
at Nain; not a ghostly apparition, as evidence, after a
fashion (but evidence always to be doubted!), of human
survival of bodily death or of the immortality of the soul.
For Mark, as for the church of his time, Jesus' resurrection meant resurrection and glorification as Messiah, as
the celestial Son of Man.[25] This is the view reflected in
all our earliest documents, in the early chapters of Acts,
and in the Gospel of Mark. It is the view which Paul "received" by tradition,[26] and which forms the substratum
of his whole teaching and theology. It is presupposed, as
the very earliest formulation of Christian teaching,
throughout the New Testament.[27] And it forms the basis
of the theology of Mark's Gospel—so far as it has a
theology—as we shall see in a later chapter.

[25] See Weiss, *History of Primitive Christianity* (1937), Bk. I, esp. pp.
23 ff. and chap. iv.
[26] I Cor. 15:1-7; Rom. 1:1-4; etc.
[27] See W. Bousset, *Kyrios Christos* (3rd ed., 1926), chap. 1; B. W. Bacon,
The Apostolic Message (1925); C. H. Dodd, *The Apostolic Preaching* (1936).

V

WAS MARK WRITTEN IN ARAMAIC?

THERE CAN BE LITTLE DOUBT, AT PRESENT, THAT THE GOS-
pel tradition arose in a Semitic milieu. Jesus himself spoke
Aramaic; his Bible was the Hebrew scriptures, our Old
Testament, whether he read it—or heard it read—in Hebrew or in a running translation later known as the
Targum; his teaching presupposed a familiarity with the
Law, the Prophets, and the Psalms, with the current
synagogue liturgy, based very largely on scripture, and
also with the traditional interpretation of scripture set
forth by the scribes; he always took for granted the religion of his people, Judaism, the highest religion in the
world of his time. Moreover, Jesus' disciples were all
Aramaic-speaking Jews, and the tradition as they and
others handed it down was doubtless in that tongue—
as we have noted, the various surviving tags of Aramaic,
such as *Abba, effathá, talithá kumi,* clearly indicate this.
The gospel tradition was originally Aramaic, though
translated from time to time, and probably from a fairly
early date, into Greek. As we have also seen, some of the
parallel sayings in the Gospels presuppose a common
Greek original, suggesting a single translation, while

others presuppose an original farther back, suggesting diversity of translation and transmission.

At first glance it might seem most probable that the Gospels themselves were composed or compiled in Aramaic, and then later turned into Greek either by one or by more than one translator. This would account for the outstanding phenomenon of interrelation between the Synoptics—namely their peculiar combination of agreement and divergence—especially if the translator of a later Gospel, say Matthew or Luke, glanced occasionally either at "Aramaic Mark" or "Greek Mark" as he proceeded. There are surely enough variables in this theory to account for almost any amount of divergence or agreement! But it is a very complicated theory—and the ancient rule of logic still holds good. "Hypotheses are not to be multiplied beyond what is necessary." [1] A much simpler explanation of the Aramaic element in the Gospels, and of their combined agreement and disagreement, lies ready at hand, namely that the oral tradition which circulated for some time in Aramaic was translated piecemeal and "as anyone was able," to use Papias' phrase, and finally came to be gathered together in the Greek writings which we know as Gospels. We owe a great debt to Professor Torrey and other "Aramaicists" for emphasizing and, to some degree, reconstructing the Aramaic original of these traditions; but I think the theory of Aramaic Gospels goes much too far.

Some of the evidence adduced for the existence of Ara-

---

[1] The rule of "economy": *Hypotheses non multiplicandi praeter necessitatem.*

maic Gospels is very questionable. For example, a passage in Tosephta Yadaim has been interpreted as evidence of the existence of Christian Gospels in Aramaic before the fall of Jerusalem, before A.D. 70. The passage reads: "The rolls [if this is what *ha-gilyônim* means] and books of the Minim do not defile the hands." As explained by the "Aramaicists," the term *gillayôn* was derived from *euaggelion,* and clearly refers to the Christian Gospels; and the term Minim ("apostates") means the Christians.[2] But, to begin with, it is most strange that a term which was not used in Greek to describe our Gospels until towards the middle of the second century[3] should have been borrowed from the Greek, given a Semitic transliteration—not a very close transliteration!—and been commonly used in the fifties or sixties of the first century in Palestine! True, there are references to the Christian Gospels in the later rabbinic tradition, after the Greek Gospels had come to be known by that name, and as a result of contact and conflict between church and synagogue in the second, third, and fourth centuries—for example in Bab. Sabbath 116a. But this is not the same thing as *gilyônim* in the passage in the Tosephta. The term used is a derisive pun, 'Awen-gillayôn or 'Awon-gillayôn—a worthless book margin(?) or a book margin(?) of iniquity. In fact, the passage in Tosephta probably does not refer to Gospels at all, or even to books, but means simply this: "The *gilyônim,*" that is, the margins,

---

[2] Charles C. Torrey, *Documents of the Primitive Church* (1941), chap. iii, "Aramaic Gospels in the Synagogue."

[3] See Justin Martyr, *Apol.* I, 66: ἃ καλεῖται εὐαγγέλια—written *c.* 150, and implying that the name was already known and used.

end pages, or blank columns, "in the sacred rolls belonging to the heretics do not defile the hands," that is, are not sacred—even though they contain sacred texts. Only the inspired text itself is sacred. If *gillayôn* had meant "gospel"—that is, a Christian book—I cannot see how there could have been any possibility of the later play on words in *'Awen-* or *'Awon-gillayôn*.[4]

The full passage of Tosephta Yadaim 2:13 reads, "The book margins and the books of the Minim [apostates] do not defile the hands. The books of Ben Sira [our Ecclesiasticus], and all the books which were written from that time on, do not defile the hands." It would be most extraordinary if, in this statement, the Christian Gospels were first described as excluded from the canon, and then the exclusion of Sirach and the Apocrypha were added! Whatever "the book margins of the Minim" may mean, here and in the similar passage in Tosephta Sabbath 13:5 where the phrase occurs, it simply cannot mean the Christian Gospels. Nor does "Minim" mean Christians, I believe, either here or in the Shemoneh Esreh or elsewhere in ancient Jewish literature or tradition where the term is used.[5] Can anyone suppose that the Minim of the Talmud, with their wrongly patterned and wrongly worn tephillin, their strange speculations about the "two powers," and

---

[4] See R. Travers Herford, *Christianity in Talmud and Midrash* (1903), p. 155. The singular is of course *gillayôn*, as in the Old Testament; *gilyôn* means a turban! Meanwhile, the word for roll, or scroll, is *megillah*, also as in biblical Hebrew.

[5] See Israel Abrahams, *Companion to the Authorized Daily Prayer Book* (rev. ed., 1922), pp. lxiv-lxv, and refs. given there.

their peculiar formulas of greeting[6] were Jewish *Christians?* Surely these were not the peculiar or—from the orthodox Jewish point of view—the dangerous features of Christianity! Nor can the denial of the resurrection and of the inspiration of the Old Testament [7] be attributed to Christianity! The "Minim" were more probably Jewish Gnostics.

The passage in Tosephta Yadaim should certainly be taken in connection with the corresponding statements in Mishnah Yadaim, which it supplements. We read there:

3:4 The blank spaces in a scroll [of the scriptures] (*gillayôn sheb^asêpher*) that are above [the writing] and that are below, and that are at the beginning and at the end, render the hands unclean.

3:5 All the Holy Scriptures render the hands unclean. The Song of Songs and Ecclesiastes render the hands unclean.

4:5 The [Aramaic] version that is in Ezra and Daniel [8] renders the hands unclean. . . . . [The Holy Scriptures] render the hands unclean only if they are written in the Assyrian character, on leather, and in ink.[9]

It is obvious that the references in the *Tosephta* to "book margins and books of the apostates" and to the writings of Ben Sira and those who came later *supplement* what the Mishnah had to say about "book mar-

---

[6] Hermann L. Strack, *Jesus, die Häretiker, und die Christen* (1910), pp. 48*, 63*. Cf. Ber. 9:5 (the name of God used in greeting), R. ha-Sh. 2:1-2 (new moon observed at the wrong date), Meg. 4:8 (tephillin worn the wrong way), Sanh. 4:5 (the two "powers"), etc.

[7] Sanh. 10:1.

[8] Ezra 4:8–7:18; Daniel 2:4–6:28.

[9] Tr. Canon Danby, pp. 781 ff.

gins" in copies of the sacred scriptures, about Canticles and Koheleth and the Aramaic sections of Ezra and Daniel. Would anyone suggest translating *Mishnah* Yadaim to read: "The Gospel in a scroll, above and below, at beginning and end, renders the hands unclean," that is, is sacred? This seems to me the very *reductio ad absurdum* of the hypothesis that *gillayôn* means "Gospel"!

Nevertheless, I would not be counted among those who entirely reject the views or the evidence adduced by the Aramaic school. Torrey's views, for example, are frequently condemned—or approved!—*en bloc,* without a careful weighing of the evidence. If anyone will take the time to go through his notes in detail, he will be richly rewarded.[10] They are the best thing of this kind we have had since Dalman, Merx, and Wellhausen. Unfortunately, the Greek text from which Torrey sets out is almost always that of Westcott and Hort, that is, the manuscripts Aleph and B. On the other hand, Wellhausen always kept his eye on "Cantabrigiensis," that is, Codex D, and the Western text generally. There is little doubt, nowadays, that Westcott and Hort held too tenaciously to their hypothesis of a "Neutral" text. As Professor Lake pointed out in his essay in the Bacon-Porter memorial volume, *Studies in Early Christianity* (1928), it is the growing conviction of New Testament textual critics that the Western text deserves far more consideration than Westcott and Hort accorded it. For the plain truth is, the

---

[10] *The Four Gospels* (1933), Notes on the New Readings, pp. 289 ff.; *Our Translated Gospels* (1936).

canons of textual criticism are not so few or so simple as they have sometimes been represented: "Prefer the shorter reading—since copyists always expand a text"; "Prefer the harder reading—their tendency is to smooth out and make easier the text they read"; "In parallel passages and in quotations, prefer the independent or divergent reading—since copyists tend to harmonize." All these rules are good within proper limits, but they must be applied with great care. Copyists do not *always* expand their texts, nor do they *always* harmonize, assimilate, or complete, nor do they *always* smooth out or simplify the hard readings. The tendency to do so was probably more general after the third century than it was before. Moreover, in the case of Mark, which was a less popular Gospel than Matthew, and probably had fewer copies made during its first century of existence than either Matthew or Luke, we must be constantly on the watch for variant readings that escaped the later process of stereotyping. At the same time, other tests are applicable, chiefly one which has never been adequately recognized, namely that of author's style. It may be thought that form criticism puts an end to such a test, the separate units in the tradition having been translated by different persons, each of them writing—or speaking—in a different style. But this is not a full account of the situation. For after all the compilers or editors of the Gospels do have each a distinctive style, which has been impressed upon the tradition; anyone can see this for himself by consulting a Greek harmony or synopsis, or by examining Hawkins' tables in *Horae Synopticae*.[11] And if the choice lies among three variants, say, of which one is demonstrably in the style of the evangelist whose text is under consideration, there can be little doubt that this is the one to be preferred. Finally, in a group of variants, that reading must be preferred which explains the others—whatever manuscript contains it, and whichever bough of the genealogical tree supports it. All our manuscripts have "mixed" texts; and a good early reading may, and often does, survive in a "late" manuscript or family; for the copyist, in this case, may quite conceivably have made use—either visually or by memory—of a very early exemplar.[12]

I have thought it necessary to mention these principles of textual criticism, in discussing the retranslation of the Gospels into Aramaic, for the reason that many of the difficulties with the present Greek text can be solved—and should be solved—on the basis of existing manuscript evidence, and even, in some cases, of warrantable conjecture, as to the original Greek readings, before appeal is taken to a purely hypothetical Aramaic original. Only when the case appears hopeless, on the Greek basis, should change of venue to another court be sought. Some —indeed many—of the retranslations into Aramaic are unnecessary, if the variant readings in the Greek manuscripts and in the early versions are taken into account. The text of Westcott and Hort is now more than sixty years old. Several ancient and most important manuscripts

[11] Second ed., 1909.
[12] See my "Studies in the Text of St. Mark," *Anglican Theological Review*, 20:103 ff.

have turned up during this interval—the Washington, the Koridethi, the Sinaitic Syriac, the Michigan-Chester Beatty and other papyri—and new editions of texts have appeared, such as those of the Old Latin and the Egyptian versions, or Sanday and Turner's reconstruction of the New Testament text of Irenaeus, also new editions of the Greek, Latin, and Syriac church fathers—all this has taken place since 1881. We now recognize, for example, that a combination of Codex D, the Itala, and the Sinaitic Syriac is in some passages equally deserving of consideration along with Aleph and B. Professor Torrey's hypothesis that D etc. reflect the influence of a corrective Aramaic tradition—a view that would have attracted Bishop Chase! [18]—is probably unnecessary except upon the assumption of the existence of a "Neutral" text. Instead of D etc. being influenced by Aramaic, they are nearer, at some points, to the Aramaic of the original tradition just because they are nearer to the readings of the autographs, beneath which at many points lay this Aramaic oral tradition. At the same time, Aramaic retranslation of doubtful readings may quite conceivably be of real help in choosing which is the more probable original reading.

Nevertheless, after all due consideration has been given to the apparatus of variant readings in our Greek Testament, it still remains true that the chief *content* of the Gospels is not Greek in origin, but Semitic. In spite of the exaggerations of earlier scholars, who spoke of bibli-

---

[18] See Frederic Henry Chase, *The Old Syriac Element in the Text of Codex Bezae* (1893), *The Syro-Latin Text of the Gospels* (1895).

cal Greek as "the language of the Holy Ghost," a peculiar
Jewish-Greek tongue not known outside the Bible, and
in spite of the reaction against this absurd exaggeration,
it is becoming generally recognized today that there is
really something unique about the language of the New
Testament, and especially of the Synoptic Gospels—something
not to be explained wholly by the parallels found in
the Egyptian papyri.

The New Testament documents were, no doubt, written in a
language intelligible to the generality of Greek-speaking people;
yet to suppose that they emerged from the background of Greek
thought and experience would be to misunderstand them completely. There is a strange and awkward element in the language
which not only affects the meanings of words, not only disturbs
the grammar and syntax, but lurks everywhere in a maze of
literary allusions which no ordinary Greek man or woman could
conceivably have understood or even detected. The truth is that
behind these writings there lies an intractable Hebraic, Aramaic,
Palestinian material. It is this foreign matter that complicates
New Testament Greek.

So Hoskyns and Davey, in *The Riddle of the New
Testament*.[14] And Fiebig, in the Preface to his *Erzäh-
lungsstil der Evangelien*,[15] may be quoted to the same
effect:

The Hebrew-Aramaic shines through the Greek. . . . . How
anyone can hope to understand the New Testament, and especially the Gospels, scientifically, without study or knowledge of
Hebrew-Aramaic, is to me quite incomprehensible. . . . . Anyone

[14] Second ed., 1936, p. 24.
[15] Leipzig, 1925.

who, like Luther, has once caught a glimpse of the beauty of the
Hebrew, and has come to recognize how it opens up a fundamentally important perspective for the interpretation of the Gospels, cannot help but inquire, again and again, about the
Hebrew-Aramaic original of the traditions they contain.

It is this inquiry into the Hebrew-Aramaic original of
the tradition that leads students to turn eagerly to Dr.
Torrey's illuminating notes, and to follow step by step,
as far as it is possible to follow, his evidence for the underlying Aramaic. If we do not go all the way with him, we
do not cease to be grateful for the light he has given us
upon many an obscure passage. Let us consider first his
proposed emendations of the Greek—many of them
shared by others, upon other considerations than that of
Aramaic translation. I shall take up, at this point, only
his proposals concerning the text of Mark.

I. Emendations of the Greek

1:2b The quotation from Mal. 3:1 may very well be viewed as a
gloss, on the basis of the parallels in Matthew 11:10 and Luke
7:27.[16] It is easier to assume a gloss here in the text of Mark
than to assume that Matthew and Luke chanced to agree in
omitting the verse in order to use it later in their Gospels!

4:31 "A grain of mustard seed, which is the smallest of all the
seeds on earth." It is not impossible that the redundant ὅν
was copied by dittography from the preceding μικρότερον. But
it is also not impossible to translate the neuter participle here;
and I should think either the first or the second occurrence of
ὅταν σπαρῇ, "when it is sown," a more probable example of
redundance—a redundance that strongly supports Lohmeyer's

---

[16] See my article on the text of Mark referred to above.

hypothesis that two variant forms of the parable have been combined by Mark. One read: "To what will we compare the Kingdom of God? To a mustard seed which, when it is sown upon the ground, grows up and puts out great branches [and becomes a tree], so that 'under its shadow the birds of heaven can build their nests.'" The other read: "In what parable will we set it forth? It is like [a mustard seed]; though it is the smallest of all seeds on earth, yet when it is sown it grows larger than all herbs, so that 'under its shadow the birds of heaven can build their nests.'"

6:22 Torrey thinks the αὐτῆς is redundant; so perhaps did the copyist of the ancestor manuscript of the Lake group—though it may be due to a form of dittography, in a series of feminine genitive endings. On the other hand, many readers, both Jewish and Gentile, would think it strange that a princess—in 6:14 Herod is a "king"—would so demean herself, and the word reflects this feeling: "Herodias' own daughter came in and danced before the banqueters!"

6:49 "They thought it was a demon"—rather than a "ghost" (R.V.). But "phantasm" is the same as δαιμόνιον, which the Sinaitic Syriac apparently read here. This is no doubt an improvement in translation.

7:7 Torrey supposes the word ἐντάλματα to be "a very ancient interpolation" from the LXX of Isa. 29:13. It would certainly ease the translation to shift it from the text to the footnotes!

8:10 Torrey's solution of the riddle of "Dalmanutha" is one of the most probable ever offered.[17] The word "Magdaloth" was no doubt easily confused, in a tradition—or by writers—un-

---

[17] The conjecture was Dalman's and is to be found even in the 1894 edition of his *Grammar of Jewish Palestinian Aramaic*, p. 133 n. He assumed that the word came from "Magdaloth" (Hebrew, "towers"), that ν was substituted for γ, and that then the first and second syllables got reversed. The inversion is not impossible, but it is a good deal more difficult to imagine a substitution of Ν for Γ in an uncial manuscript than when the letters are written lower case! The expression "Migdaloth Chinnerim" occurs in Meg. 70*a*.

familiar with Palestinian topography, and especially with Galilee.[18] The queer variants in B N W 28 sy^s p^{45} D* ⊕ λ φ and the Itala manuscripts may be seen in Nestle or Legg; they were all guesses! Somewhat the same variety in readings may be found in Matthew 15:39. But, after all, more than half of the variants come down for something beginning with "Mag"— for example "Mageda," "Magedan," "Magdala," "Magedam," "Magadan," "Magdalan"; and one thinks of the LXX, which got "Magada" out of "Migdol" in Josh. 15:37. And let us not forget that the Caesarean text (⊕ λ φ) had "Magdala" all the time, both here and in the parallel verse of Matthew!

9:13 This is one of the most difficult verses in the Gospel, as Lohmeyer and other commentators recognize. Turner proposed a rearrangement of the order, inserting vs. 12*b* after vs. 10.[19] Another possible arrangement is vss. 10, 11, 12*a*, 13*c*, 13*ab*, 12*b*. Torrey proposes the restoration of a sentence, following Matthew. Lohmeyer views vs. 12*b* as a gloss. The sense of the whole paragraph, which many scholars suppose to be derived from later debate over the significance of John, is that Jesus, like John, must suffer many things. (Luke significantly omits the section, while the Fourth Gospel flatly denies the identification of John with Elijah, 1:21.) Torrey's conjecture is surely in line with the most probable meaning of the passage.

10:19 "Do not defraud" is omitted by Torrey, as due to dittography after ψευδομαρτυρήσῃς. This is not unlikely, and is, I think, more probable than Lohmeyer's conjecture, deriving it from a hypothetical "Christian Galilean" form of the decalogue.[20] But note that B* W sy^s and many other MSS omitted it—perhaps not simply out of regard for the wording of the Ten Commandments; that is, they either omitted it or, possibly,

---

[18] See the series of articles by C. C. McCown, "Studies of Palestinian Geography in the Gospels," *Journal of Biblical Literature*, 50:107-29; 57:51-56; 59:113-31; 60:1-25.

[19] *The Study of the New Testament, 1883 and 1920* (3rd ed., 1926), p. 61.

[20] *Galiläa und Jerusalem*, pp. 72 f.

had never heard of it! The command may even seem to be Pauline—cf. I Cor. 6:7, 8; 7:5; and also I Tim. 6:5. But in reality it was good ordinary Jewish and Old Testament teaching. Its omission by both parallels here strongly suggests that it is a later gloss, like some others—from the Pauline viewpoint—in the Gospels.

12:4 "Again he sent to them another servant, and him they covered with blows," instead of "wounded in the head." Torrey builds upon Burkitt's conjecture, ἐκολάφισαν; his translation is that of Swete, who took the Greek as it stands. Probably exegesis had something to do with textual transmission at this point: "wounded in the head" was taken to be a reference to John the Baptist, as in the Old Latin (k) decollaverunt, modified later to in capite vulneraverunt.

12:30 Torrey omits "and with all thy mind"—as do Codex D and the Itala. But it could readily be omitted by homoeoteleuton, or because of its omission in vs. 33. Both parallels have it, and so has Deut. 6:5 LXX Bγ. Why must it be viewed as "a very early interpolation from the LXX"?

13:15 Torrey omits the words "go down, nor" and reads: "Let him who is on the housetop not go in . . . ." The omitted words are ascribed to a careless recollection of Matt. 24:17. But it is difficult to see why the words are "quite impossible" here, and not in the passage in Matthew! Would the verb "enter in," taken alone, presuppose a western or Egyptian house with an inside stair, whereas the Palestinian stair was outside? I confess I feel as much difficulty without the words that Torrey omits as I do with them. Perhaps the reading of D Θ etc. would help: "Do not go down into the house." If only we could read "and" or "or" instead of "neither" (μηδέ)! At any rate, the καταβάτω is certainly suspect, and the present text of Mark looks like a conflate of Matthew's καταβάτω with Mark's εἰσελθάτω. Luke is no help, for he alters to fit the situation of the siege of Jerusalem. Luke 17:31 reads μὴ καταβάτω; but there the point is the suddenness of the Parousia, like the destruction of Sodom, and the futility of going down to gather up one's goods. Here the command is to flee to the hills—and no one could do that without first going down from the roof. I agree with Torrey that the words are a Matthean gloss and should come out—I have had them bracketed in my copy for several years!

13:27 Torrey adopts Blass's conjecture that "heaven" at the end of the verse is an accidental accretion, easily suggested by the parallel in Matthew. The resulting translation is certainly smoother: "from one end of the earth to the other." [21] But there is evidence in Jewish literature not only for this expression (Deut. 13:7; Jer. 12:12) but also for "from one corner of heaven to the other" (Deut. 30:4; Ps. 18:7; etc.). Lohmeyer suggests that Mark has mixed the two idioms, and thinks of an ascension of the elect from the center of the earth to the height of heaven. The idea reminds one of the ascent of Israel to the stars in the Assumption of Moses (10:8 f.), and Paul's conception of the ascension of Christians (I Thess. 4:17). Perhaps if we had more of the Little Apocalypse than the two or three fragments embedded in Mark 13, we could solve the problem.

14:72 Torrey is not alone in omitting "the second time" and reading simply: "Thereupon a cock crew." Aleph and c have omitted the phrase for a long time! But we might go further; the textual evidence in vss. 30 and 68, and the parallels, seem to warrant but one cockcrow. I cannot see the deep significance in the double cockcrow that Lohmeyer does.[22] Probably some proverbial expression lies back of the words, the point of which is merely "by cockcrow," that is, before dawn; cocks usually crow several times at dawn! Or, possibly, "Before the cock can crow twice, you will deny me three times over!" Torrey's explanation of the origin of the gloss is very convincing. It is the location of the numeral in the sentence that gave rise to all the trouble: "Before the cock crows thrice you will deny me." Of

---

[21] Cf. Wellhausen, *Skizzen,* vi, 190 n., who has this translation.
[22] *Commentary,* p. 313.

course the sentence demands a comma—but where are you placing it, before "thrice" or after it?

15:34 Torrey has a very good note on the cry of desolation, "My God, my God, why hast thou forsaken me?" But it is doubtless the tradition in *Greek* that accounts for the wide divergence in spelling. Crude as it is, the Gospel of Peter seems to stand closer to the Semitic original than do our canonical Gospels—even in mistaking the word "God" for the word "strength" or "power." Codex D seems to be influenced by the Hebrew of Psalm 22, not by Aramaic; while Codex B seems to suggest no knowledge of either Semitic tongue—or if B interprets it to mean, "Why hast thou sacrificed me?" the interpretation is clearly wrong.

II. EMENDATIONS INVOLVING ARAMAIC

1:43 The Greek participle ἐμβριμησάμενος, "being very angry," has caused commentators no end of trouble. It should be taken in connection with the reading of D *a ff*² *r* in vs. 41, ὀργισθείς, and both with 3:5 μετ' ὀργῆς. "Charging sternly" is much too toned-down a translation, both in R.V. and in Torrey's version. I should not wonder at all if *r'gaz* lay at the heart of the expression, and that the Greek translators took it in too strong a sense. At the same time, what Lohmeyer says on 3:5 is important: "Wherever in the evangelic tradition we come upon words describing Jesus' emotions, they have nothing whatever to do with the 'genuinely human' traits of the man Jesus [as the exegesis of forty years ago maintained!], but with the *genuinely divine* reactions of the [supernatural] Son of Man, as most notably in the Fourth Gospel. Every word points to his 'anger and grief' or his 'anger and compassion'—both are characteristic of the divine Figure sojourning upon earth, who came hither for man's sake and by sinful man was met with hatred." [23] *That* doubtless goes too far in the other direction. But there

[23] *Ibid.,* p. 69.

was probably in Jesus—and in Mark's conception of him—
something strange, overpowering, and awe-inspiring, and on
occasion even terrifying; he was no genial, ordinary man, this
one who commanded the demons and they obeyed him, and
who quieted the thunders and raging storms at sea with a
word; and we must expect to find traces of this conception in
other passages than those in which he beards the roaring elements and calms the witless maniacs. It is of interest that Lohmeyer thinks the story of the healing of the leper in 1:40-45
has come down in two forms, one in which Jesus reprimands
him, the other in which he pities him—and in both heals him.
Lohmeyer accounts for the divergence, and the variants, as due
to local oral tradition, which by no means died out at once
after the Gospels were written.

3:17 "Sons of the thunderstorm" for "sons of thunder," as the
byname of James and John. This is an interesting conjecture—
though the real significance of the epithet is still as obscure as
ever. *Regesh* is of course a familiar *Hebrew* word for "a noisy
crowd"; so is *rogez,* "tumult." Some Greek MSS have
Βανηρεγές, which the Syriac clearly presupposes.

3:31 f. "They sent to call him, for a throng was seated about
him." Mark's Greek can *almost* be phrased as Torrey supposes
the Aramaic to have read. Mark's καὶ and his ὅτι are sometimes picked up by mistake and then laid down—like a carpenter reaching for a chisel and instead picking up a gouge,
and then quickly laying it down for the proper tool!

4:4, 15 "Some seed fell upon the highway"—instead of "by" or
"beside." Torrey insists that Mark's παρά is "flat mistranslation"
of ʿal. But Mark has some peculiar uses of παρά—see 3:21; 5:26
—and Lohmeyer translates "on the road" without appeal to
Aramaic!

4:8, 20 "Thirtyfold" etc., reading ἕν, "one," each time. So do
D ⊙ and the Latin version. Of course the earliest MSS did not
distinguish EN with a breathing from EN without one! Torrey
would not have had to clear up so much debris if textual study

had not come to a halt, in many quarters, with Westcott and Hort—or if English and American students had studied not only Westcott and Hort's text but also their notes![24]

4:12 This is, for exegesis, probably the most important correction of Mark.

> "The parables are for those who are outside;
> those who 'indeed see, but without perceiving;
> who indeed hear, but without comprehending;
> lest they should turn and be forgiven.' "

Torrey explains Mark's ἵνα as a translation of "the frequently ambiguous *dî*," which was here only a relative pronoun, not the conjunction "in order that." This is a very simple explanation, and let us hope it can be maintained; but it is also true that Matthew used ὅτι in his parallel, and also—in spite of the views of Wernle, Windisch, and others—that Koine Greek had weakened the word ἵνα, so that it sometimes bore the meaning of "that" rather than "in order that."[25] How much has been read into this verse, into this single particle! Johannes Weiss was sure that it reflected the *Verstockungsgericht* or "judgment of stubbornness" which Mark believed to have overtaken the Jewish people. That theory may still belong to Mark, but, as Lohmeyer maintains, it can find no support in the conjunction ἵνα. Of course there is some support for the word, and more

---

[24] But on the question as a whole see Wellhausen, *Skizzen*, vi, 193, who takes EN as a preposition (with B), not a numeral.

[25] See W. D. Chamberlain, *An Exegetical Grammar of the Greek New Testament* (1941), pp. 182 ff. Although it remains true, as Robertson maintained (*A Grammar of the Greek New Testament in the Light of Historical Research*, 3rd ed., 1919, p. 985), "With all the wide extension of ἵνα in Western Hellenistic, at the heart of it there is the pure telic idiom," still a glance at the lexicons, even Thayer's, will show the weakening of the purposive meaning and its wide variety of use in colloquial Greek. See also Robertson's article in the Bacon-Porter volume, *Studies in Early Christianity*, ed. S. J. Case (1928), pp. 51-57. Cf. H. Windisch, "Causal ἵνα in Later Koine," *ZNTW*, 26:203; C. H. Turner, "Notes on Marcan Usage," x (4), *Journal of Theological Studies*, 29:356-59.

for the idea, in Isa. 6:9-10, though it does not harmonize with the rest of the Book of Isaiah.

4:13 "Any parable." This is hardly necessary if 4:10 is corrected: "They asked him about the parable"—a reading which I believe is the right one (see 7:17). The whole point of vs. 13 is that the disciples inquire about *this* parable, not parables in general, or Jesus' parables as a whole. It is generally recognized that vss. 11-12 are an editorial insertion into the pericope—which is secondary to vss. 3-8, in any event. But even without bracketing the editorial insertion, the singular is required in vs. 10. The plural probably crept in from vs. 2 or vs. 13. As it stands, vs. 13 undoubtedly has reference to the whole little collection of parables that is to follow in chap. 4.

5:1 The reading "Gadarenes" is of course perfectly respectable in Greek, without support from Aramaic. If Mark wrote "Gerasenes"—and he may well have done so; his Palestinian geography is not first-class—then Matthew probably corrected it in his parallel, and the corrections got back into the text of Mark sometime later. Origen's "Gergesenes" may be only a guess,[26] though there are good scholars who support it—as also do Θ sy^s bo.

5:21 "While he was still at the lakeside, ..." Here an appeal to Aramaic is unnecessary. Mark's Greek can be pointed with a period after αὐτόν, and a free translation would give what Torrey requires (cf. 3:31 f.). It is to be noted that the editorial "frames" of the tradition—introductions and conclusions of pericopes—are the least fixed of the gospel materials, even in translation!

6:3 Torrey's note is sound, though he has not emended his translation. Lohmeyer seems to overlook Luke's agreement with Matthew against Mark. I believe that what Mark wrote was something like this: "the son of the carpenter, the brother of James and Joses . . . ."—a reading to which I believe a large number of textual critics would now be inclined to subscribe.

[26] Perhaps based on the O. T., e.g., Gen. 16:16.

6:8 f. "Take . . . . no staff." [27] Torrey's discussion of the text of Mark at this point, as compared with that of Matthew and Luke, is most illuminating. I do not doubt that the difference between Mark and the parallels may be explained by recourse to the probable Aramaic form of the saying, either as Wellhausen proposed, *illâ* for *lâ,* or as Torrey proposes, the aleph carried over from the preceding word, *arkhâ.* That there was a common underlying tradition at this point in all three Synoptics seems undeniable, and is now generally recognized. Mark himself is dependent upon this common tradition, more fully given in Matthew and Luke.[28] But the variation may quite conceivably have taken place in Greek, by inserting ϵi before $\mu \acute{\eta}$ and then spinning $\mu \acute{o} \nu o \nu$ out of the preceding $\dot{\rho} \acute{a} \beta \delta o \nu$ or its second syllable. If one were given to dreaming, he might even guess that $\mu \acute{o} \nu o \nu$ came from a lost $\mu \grave{\eta}$ $o i \nu o \nu$, or even $\mu \grave{\eta}$ $\check{o} \nu o \nu$—"no wine, no bread," or "no staff, no ass"! But it is surely not dreaming to recognize other factors at work here than the Aramaic original. One is the difference in conception—a brief journey during Jesus' lifetime in Mark, the continuous later Christian mission in Palestine in Matthew, both the Jewish and the Gentile missions in Luke. Another is the influence of the Old Testament, especially the Passover regulation in Exod. 12:11: "Thus shall ye eat it: with your loins girded, your shoes on your feet, and your staff in your hand; and ye shall eat it in haste." The early Christian, and even Jewish, interpretation of the Passover in an eschatological sense—the final Passover to introduce the consummation, the final redemption of Israel, the "latter days" to be like the "former days" with a repeated exodus from "Egypt," that is, from present bondage—this idea might also influence the tradition of Jesus' commands regarding the mission of his disciples and their constant state of preparedness for the coming of the end.

[27] *Our Translated Gospels,* pp. 143, 144 ff.
[28] I once argued that this common element was from Q—"The Mission of the Disciples," *Journal of Biblical Literature,* 35 (1916): 293 ff.

6:14 "He said, John the Baptist has risen from the dead." In spite of Torrey and the R. V., I am sure we should read ἔλεγον, "they said," with B (D) it etc. That was the point of the popular rumor. And it makes better sense in view of the verses that follow, especially vs. 16. On the clause, "therefore these powers work in him"—which, by the way, Johannes Weiss proposed to insert at the end of vs. 16—Torrey is surely right. "Powers," in Mark's use of the word, do not "work" but "are wrought," by God, by Jesus, or by the Spirit. I think we may recognize that Torrey's brilliant conjecture—see his note on Matt. 14:2—is the most probable solution of the problem: the Aramaic passive verb, not being vocalized, was misunderstood as an active verb. The error must have occurred in reading a written copy—though not necessarily a gospel. On the other hand, it should be noted that it is a superstitious, half-heathen "king" who is speaking, and Mark—or the tradition—may have represented him as speaking in proper character. He scarcely shared the theological viewpoint of the Jews or Christians in his territory! [29]

6:15 Torrey's suggestion has weight, of course, only if we are sure that ὡς belongs in the text of Mark. It seems impossible that Mark could have written προφήτης ὡς εἷς, and we are not surprised that the Western text omits the προφήτης ὡς. One cannot help suspecting that Mark's true text at this point is preserved, under modification, in Luke—as sometimes happens!— and that he wrote προφήτης τις; also that an early variant, perhaps an alternative translation from oral tradition, was εἷς τῶν προφητῶν—see Mark 8:28. The expression ὡς εἷς, though it would be good idiom in English, "like one," in Greek suggests "about," "nearly," "approximately"—ὡς with a numeral, as in 5:13; but cf. Judg. 16:7, 11 LXX, Lohmeyer. In rabbinic usage k'akhadh may mean "at once," "at the same time"; but in the O.T. it is often, and properly, translated by ὡς εἷς. Wellhausen

[29] On the whole conception of the Baptist *redivivus* see Carl Kraeling's article, *Journal of Biblical Literature,* 59 (June, 1940): 147-57.

took it for a Semitism, "one prophet like another." Semitism
it doubtless is—perhaps mediated by the LXX—as Blass-
Debrunner hold;[30] but its meaning is surely "like one." As it
stands, the reading in Mark is extremely crude—even for Mark!
—and fits the context miserably: "But others said, It is Elias.
But others said, It is a prophet, perhaps [k'] one of the prophets"—or, with the LXX, "like one of the prophets." Only familiarity induces us to acquiesce in such literary crudity as the R.V.,
"It is a prophet, even as one of the prophets." One might even
suspect that 15a and 15b are doublets, and that *both* προφήτης
[τις] and εἱς τῶν προφητῶν are two early glosses to "Elias,"
added earlier than Luke's use of Mark. The ἄλλοι δὲ ἔλεγον ὅτι
then naturally got repeated. Such explanatory glosses would
of course not be required in a Christian—or a Jewish—community, but were here intended only for non-Christian Gentile
readers. With such a complicated text of Mark before us, the
true sense of the passage, and the wording as well, must be
recovered from Luke: "Some said John was risen from the
dead, some that Elias had appeared, and others that one of the
prophets of old had risen"—Elijah was expected to *appear* at
the end of the age, but an ancient prophet arising from the
grave was something else. Heretical as it sounds, I believe it
might even be argued that Mark originally read προφήτης τις
τῶν ἀρχαίων—with 61 bo geo² 33, late as they are! This would
explain the reading of Luke, who added ἐφάνη and ἀνέστη, quite
correctly, and it would also explain the present text of Mark.
The omission by D Itala took place after the text had been
corrupted into its present form, that is, fairly early, when
προφήτης ὡς (or τις) looked like a variant for εἱς τῶν προφητῶν.
One final possibility ought to be considered—that ΩΣ is itself
a corruption of ΕΙΣ. Torrey's solution may be the best, in the
end; but it should be noted that it is one among several competing solutions, and that we do not have an unquestionable
Greek text to work from.

[30] *Grammar,* §306. 5. 5.

6:20 "Herod feared John, whom he knew to be a just and holy man; and he treasured up many things which he had heard from him, for he heard him gladly." Something like this may certainly have been Mark's original, though the present text is not impossible: Herod feared John, knowing he was a saint, and was fascinated by him, but was much perplexed, both by what the prophet said and by the problem on his own hands, namely what to do with a prophet who was also a popular leader, one whom he must keep in custody and could neither release nor put to death without risk of a public revolt. Schmiedel conjectured, on the basis of Luke 9:7, that the "perplexing" clause in vs. 20 should go back to vs. 16, and be translated: "And when Herod heard it he was much perplexed and said, The one I beheaded, John, that one has risen from the dead!"

6:51 Surely this looks like a conflated text! The expression ἐκ περισσοῦ is found here only in the N. T., though Mark 14:31 has ἐκ περισσῶς, also unique. Some MSS omit λίαν; others omit ἐκ περισσοῦ—and they look like real omissions, not "non-interpolations." Torrey gives us good ground for keeping the double expression, which is not unlike Mark's style elsewhere— 1:32, 35, etc.

6:53 "When they came to land on the other side, at Gennesaret, they moored to the shore." The present text is not impossible, though the phrase διαπεράσαντες ἐπί is strange:[31] (Where does Lohmeyer get εἰς? It must be an oversight.) Of course Mark's geography is obscure, especially in these chapters (6–8); and yet the general sense is clear. If we take "to land" with the verb "came"—as Torrey does, and as anyone may do, reading the Greek just as it is—we obtain a sensible translation; so also if we take "came" with "Gennesaret": "And when they had crossed over to the land [from the middle of the lake, vs. 47], they came to Gennesaret and moored." It may be reading in too

[31] Grinfield, *Novum Testamentum Graecum, Editio Hellenistica,* I (1843), 226, notes a similar usage in Isa. 23:2 LXX.

much of a meaning to suppose that Mark always supposed τὸ πέραν meant the eastern shore—as Lohmeyer seems to think.[32]

7:3 "Wash with the fist" is certainly, as Torrey observes, "curious and impossible." [33] The Sinaitic Syriac, the Sahidic, and some Greek MSS omit the word—perhaps as meaningless. Most of the variants are mere guesses, though one of them, found in the Old Latin, is so intrinsically probable that one might almost suppose that it underlies Torrey's translation: *primo*, found in d.[34] Lohmeyer accepts Torrey's conjecture, "do not eat at all," though it presupposes an Aramaic Gospel, and these two verses (3 and 4) are very difficult to imagine as part of an Aramaic book—readers of Palestinian Aramaic would scarcely need to be informed of Jewish customs, and might indeed take exception to the statement as applying to "all the Jews"!

7:11 f. The "korban" saying is surely one of the "oldest"—that is, in form—and most unquestionable sayings in the evangelic tradition. Torrey's argument for an Aramaic basis is most convincing.

7:19 "Which purifies all foods," instead of the R.V., "This he said, making all meats clean." Editors and commentators have wrestled with this clause for centuries! I still think, with Rawlinson and others, that the clause is a gloss, and is best translated somewhat as the R.V. does. What is the sense of the words, "the bowel, which purifies all foods"? Treated thus as a sub-

---

[32] *Commentary*, p. 100 n.

[33] The rule in the Mishnah is similarly obscure: "The hands are susceptible of uncleanness, and they are rendered clean [by the pouring over them of water] *up to the wrist*" (? *adh happarek*, which means either "up to the wrist," or perhaps "to the second joint of the fingers," or "to the knuckle"; the term is variously interpreted). It is interesting to note that Franz Delitzsch used the phrase in his Hebrew New Testament, *ad loc.*

[34] Where the Greek has the curious πυ κμη (sic). Can this be the clue we are looking for? Does the final μη merely repeat the preceding one, while the intervening letters, and space, are all that is left of some glossator's note based on *adh happarek*? The Greek can of course be read without the word.

ordinate clause, it seems to take for granted a common view which the reader will not question. But where is there any evidence for such a theory of the function of the intestinal tract? [35] Moreover, it gives the argument of vss. 18-19 a most banal and pedestrian conclusion: the secondary verse, 19, must have struck some ancient readers as it does some modern, as vulgar and prosaic. Viewed as a gloss, the final clause reflects the view of the Hellenists, as against that of strict observants of the Jewish food regulations.

7:26 "The woman was a foreigner, a Phoenician by birth." There are certainly variants enough to choose from at this point! "Hellene" is undoubtedly used in the sense of "foreigner," "Gentile," here as often elsewhere in the N. T.—not "a Greek" but one who spoke the Greek language. Torrey's translation presupposes the reading of B etc., "a Syrian, a Phoenician," whereas the majority of MSS, including now p[45], read "a Syrophoenician"—that is, presumably, a *Phoenician* Syrian, a coastal Syrian, by birth (or race).

7:34 "Ethpatha!" The correction of the Aramaic is interesting— but it is not surprising that Greek MSS should have altered the form of a word in a tongue unknown to their transcribers.

8:24 "I see the men, *whom* I see as trees walking." Here again we are faced with a complicated textual problem, where the original text is probably buried among the mass of variant readings. The same is true of vs. 26. Torrey's translation can easily be got out of the Greek—even the modern editions, without recourse either to textual criticism or to a reconstruction of Aramaic. As already noted, Mark's use of ὅτι is rather free, and may well reflect either the Aramaic *dî* or the non-literary Koine usage.

8:33 "Away with you, Satan!" literally, "get behind yourself"—as the Sinaitic Syriac reads in Matt. 4:10 and as Blass conjectured here and in Matt. 16:23 on the basis of that reading. Torrey's reconstruction and translation support this reading. That it

[35] See Loisy, *ad loc.,* and Lagrange.

was a difficult expression is clear from the efforts of translators and commentators, for example Epiphanius: ἀπόστα ἀπ' ἐμοῦ κτλ. Some have proposed to omit "Satan," and view it simply as a command to obedience. If the σου was original, it would easily be conformed to the other cases of ὀπίσω μου in the Gospels.[36] The proposal seems a probable one, and the testimony of the Sinaitic Syriac is strengthened by its clear presupposition of ὀπίσω μου in Matt. 4:19 and elsewhere.

8:34 "Take up his yoke," instead of "cross." This is an interesting conjecture. But it sounds like patristic exposition, and rather homiletical at that. And how was it possible to lose one's life (vss. 35 ff.) in bearing a yoke?

9:10 Why is the phrase "among themselves" superfluous? Only if it is taken with the preceding finite verb, rather than—as Mark's style certainly allows!—with the following participle. In fact it is needed, as the motivation of vs. 11. Cf. vss. 33 ff., for both order and motivation.

9:12 "Is indeed Elijah, coming first, to set everything in order? How then is it written of the Son of Man that he must suffer many things and be despised?" This certainly makes sense of the passage, in its present order, as the common interpretation, taking 12a as a statement, does not. But many commentators and some editors—for example, von Soden, in Matt. 17:11— so take the Greek; and so did D 565 etc., who read εἰ before Elias. (This EI might easily be lost before ΗΛΙΑΣ—or ΗΛΕΙΑΣ.) If it were not for the identification of John with Elijah in vs. 13 and in Matt. 11:14; 17:12 f.; and elsewhere— contrast the tradition reflected in John 1:21—the sentence would probably always have been taken as a question. Torrey's solution seems to me definitely superior to that of Lohmeyer, who brackets 12b as an intrusion, a gloss that has got into the text. It *may* be a gloss, either upon Mark or upon the tradition;

---

[36] On the usual meaning of the phrase see Kendrick Grobel, "He That Cometh After Me," *Journal of Biblical Literature*, 60:397-401. On the reading in the Sinaitic Syriac, see A. S. Lewis, *The Old Syriac Gospels* (1910), p. xvii.

the sequence of 12*a*-13, omitting 12*b*, seems clear, and the phrase "as it is written concerning him" reflects no prophecy but only the stormy career of the Tishbite as related in the Old Testament. Torrey's bracketed insertion in vs. 13 I think unnecessary. Contrast 9:13 above, page 101.

9:15 "In excitement," rather than, "were greatly amazed." But Mark is the only writer in the New Testament to use this verb, and he uses it four times; Acts uses the noun, just once. I wonder if Exod. 34:30 has not influenced the tradition—in spite of vss. 8-9, which Lohmeyer cites against this view. The Old Testament background of the Transfiguration narrative is strongly evident. Unlike the Israelites at Sinai, the people did *not* fear to approach Jesus!

9:23 "If *you* are able!" This is good translation, and the Greek warrants it, without reference to Aramaic. D ☺ and other MSS omit the τό, and so now does p⁴⁵, a very respectable group. The article may in fact be only an introduction to Jesus' quotation of the man's words—as Old Latin *a* took it, *"quid est si quid,"* and as do various modern editors and commentators. I only suggest that not "you" but "able" should be in italics— *Jesus* is the one who has the necessary faith!

9:29 "Not even by prayer," rather than "save by prayer." But could *Mark* have meant what Torrey makes him say? Contrast 11:22-24, not to mention vs. 23 just above and the anticlimax the new translation provides!

9:42 "One of the least," not "these least." In this series of masculine genitive plurals—five successive endings in -των or -ων—the τούτων might be more reasonably suspected of being a product of dittography, if it is thought superfluous. But text and context alike require it, and the parallels strongly support it—Luke with a flying buttress anchored at the end of the next verse, twenty-seven words distant!

9:49 f. "Whatever would spoil, is salted." Torrey's conjecture is again a brilliant one, and throws real light upon this utterly obscure verse. Moreover, an antecedent is now supplied to αὐτό in verse 50, which otherwise is left dangling, and inexplicably so. Perhaps the πυρί was suggested—at least to some copyist—by the preceding πῦρ, vs. 48. The final clause in vs. 50 looks very much like an editorial addition, referring back to the pericope with which the section opened, vss. 33-37, the contending of the disciples.

9:50b "Have salt in yourselves, and pass it on to your fellows." One may suspect that this was perhaps originally a play upon words, occasioned by the similarity of malakh, "to salt," and malak, "to rule" or "to counsel"; so that the original meaning was simply, "Control yourselves"—or "take counsel among yourselves"—"and be at peace one with another." I suppose the verb would be an Ithpeel imperative, perhaps ithmalak(h)ûn. The command "Be at peace" referred back, as I have suggested, to vss. 33 ff. Then the words "Salt is good; but if the salt has lost its savour, what will you do for seasoning?"— or, "Wherewith will you salt" . . . . anything that requires salt?—give another saying introduced here editorially; while "Every sacrifice is salted" is only a gloss (from Lev. 2:13) and "salted with fire" is a gloss upon a gloss, the idea being derived from the preceding pericope! I wonder, therefore, if the original was not simply, "*Take counsel* among yourselves [as in the Syriac of Matt. 26:4, Acts 4:26, where the Ethpael of malak is used], and be at peace with one another." [37]

10:6 The current text reads simply "he made them," and this presupposes mention of the Creator—or would, in Aramaic. But does it not do so equally in Greek? Moreover, there is strong textual evidence for ὁ θεός. It is much easier to suppose it was lost after αὐτούς (--ΟΥΣΟΘΣΕΝ--) than that it was supplied from the LXX by some copyist, for in the LXX the noun ὁ θεός comes much later in the verse (Gen. 1:27). In fact, the verse in Mark would cause no difficulty for an early Christian reader, familiar with the LXX—his Bible!—since

---

[37] On the close association of "rule" and "take counsel" see A. Merx, *Chrestomathia Targumica* (1888), pp. 230 f.

the words are quoted literally and "God" was most certainly understood. The difficulty requires no appeal to Aramaic—indeed there is, and was, no difficulty!

10:12 Although it is often said, as here by Torrey, that at that time the Jewish woman *could not* divorce her husband, still there were ways of getting around the situation—for example by the wife's family's compelling the husband to divorce her. In addition to the reference to Josephus which Torrey gives, *Ant.* 15. 7. 10, there are others, for example *War* 1. 25. 5; *Ant.* 18. 5. 4; 20. 7. 2-3. Moreover, most commentators take this verse as a *Roman* corollary to vs. 11—a view which Torrey comes near to sharing in his rendering, "if she . . . . marries another." A Roman woman could "marry"; a Jewish woman "was married to" her husband—a distinction still recognized in the Anglican Prayer Book: "Who giveth this woman *to be married to* this man?" And how can we be sure that the subject of μοιχᾶται is "he"? Why not read "*she* commits adultery"?—except that in Jewish idiom adultery was the act of the man, and that the sentence may be taken in strict parallelism to vs. 11. As for the original form of the *saying,* Luke 16:18 may well be a better rendering than Mark 10:11 f.

10:30 Torrey brackets vs. 30*b*. This may easily be either a gloss or a textual duplication—in the latter case the phrase "with persecutions" has been added as a gloss!

10:32 "Jesus . . . . was in deep distress." Turner came to the same conclusion without reference to Aramaic.[88] It is another of Mark's "psychological" touches. The omission by D etc. was probably occasioned by homoeoteleuton—after the preceding verb had become a plural.

11:1 Torrey brackets "and Bethany," I think rightly. It was an easy addition, in view of vs. 11.

11:9 f. Torrey's conjecture, "God save him!" for the obscure "Hosannah," and "God in heaven save him!" is a brilliant solution of a vexatious problem. See his note on Matt. 21:9. It is a

[88] *The Study of the New Testament,* p. 62.

question if Mark, who was not familiar with Hebrew, I feel certain, understood what was meant by the cry "Hosannah" any more than he understood "korban" in chap. 7. (The word of course means "gift," but here in the sense of "offering," that is, to God.)

11:14 "Not (yet) the time for figs." This addition is surely justified, as understood in the text.

11:19 The "every evening" is too literal—see other instances of ὅταν, 2:20; 4:29; 8:38; 9:9; 12:23; 13:4; etc. This is worth noting, as the R.V. margin is quite misleading. See Souter's *Lexicon*.

13:19 "Such" tribulation. Torrey suggests that the equivalent of τοιαύτη had already been inserted into the free rendering of Dan. 12:1. It could easily get inserted from such a passage as Exod. 9:18, and the sense of the passage certainly requires it. Even in *Greek* it could get inserted by a careless or tired copyist from the line above:

$$\text{ΟΙΑΟΥΓΕΓΟΝΕΝ}$$
$$\text{ΤΟΙΑΥΤΗΑΠΑΡΧΗΣ}$$
$$\text{ΚΤΙΣΕΩΣ} \ldots$$

Appeal to a Semitic original of Mark is scarcely necessary.

14:3 "Jar-merchant" for "leper" is an interesting conjecture. If he was a "leper," it must have meant one who had been already "cleansed" of his leprosy.

14:33 Jesus was "deeply agitated and distressed." This strengthens the conjecture in 10:32—but in the area of Greek textual transmission, not of Aramaic MSS or tradition.

14:36 "*Abba* (Father)." But Mark regularly translates the Aramaic terms he gives—though not always! cf. "Hosannah," 11:9 f.

14:37 "One brief space," instead of "one hour." Is this necessary? We need not debate the length of time Jesus' prayer continued. "Hour" is a flexible measure of time in the Bible—including Mark! See vs. 41.

14:38 "Not to fail in the (approaching) trial." Torrey's note (on Matt. 6:13) is interesting and valuable. The phrasing of the verse—the punctuation is not certain; see R.V. margin—may be influenced by the Lord's Prayer, which was probably as well known by Christians of the first century as it is now, and the most familiar passage in the Gospels. The contrast of πνεῦμα and σάρξ is especially suggestive of later formulation. Torrey's translation "the (approaching) trial" is pure interpretation—perhaps influenced by Schweitzer's? Mark reads simply "into trial," or "into temptation." Even so, Torrey's main contention here is most attractive: "pray not to fail."

14:41 "Will you sleep now, and take your rest? Already the time has come. . . . ." This is a decided improvement! As for (τὸ) λοιπόν—several MSS omit the article, but even with it the adverbial sense is obvious—the word has probably too often been translated, here and elsewhere in the N.T., without regard to its history; in modern Greek it means "now," "then," "well," or "therefore," and is a useful connective in discourse. Though the modern editions of the Greek N. T. do not take 41*b* as a question, it surely ought to be so taken—as Torrey does, with the R.V. margin. But it is the strange and bewildering ἀπέχει that is the field of Torrey's real triumph here—so strange that the latest commentator, Lohmeyer, gives up trying to translate or interpret it! According to Torrey, it renders *kaddû*, which in Palestinian Aramaic means, not "enough" but "now" or "already." [39] If so, it looks like another double adverb—like 6:51. Though the reading of D ⊕ it and syr : ἀπέχει τὸ τέλος, is suspected of conflation with Luke 22:37, it may need to be taken into fuller consideration before a final solution of the

---

[39] The usual translation, "It is enough," is supported by Field, *Notes on the Translation of the New Testament* (new ed., 1899) and also by Moulton and Milligan, *Vocabulary of the Greek New Testament*, Pt. I (1914). But see Alexander Pallis, *Notes on St. Mark and St. Matthew* (new ed. 1932), pp. 47 ff. Pallis' notes are always stimulating and sometimes richly rewarding; he approaches the study of New Testament from the vantage point of modern Greek, both literary and colloquial.

riddle is found—and it would not be impossible in combination with Torrey's interpretation of the verb: "The end has come already!" "The hour" in vs. 41 must have some relation to "the hour" in vs. 35. Perhaps this is Jesus' acknowledgment that his prayer has not been answered—that is, it has been heard, but not answered as he had hoped.

14:55 "But (at first) they found none." This is of course interpretation, perhaps justifiable in view of the present context. But it may not be implied in the oldest form of the passion narrative, which, as many scholars suppose, did not contain vss. 61b-64.

14:68 "I am neither an acquaintance . . . . nor do I know him at all." Torrey's conjecture seems very involved. If there is any difficulty here, that is, with the Greek as it stands and as it is printed in most modern editions, Hort's proposal is certainly a simple enough solution! Translate: "I don't know nor understand! What is it you are saying?" As part of the story, this seems not improbable.

14:72 "As he thought upon it, he wept." Many are the conjectures that have been hazarded to account for ἐπιβαλών! But the papyri now make it clear that the R.V. margin—not the R.V. text, which Torrey follows—gives an adequate translation: "And he began to weep." This was the reading, in fact, of D ⊙ 565 it syr sah arm!

15:21 "Simon the farm labourer" instead of "the Cyrenian" is an interesting conjecture which can neither be proved nor disproved. It is like Simon the Cananaean, or "trader," as some conjecture!

15:42 "Late in the day." This too is an interesting and not improbable conjecture, like Blass's γινομένης; but after chap. 7 we are not so sure that Mark—"Greek Mark," as Torrey calls him—knew Jewish customs thoroughly well, nor can we be sure that he *meant* a time *after* sundown (see 1:32). Perhaps he thought it was *about* sundown.

16:2-4 The text *is* complicated, but it is a question if the fault is mistranslation from Aramaic. The first and the final columns of MSS are notoriously full of variants, for obvious reasons, such as wear and tear, fading, breaking off of ends of rolls, or first and last pages of codices, and then the attempts of copyists to restore what was either obliterated or missing. A glance at Nestle or Legg or Tischendorf will show the abundance of variants at the end of Mark. Torrey's repunctuation helps—but it leaves him with the necessity of treating 2b-3a as a participial clause plus a finite verb: "When the sun had risen, and they were saying to one another . . . ." This is a heavy strain even on Mark's style! And it is doubtful if the sense of the passage is any clearer. Would they wait until sunrise to ask their question? or to discover that the stone was already rolled away? Turner conjectured that the opening sentence of the pericope repeats from 15:47, perhaps as the beginning of an Easter lection;[40] and it is not impossible that vs. 3 is an editorial insertion, not so much to give continuity with 15:46 as to motivate vs. 4, if vss. 1-8 formed an independent lection. Both parallels omit the verse. The reading of D etc. at the end of vs. 2 may be something more than the result of an effort to ease the reading; on the other hand, λίαν at the beginning seems to be definitely in Mark's style (cf. 1:35 etc.); so is the double dating (cf. 1:32 etc.). If vs. 3 is editorial, as I suspect, the original may have run: "And very early on the first day of the week they came to the tomb. [Period, as in Torrey!] When the sun had risen they looked and saw that the stone was rolled back"—two participles, as often in Mark, for example five verses back, in 15:46. *We* should say, "When the sun had risen, and they could see, they discovered that. . . . ." But Mark wrote in his own style, not in ours!

I have taken the time—and now the space—to examine Dr. Torrey's evidence in detail, believing that if his case is

---

[40] *The Study of the New Testament*, p. 60.

proved for Mark it will carry the whole "Aramaic Gospels" hypothesis with it. The full evidence seems to me to fall somewhat short of demonstrating the existence—or even the probability—of an Aramaic Gospel, but it is by no means without value or significance. To begin with, (1) there are some passages that, so far as I can see, are in no need of "retranslation," but are perfectly acceptable as they stand. In the next place, (2) there are obscurities in the present text of Mark, and the obscurities persist even after retranslation into Aramaic—for example Mark 7:3; 8:34; 9:29. (3) A great many of the obscurities and other difficulties in the present Greek text of Mark are due to careless copying, and that they still survive in modern printed editions is largely due to the fact that the task of textual criticism has not been completed. In the English-speaking world, textual criticism more or less came to a halt with the publication of Westcott and Hort's Greek Testament. The main lines of their solution are of course sound, but a great deal of work still remains to be done. Many of the obscurities in the present text of Mark can be explained and cleared up from the present textual apparatus of variant readings—in both manuscripts and versions—without recourse to translation into Aramaic. (4) Some of the "retranslations" lack that quality of intrinsic probability which, taken alone, might be their sufficient support; they do not "click" in the way which Torrey himself has led us to expect, with many of his conjectural emendations of Old Testament passages. For all this, (5) there are a number of passages which Dr. Torrey has effectively cleared up—for the first time in the whole long history of exegesis. Some of these passages are found in the Gospel of Mark, others in the other Gospels. As a rule, (6) those "retranslations" which are most thoroughly self-authenticating are found within the body of the pericope under consideration or have to do with one of Jesus' sayings. In other words, the retranslation of the material which *ex hypothesi* was originally in Aramaic naturally throws most light upon the present text; as Professor Sherman Johnson has pointed out, "Where Dr. Torrey's conjectures ring truest and most naturally, the passages in question belong either to Q or L or to the oldest pericopes in Mark—in almost no case to the editorial framework." [41] (7) Even though retranslation clears up a large number of passages, it does not follow that the theory of original Aramaic *Gospels* is sound; nor, finally, (8) does it follow that the early dating of the Gospels is sound. In fact, the best solution of the problem of the gospel tradition is not the early dating of the Gospels, on the theory of their composition in Aramaic and their later translation into Greek, but the form-critical one of stereotyped oral tradition, of course in Aramaic as well as in Greek—originally no doubt in Aramaic and then translated sooner or later into Greek— the translation being carried out by different persons at different times, "each one translating as best he was able,"

[41] *Anglican Theological Review*, 19:223. In the *Journal of Biblical Literature*, 48 (1929): 117-23, Professor Millar Burrows has argued that Mark's transitions are quite as "Aramaic" as the content of his pericopes. But (*a*) some of the pericopes were already linked together, or provided with settings, in the oral tradition; and (*b*) the style of the tradition may have influenced its editor—as we may observe in the other Gospels, and even outside the New Testament.

as Papias said of Matthew's *logia* in the "Hebrew dia-
lect." Some of these pericopes and sayings may even have
been written down in Aramaic before translation into
Greek. But it looks as if Q was a Greek document or
cycle; the Aramaic must have lain some distance behind it.

This attempted evaluation of a small section of Dr.
Torrey's work must not close without a final word of
acknowledgment and of deep gratitude to him for the
stimulus and suggestion which his studies have given
the whole world of modern New Testament scholarship.
Even though many students of the New Testament are
not able to go the full way with him and accept his
theory of Aramaic Gospels, this does not in the least
minimize the debt which we all owe him.

VI

JERUSALEM OR GALILEE?

GALILÄA UND JERUSALEM," BY ERNST LOHMEYER, IS A
study of the Jerusalemite and Galilean traditions of the
resurrection. It grew out of the author's work upon the
Synoptic Gospels and appeared as a prolegomenon to his
commentary on Mark, which was published a year later,
in 1937. The study leads to a number of conclusions which
are of cardinal importance for the interpretation of the
Gospels, especially of Mark.[1]

Its main thesis is that there were two main centers of
primitive Christianity in Palestine, one in Jerusalem, the
other in Galilee. This is, of course, very different from the
ordinary view, according to which there was no early
church in Galilee: Jesus' work there came to naught, and
the Twelve—or rather, the Eleven—removed from Galilee
to Jerusalem either soon before or soon after the day of
Pentecost. The late Professor Burkitt, in his little book
Christian Beginnings (1924), advocated this view in all
seriousness, improbable as it seems upon a further recon-
sideration of the evidence and especially in the light of

[1] R. H. Lightfoot called the attention of English and American students to
this work in his *Locality and Doctrine in the Gospels* (1938), chiefly to its
contribution toward solving his problem of the conclusion of Mark.

Professor Lohmeyer's interpretation. It is not at all probable that Jesus' work in Galilee left no trace behind, especially if, as some of us hold, his following was much greater than even the Gospels assume.[2] Their interests are very largely centered upon the apostles, but at the same time the surviving tradition within them makes it clear that Jesus' influence upon the populace of Galilee resulted in "multitudes" following him about and hanging upon his words.

It is true that Galilee is omitted in the list of stages in the expanding mission field of the early church set forth in Acts 1:8; but this is to be explained, according to Professor Lohmeyer, by the hypothesis that Galilee was already *terra Christiana*, as the result of the work of Jesus himself. On the other hand, Mark 16:7, "He goeth before you into Galilee," presupposes that Galilee, not Jerusalem, was to be the center of the messianic Kingdom, the location of the Parousia of the Son of Man. It would seem that Jerusalem was the center of expectation in the more or less nationalistic messianic hope which *Luke* takes for granted; and it is certainly obvious that Luke assumes that primitive Christianity set out from Jerusalem upon its career of world expansion—his second volume might be entitled, "From Jerusalem to Rome." But the "Son of Man" eschatology, as distinguished from that which centered in the conception of the "Messiah," was a northern product, as we may gather from the books

[2] A point which I have attempted to argue in *The Gospel of the Kingdom* (1940).

of Enoch.[3] It was nonnationalistic and universal, transcendental rather than political. And it presupposed, in its Christian form, no particular ecclesiastical theory, as did the Christology of Luke. Finally, Galilee—or Deccapolis—was the home of Jesus' family after the destruction of Jerusalem; and accordingly, so Lohmeyer assumes, his brethren carried on missionary work there for some time, although later on we find James residing in Jerusalem and presiding over the church in Judea.

This is a very interesting thesis and deserves careful consideration. Some problems, of course, still stand in the way. For one thing, if Galilee was *terra Christiana*, how are we to account for the woes upon the Galilean towns which we find in Q? And is προάγω unquestionably used by Mark in the sense of "precede" rather than "lead"?[4] Furthermore, in view of Luke's geographical terminology in both the Gospel and Acts, is it so certain that Galilee is *not* included in Acts 1:8? He sometimes uses "Judea" for the whole Jewish-populated territory of Palestine.[5] "All Judea and Samaria" probably means "all Palestine, both Jewish and non-Jewish territory."

In view of the scarcity of the historical evidence, it is surely legitimate to indulge in hypothetical reconstruction of the provenance of the tradition, even though much

[3] See Chaim Kaplan, "Angels in the Book of Enoch," *Anglican Theological Review*, 12 (1930): 423-37; "The Pharisaic Character and the Date of the Book of Enoch," *ibid.*, 12:531-37. Even Daniel may have been northern; see G. A. Barton, "Danel, Pre-Israelite Hero of Galilee," *Journal of Biblical Literature*, 60:213-25.

[4] Mark 14:28; 16:7; see Johannes Weiss's commentary on 14:28 in ed. 8 of Meyer (1892); also his *History of Primitive Christianity*, I, 14 ff.

[5] E. g., Luke 6:17; 7:17; 23:5.

of the hypothesis, brilliant and attractively presented as it is, remains a matter of speculation—that is, it is an interpretation of the surviving evidence rather than a discovery of further evidence. It does help us to see how the tradition continued to circulate—and to grow—in the period between the Crucifixion and the composition of the Gospel of Mark. It may be well, then, to attempt to sum up the chief contributions which Lohmeyer's little book throws upon our study of the tradition.

The book begins with a clear recognition of the difference between the resurrection narratives in Luke 24 and John 20 on the one hand and those in Matthew 28, John 21, and what must be presupposed as the tradition underlying Mark on the other hand. These divergent traditions no doubt point back to different localities of origin and transmission. Johannes Weiss dismissed the Galilean tradition as an old error of Mark, but this solution is inadequate. It does not account for the existence of traditions which point specifically in the direction of Galilee. Mediating views, which maintain that Peter saw the Lord in Galilee but immediately returned to Jerusalem, likewise fail to recognize the possibility of a Galilean tradition. It is much more likely, Lohmeyer maintains, that the Galilean community looked upon itself as the future center of the Kingdom of God. Galilee, rather than Jerusalem, was the land of revelation and of promise. Jesus' words to the disciples in Mark 14:28 and 16:7 presuppose that the Parousia will take place in Galilee and, presumably, that it will be the dawning point of the New Age.[6] The same presupposition seems to underlie—but more remotely—the accounts of the Resurrection in Matthew and in John 21.

Accordingly, the Galilean appearances are to be distinguished from those in Jerusalem not simply by external circumstances of time or place or persons concerned;[7] instead, entirely divergent theological developments of primitive Christianity are involved. No Galilean narrative undertakes to prove the actuality or the scriptural authority of the Resurrection. Indeed, Matthew even notes that "some still doubted."[8] It was the evangelist Mark who preserved in purest form the expectation that the Parousia was to take place in Galilee, and he did not water down this expectation by a description of actual appearances of Jesus. On the other hand, the Lucan narrative undertakes to prove that all this was in accordance with the scripture, including the prediction that Christ would rise on the third day, and it is concerned with the spread of this message among all peoples.[9] Lohmeyer sets forth this distinction in epigrammatic style: The Galilean story presupposes the doctrine *Kyrios Iêsous,* Jesus is Lord; the Jerusalemite presupposes the other, *Christos Iêsous,* Jesus is Christ.

---

[6] This holds true even if, as some believe, these two verses are glosses upon Mark or late additions to the pre-Marcan tradition. Their point of view certainly centers in Galilee. See my "Studies in the Text of St. Mark," *Anglican Theological Review,* 20:103 ff.

[7] P. 23.

[8] Matt. 28:17.

[9] Luke 24:25-27, 44-49.

He now goes back and discusses the relation between Galilee and Jerusalem in the ministry of Jesus. Galilee had become a Jewish territory once more, by the lifetime of Jesus; and although it still had a large gentile population, the dominant element in the population was a type of Jews who in their origin and in their religious outlook had strong affiliations with Jerusalem. In spite of certain scornful references to Galilee and Galileans, even within the New Testament, there are traces of a higher estimation. Shammai was a Galilean, and taught there; his rigorous views of marriage and those of Jesus are fairly similar. So also the repeated messianic outbursts in Galilee, culminating with Bar-Kochba in A.D. 132, clearly point toward a genuinely Jewish religious loyalty on the part of the leading element in the population of Galilee.[10]

Mark names Galilee a dozen times, and it is clear that he assumes Jesus made Capernaum his headquarters, the center of his ministry about the shores of the Galilean lake. This ministry, far from being a failure—as Maurice Goguel[11] and other writers on the life of Christ have assumed—was a great success. The account of Peter's denial almost assumes it as self-evident that to be a Galilean and to be a follower of Jesus were identical.[12] I think this is pressing the words too far—but the idea may have been somewhere in the back of Mark's mind. Further, according to Mark, Jesus goes to Jerusalem not to carry on a ministry there but only to die; Galilee is

[10] See *The Gospel of the Kingdom*, chap. v, "The Background of Jesus' Message."
[11] *The Life of Jesus* (1933), chap. xiii, "The Crisis in Galilee."
[12] Mark 14:70.

the scene of the beginning and the middle of his career,
Jerusalem only of its end. Galilee is accordingly the
"holy land" of the Gospel, the anticipated scene of the
final eschatological fulfillment. This theory—for theory
it is, and it ignores some facts that even Mark relates,
for example, that Jesus has friends in Bethany—this
theory really controls Mark's narrative. The whole story
of the ministry, as presented by Mark, begins with the
announcement of the coming salvation in Galilee: here
the eschatological gospel was to have its fulfillment, its
final realization. It was in Galilee that Jesus undertook to
gather together the outcasts of Israel, the lost sheep, and
reunite the nation once more under its true King, as the
"eschatological community." Here the Twelve were to
be the heads of the New Israel. And the expectation
still held good, even after Jesus' death: if as a matter of
fact it had *not* been realized during Jesus' lifetime, and
he had left Galilee to go to Jerusalem and die, this had
only postponed the day of triumph, the final consummation; presently he would return, and the Parousia would
take place in Galilee. This was the outlook of the primitive Galilean community, and it is reflected in its tradition; the later view, which centers in Jerusalem, or even
in a world-wide manifestation of Christ in glory, is the
result of later reflection and editorial revision. The oldest
tradition bears the stamp of Galilee—and Galilee is the
anticipated center of the Kingdom of God upon earth.

All this throws light upon the Marcan presentation
of the life of Jesus. The apostles are not chosen in Jerusalem—they have nothing to do with the capital city, now

in the hands of the Romans. The Transfiguration, the preliminary appearance or epiphany of the Son of Man in glory, takes place not in Jerusalem—contrast Malachi 3:1 and other prophecies—but in a secret mountain fastness in the remote north, in Galilee, a land despised by men but graciously favored and chosen by God. It is true that Mark recognizes the existence of opposition to Jesus in Galilee but this is only because Mark is faithful to the tradition, in spite of his theory; and he notes that the opposition was inspired by "the scribes who came down from Jerusalem."[13] The real center of opposition to Jesus is in Jerusalem, not Galilee—and this, we may grant, is probably not only Mark's theory, or Lohmeyer's theory about Mark's theory, but the historical actuality. If Jesus had been content to remain in Galilee he might never have gone to the cross. Why he went to Jerusalem belongs to the "superhistorical" motivation of the story. It is part of the divine plan: the Son of Man *must* suffer . . . . at Jerusalem, the city of sin and of death.[14] This is the point of the three mysterious passion announcements,[15] and of the secrecy of his movements after Caesarea Philippi. The preliminary vision, the foretaste of glory, has established the certainty of the future realization of his divine rule.[16] What follows now is the divinely decreed process—$\delta\epsilon\hat{\iota}$ . . . . $\pi\alpha\theta\epsilon\hat{\iota}\nu$—by which Jesus "dies and enters into his glory." That it was necessary is clear from the history: certainly (*a*) it took place,

[13] Mark 3:22.
[14] The same view reappears in the Apocalypse of John—Rev. 11:8.
[15] Mark 8:31; 9:31; 10:32-34.
[16] Mark 9:1.

and certainly (b) it would not have taken place unless
God had willed it; but (c) why it took place was as
deep a mystery to Mark as it was to Paul or as it is to us.
Somehow it was related to the ransoming of "the
many"[17]—that is as far as Mark goes toward a doctrine
of atonement.[18] Some scholars have seen in Mark the
pattern of a Greek tragedy, and indeed with some probability.[19] In that pattern, the course of the action from
Caesarea to the still-anticipated Parousia leads on steadily
to the grand *katastrophê,* resulting in the divine *peri-
péteia:*[20] the Resurrection is an episode indispensable to
the total action, but still an episode. For the Resurrection is the *beginning* of the great reversal, not the whole
of it. That episode takes place at Jerusalem; but Galilee
is still the scene of the main action, both past and future,
for it is the place chosen by God for his own "eschatological work" and for the beginning and the center of the
proclamation of the gospel.[21]

This Marcan scheme obviously rests upon a theological
idea; and it is not strange if later Gospels, resting upon
quite other theological convictions, have done violence to
Mark, often without realizing it. And this conviction of
Mark's is also, obviously, connected with the idea of the

[17] Mark 10:45.

[18] Cf. Mark 14:24.

[19] See Ernest W. Burch, "Tragic Action in the Second Gospel," *Journal
of Religion,* 11:346-58; Walter E. Bundy, "Dogma and Drama in the Gospel of Mark," *New Testament Studies,* ed. E. P. Booth (1942); also, Henry
Beach Carré, "The Literary Structure of the Gospel of Mark," *Studies in
Early Christianity,* ed. S. J. Case (1928).

[20] On these terms, see Aristotle, *Poetics* 1452*A,* 1454*B.*

[21] P. 34.

Son of Man. Mark assumes that "the Son of Man" was the secret title which covered and hid within its shadowy folds the other name by which Christian faith more clearly expressed itself, namely "the Son of God." [22] In the other Gospels, this distinction is no longer maintained—nor is the location of Jesus' "manifestation of his glory." John specifically located this in Galilee, at Cana; [23] but there is no attempt to limit the manifestation to the Transfiguration, as we might expect—indeed Mark does not do so—nor is it limited to Galilee: Jesus performs miracles repeatedly in Jerusalem and elsewhere outside Galilee. [24] Nevertheless, it is in one of the other Gospels, Matthew, that we find a clue to the basis of the eschatological estimate of Galilee—the passage quoted from the Book of Isaiah:

Land of Zebulun and land of Naphtali . . . .
In the latter time hath he made it glorious,
  By the way of the sea,
  Beyond the Jordan,
  Galilee of the nations.

The people that walked in darkness
  Have seen a great light;
They that dwelt in the land of the shadow of death,
  Upon them hath the light shined. [25]

[22] P. 35.
[23] John 2:11.
[24] Although Mark has only two miracles in Judea, the healing of Bartimeus at Jericho (10:46-52) and the cursing of the figtree at Bethany (11:12-14, 20)—and none in Jerusalem.
[25] Matt. 4:12-17, from Isa. 9:1-2.

This was the main text, so to speak, of Galilean eschatology, a prophecy of the cleansing of the territory from heathen defilement, and of the beginning of the New Age—one thinks of a modern and somewhat remote parallel, the Bahaist "Dawning Point of the Praises of God." Here in Galilee the Sun of Righteousness is to dawn, "with healing in his wings." Here the Son of Man is to appear, "the dayspring from on high," the celestial judge and ruler of the world who was—and is— also a man among men, the holy among sinners, the sinless among the sinful, the light in the midst of darkness.[26] The theology underlying Mark's presentation is clearer from Matthew than it is from Mark, because Matthew uses the Old Testament far more; but the presentation of the Galilean theory is clearer from Mark, for he stands closer to the primitive stream of tradition than does Matthew. At the same time Matthew has combined the *Kyrios* conception with that of the Son of Man—the title "*Kyrios*" is the one which later came to express openly all that the other had held back as a secret.[27] But it is clear that Matthew at the same time preserves in full strength the conception of the Galilean location of the expected Parousia, though now the delay is occasioned not only by the episode of Jesus' death at Jerusalem but also by the whole Gentile mission.[28]

It is evident that John and Luke have each a totally different view of the course of Jesus' ministry from that

[26] Cf. Matt. 28:18; 25:31-46.
[27] P. 38.
[28] Matt. 28:19-20; cf. Mark 13:10.

of Mark—even though almost the whole of Mark is incorporated, under modification, in the Gospel of Luke. The real center of Jesus' ministry in Luke is "Judea," that is, the Jewish-populated part of Palestine, without too much attention to geographical distinctions between Galilee, Samaria, and Judea proper. In John it is notorious that Judea, indeed Jerusalem, is Jesus' headquarters, as Capernaum is in Mark. Indeed, one passage almost says that Judea—or perhaps Samaria?—was Jesus' native land: "After two days he went forth . . . . into Galilee. For Jesus himself testified that a prophet has no honor in his own country." [29] Here, in John and in Luke, we see the triumph of the age-old, inherited conception of the Jewish Messiah who must complete his work in Jerusalem, in utter disregard of the Galilean tradition which centered not only his ministry but also his coming Parousia in Galilee.

Thus emerged two different outlines of the life of Jesus, equally significant in their results upon the narration of the incidents of his biography and for the general theological presuppositions. They are most clearly recognizable in the Gospels of Mark and Luke. In Mark, Galilee is the main scene of Jesus' activity; only here does he exorcise demons, which was his chief eschatological work; only here does he deliver an extended discourse to the people (chap. 4). And this situation is not only a historical fact but also a theological—or, more accurately, an eschatological—postulate: it rests upon the thought of Jesus as the Son of Man.[30]

As he is both the hidden and the revealed Son of Man,

[29] John 4:43-44.
[30] P. 45.

so likewise the eschatological significance of Galilee is both hidden and revealed. And as in the future he will be revealed "in power and glory" as the Son of Man, so also will Galilee be revealed as the land of eschatological fulfillment. That is the whole point of the saying: "He goes before you [that is, precedes you] into Galilee; there will you see him," as the manifested Lord and Judge. *Matthew* takes this concept and gives it an Old Testament basis, but he adds certain features to the Appearance in Galilee which are derived from the expectation of the Last Day. *John* acknowledges the significance of Galilee as a fact in the story of the Son of Man, but adds another feature, secret and sacred, the institution of the Supper,[31] though his peculiar mode of presentation often obscures the significance of the topography. He also makes the shore of the Galilean lake the scene of Peter's installation as "shepherd of Christ's sheep"[32]—though the primitive conception of Jesus as the Son of Man is greatly weakened in John, since another conception, and title, take its place. *Luke* tells the story in such a way as to make the whole of Palestine the locale of Jesus' ministry: as in Acts 10:37, the scene is "all Judea."[33] Galilee is for Luke only the opening scene; the full development and climax of Jesus' ministry is at Jerusalem, where also the resurrection appearances all take place. "And this biographical datum rests upon the eschatological conviction that Jesus is the lawful

[31] John 6.
[32] John 21.
[33] Cf. Luke 23:5.

King of Israel, the restorer of the throne of his father
David, the redeemer of Israel."[34]

It is this difference in theological outlook, according
to Lohmeyer, which explains the alternation of Galilee
and Jerusalem as the scene of the appearances of Jesus
after his resurrection; and the probability is now en-
hanced and supported by his study of the traditions relating to the two centers in the apostolic church.[35] The
Book of Acts naturally follows the Lucan scheme and
carries out its underlying conviction: Jesus is the Christ,
the Anointed, the true King of Israel; and the founding
of the church, the spread of the gospel, the mission of
the apostles must all take place in and start from the
nation's capital—not from Galilee. Everyone recognizes
that this ecclesiastical theory is dominant in Luke-Acts;[36]
no one heretofore has pointed out, as clearly as Lohmeyer
does, how this theory ignores facts which even Luke
himself has to admit—the presence of disciples like
Ananias in Damascus and the "old disciples" in Galilee.[37] Still further evidence is found in the traditions of
the relatives of Jesus, the *Despósynoi,* recounted chiefly
by Eusebius—from Hegesippus, a second-century Palestinian, and from Julius Africanus, who lived in Palestine
in the third century. Indeed, the fluctuating designation
of the "Apostles," "the Twelve," "the Brethren of the
Lord" may very likely go back to an interchange in

[34] Pp. 45-46.
[35] Chap. 4.
[36] See esp. Henry J. Cadbury, *The Making of Luke-Acts* (1927), and
Burton S. Easton, *The Purpose of Acts* (1936).
[37] Acts 9:10, 19*b,* 25; 21:4, 7, 8, 16.

leadership between Jerusalem and Galilee during the opening decades in the history of the new faith. And a later designation of the Christians as "Nazoraeans"[38] probably points back to a Galilean usage in the first century: the later term still points to the "Nazarenes" as the originators of the sect—not as "from Nazareth," but as observers of the *Nazirite* vow as a duty, not merely as a work of merit.[39] Along with this went the term *"Ebionim"*—not a later sect, but a name for the primitive Galilean Christians, who made poverty (*ebionim* means "the poor") a Christian duty.[40] Jesus was still looked upon as the Son of Man, as the legend of the martyrdom of James makes clear. When asked by his persecutors, "What is the gate of Jesus?" he replied, "Why do you ask me about the Son of Man? He sits in heaven at the right hand of the Power on high, and is to come on the clouds of heaven."[41] Jesus is still the hidden Son of Man, as in Enoch,[42] and his Parousia will reveal him to the world in his true supernatural dignity and worth.

Thus a common Christology underlies all these fragments of old tradition regarding the martyr James, the Nazoraeans, and the descendants of the family of Jesus. . . . . Jesus is the eschatological Teacher, who upon the foundation of the sacred Jewish Law but with special commandments (relating to poverty and obedience) and with divine power leads his followers to the gates of the Kingdom of God; he is now exalted at the right hand

[38] So Jerome in the fifth century—see Guthe in *PRE*[8], XIII, 677.
[39] P. 64.
[40] See also the Epistle of James, and the reflection of this view, under modification, in the Book of Acts.
[41] Eusebius, *Eccl. Hist.* 2. 23. 8-18.
[42] En. 46:2–48:10.

of God, and is soon to come "on the clouds of heaven" as the judge of all mankind.[43]

It is this Christology, with no reference to the Holy Spirit, and no outlook of world mission (though not opposed to the world mission), which lies behind the Galilean tradition—very different from the richer and more colorful tradition of Jerusalem which Luke enshrined, with its emphasis upon Jesus' Messiahship (as King of Israel), upon the Spirit, and upon the world mission of the church. The one is centered in the conviction that Jesus is Son of Man and Lord (*Kyrios*); the other in the conviction that he is the Messiah, the Redeemer of Israel—and of the world.

On the basis of this hypothesis it is easy to see how the evangelic tradition received the form and emphasis it possesses in the Gospels. Instead of one uniform tradition, all from one point of view, there are different points of view and different resulting emphases. There is not one, and only one, "Christology of the Synoptic Gospels"; there are at least two—possibly three or four Christologies. And they reflect the convictions of those who handed down the tradition, in different localities— certainly in two, Jerusalem and Galilee, probably in three or four, if we include Caesarea and Antioch, possibly in many more. The conclusion is inescapable that there was in general a twofold origin of the church, with two centers in Palestine from the lifetime of Jesus down at least to the war under Hadrian, in Galilee, and

43 P. 74.

down to the war under Nero and later, in Judea—and then on into the following centuries, when successive conquest and exodus scattered the little Christian communities far and wide, down to the Mohammedan conquest in the seventh century, and even to this day. There are Galilean Christians today who at least claim to be descended from early bishops, saints, and martyrs.

As we shall see, this hypothesis of Lohmeyer's not only enables him to write the most penetrating of commentaries on the Gospel of Mark; it also enables us to reconstruct—in further hypothesis of course, since hypothesis is all we can hope to achieve in this area—to reconstruct one or two of the stages through which the gospel tradition passed before it reached Mark, the writer of the earliest account of what Jesus said and did.

The main result of Professor Lohmeyer's investigation is to establish the probability that early Christian communities were found in Galilee, taking Galilee in the wide sense as extending east of the Jordan, north to include Mount Hermon, and northeast to include Damascus. "Of the early history of Christianity in this district we know little enough, but its existence is assured, from the period of the earliest proclamation of the gospel to the beginning of the second century; of its wide extent and strength we have the testimony of Origen in the third century, of Epiphanius in the fourth, and of Jerome in the fifth." [44] It was Jerome who copied "the Hebrew Gospel of Matthew" at Aleppo and wrote

[44] *Ibid.*

to Augustine that "to this day throughout all the Jewish synagogues of the east is spread that heresy which they generally call the Nazoraean." [45] These Christian communities go back for their origin to the ministry of the Lord himself and his apostles and brethren, though the traditions of the apostles and brethren are very fragmentary. That there were martyrs among them seems clear from Hegesippus, quoted by Eusebius.[46] Their missionary efforts in neighboring regions were not without success, though Galilee remained the center of this northern propaganda—only so can we explain the flight of the Jerusalem Christians thither shortly before the siege of the city in the year 68. Jerusalem was accordingly the second, not the first, center of the primitive church. As represented in Matthew—not in Luke—the great commission to evangelize the nations is delivered in Galilee, not in Jerusalem. Significantly, this legend was written down at a time when Jerusalem had in fact long been the actual center of Jewish Christianity.[47] How and when the transfer to Jerusalem took place we do not know; but it is clear that contact with Galilee was still maintained when the Gospel of Matthew was compiled. This inference, according to Lohmeyer, is further supported by the position of James, the Lord's brother, in the Jerusalem community. It was because he came from Galilee, and was Jesus' blood relation, that he was made head of the "apostles and elder brethren" at the capital.[48]

[45] *Ep.* 112. 13.
[46] *Eccl. Hist.* 3. 32. 6.
[47] P. 81.
[48] See Acts 15.

These apostles were not missionaries, in Judea, but leaders of the Jerusalem church;[49] the actual mission was conducted by their emissaries; and probably James came to the city at the time Peter and John first left it and went to Samaria, during the persecution that followed the martrydom of Stephen. This was the very time when Saul was engaged in carrying the persecution farther afield, to the very headquarters of the new sect in the north and as far away as Damascus.[50] James came to Jerusalem, then, as the representative of Galilean faith and piety; and it is James' views, not Peter's, that are authoritative and decisive at the Jerusalem council.[51] Here we have a phenomenon not without parallel in the history of other religions, as Lohmeyer notes—for example in Islam and in Mormonism—namely a shift from a first center to a second within the first generation of believers; and it is all the more striking that the evidence is preserved in Acts, whose whole interest and orientation centers in Jerusalem, not in Galilee, and whose earliest traditions are almost exclusively those of the capital city.

That there was a theological difference between Galilee and Jerusalem is, I believe, most probable. Jesus had arisen among the circle of "the poor," and it was among these Galilean *anawim* that his message had taken deepest root. The Galileans were loyal Jews, that is, loyal to the Torah—though the Talmudic evidence which Lohmeyer cites may refer mainly to conditions in the second

---

[49] Cf. Acts 8:1.

[50] See H. E. Dana, "Where Did Paul Persecute the Church?" *Anglican Theological Review*, 20:16-26.

[51] Acts 15.

century, after the Pharisaic schools had removed from the south and relocated here. At least there were no "Hellenists" in Galilee, that wing of the early Jerusalem church which the Book of Acts may be interpreted to imply as the origin of what later became world-wide Gentile Christianity. There were certain characteristic emphases in Galilean Christianity, Lohmeyer maintains. One was the form of the Decalogue which substituted "Thou shalt not defraud" for "Thou shalt not covet"—a formulation which Jesus himself apparently shared.[52] Another was the requirement of poverty, since only the poor are pleasing to God.[53] Still another feature of Galilean Christianity was the expectation of a heavenly figure at the end of days, not the national Messiah but a figure patterned upon Daniel's vision of "one like a son of man" coming on the clouds of heaven. And it is characteristic that whenever the apocalyptic expectation is centered in the "Son of Man," there the poverty ethic is also emphasized—as we may see from the Book of Enoch. These elements are clearly present in Galilean Christianity from the beginning, and they survived long after, in the doctrines of the Ebionites. There was also far less emphasis—to say the least—upon the sacrificial cult than was to be found in Judean Christianity.

Now these characteristic theological emphases were of great importance for the preservation and formulation of the gospel tradition, even prior to its incorporation in the earliest written Gospel, that of Mark. The

[52] Mark 10:19.
[53] Mark 10:21, 23-31.

whole conception of Jesus' earthly ministry is influenced
by them: "Jesus is the Savior, but only as combining in
himself the office of a Jewish teacher and that of the
hidden Son of Man, by virtue of which twofold office
he is able by word and deed to bring men to the 'gate'
of the Kingdom of God. He is the Savior, who holds to
the sacred Law but also adds the further requirements—
which lead to 'life'—of voluntary poverty and obedience to himself." [54] These features characterize not only
the later Nazoraean belief and practice, but also the
earliest traditions preserved in the Gospel of Mark—for
example the words to the rich man, and the narrative
of the Transfiguration. And the apocalyptic outlook,
centering in the coming Parousia of the Son of Man in
Galilee when that land will become fully and forever
the land of promise, the center of the New Age, is likewise reflected in Mark, especially in the two verses 14:28
and 16:7. Jesus has already appeared in Galilee, as the
hidden or secret Son of Man; his divine deeds and words
are related in the traditions which the earliest preachers
of the gospel used, and yet he remained unrecognized
save by two or three intimate disciples; but he will come
again in glory, fully revealed as the transcendent figure
of the Danielic-Enochic hope, as "the Son of Man from
heaven." Mark's theory of the messianic secret was therefore only a dogmatic formulation of something which
was basic to the whole of the earliest evangelic tradition. [55] One might almost, Lohmeyer suggests, venture to

[54] P. 85.
[55] P. 87.

reconstruct the Galilean theology—or, rather, the primitive Galilean piety—from the pieces of tradition which Mark records; though not every "Son of Man" saying in the Gospel is primitive, and in its present form the conception has been influenced by the later identification of the Son of Man with the Suffering Servant figure depicted in Second Isaiah.[56] The Nazoraean theology—or piety—was of course only one among several streams of tendency and tradition in the early church. Such later developments and interpretations of the primitive belief and practice as we find in Luke, in Paul, in John—these followed in due course, and partly as the result of the transfer of leadership to Jerusalem; in particular the emphasis upon the idea of Jesus' Messiahship, as the future Anointed King of Israel, was characteristic of the Jerusalem outlook. The older, more primitive identification of him with the celestial Son of Man had sufficed in Galilee.[57] It is clear that the Messiah idea is secondary; it is really supported and maintained by the underlying conviction that Jesus is the heavenly Son of Man. Its importance for later Christian thought is obvious—but in its origin it is not so primitive as the Galilean faith.

Where, then, did the earliest resurrection appearances take place, in Galilee or in Jerusalem? To that first and also final question Lohmeyer can find no answer. We do not even know where the appearance to Peter took place, the first one in the earliest list.[58] Nor is it unlikely

[56] See *The Gospel of the Kingdom*, pp. 157 ff.
[57] P. 94.
[58] I Cor. 15:5-8.

that, in the communication back and forth between the
two localities during the earliest days, appearances took
place in various localities. From the theological point of
view, I can see no reason why the appearances should be
limited to one place or even to one time. Certainly Paul
assumes that his own vision of the Risen Lord was
completely on a par with those that preceded.[59] What is
remarkable—and Lohmeyer has made this abundantly
clear—is that the appearances were *interpreted* differently
by various groups, and in the traditions of different localities and persons, chiefly in Galilee and in Jerusalem.
Each interpretation presupposed a particular pattern of
eschatological outlook; and it is clear that the earliest
Christology was really, as the term suggests, *an eschatology,* in which the central figure was the same—the
risen, glorified Christ who had lived and talked and
done mighty works in Galilee but had died on a cross outside Jerusalem, who was now at the right hand of God,
and was soon to come in glory to inaugurate the New
Age. Whatever we may think of some of the details in
Lohmeyer's argument, his investigation has thrown a
flood of light upon the earliest gospel tradition; and his
book will remain one of the most important ever written
upon this subject.

[59] I Cor. 15:8.

VII

THE THEOLOGY OF MARK

MARK TAKES FOR GRANTED THE PRIMITIVE CHRISTIAN TRA-
dition about Jesus. What he aims to do is to tell "the
Christian story as it was known and believed in the
churches of the Hellenistic world a generation after
Jesus' death."[1] He also takes for granted the apostolic
faith; for he writes as a Christian, a believer, not as an
outsider or critic—and not even as an historian or biog-
rapher. Hence his "theology," so far as he has a theology,
is not his own, but merely the theological interpretation—as far as it had gone in his day—of the tradition
as held by the contemporary church. Professor Branscomb truly says: "Fact and theology had already been
combined in this tradition, and what is often described
as Mark's theology is really the early Christian belief as
to the historical facts."[2] The contrast with Paul, for
example, is very marked. Paul lives in a realm of ideas—
revelation, law, grace, justification, glory. By Paul the
tradition is taken for granted—but left behind. Mark,
on the contrary, still moves upon the level of the received
tradition, and makes almost no effort to interpret it in
terms of general ideas. He is not a theologian—not even
in the sense that Paul may be described as one—and he

[1] B. H. Branscomb, *Commentary*, p. xxii.
[2] *Ibid.*, p. xxi.

148

has scarcely the most elementary idea of what it would require to be a theologian, or how a theologian would go about his task. It is fortunate for us, that is, for the whole later church, that this was so! Upon the basis of Paul's teaching, taken alone, Christianity might possibly have foundered a century later in the rising sea of Gnosticism; possessing Mark's compilation of the historic traditions, later amplified by the other evangelists, the church held true to its course, steering with firm, unslackened grip upon the historic origins of its faith.

And yet Mark has often been represented as so greatly influenced by Paul that he introduced Paul's ideas everywhere into the tradition he records. Paul's influence, not Peter's, is the modern theory! On the other hand, Professor Martin Werner has studied the evidence for this supposed influence of "Paulinism" upon the Gospel of Mark, and concludes that instead of "Paulinism" Mark presupposes only the common Christianity, the generally accepted Christian doctrine, of the Gentile churches at the middle of the first century.[3] This view is very similar to that of Professor Branscomb, just quoted. And yet there must have been some influence of Paul upon the Christian community in Rome, as elsewhere in the West following his years of missionary preaching and teaching in Asia Minor, Macedonia, and Greece, and his final visit to Rome, where he preached and taught for at least two years, as we learn from the last lines of the Book of Acts: "preaching the Kingdom of God and teaching

[3] See chap. ix below, "Was Mark a Pauline Gospel?"—also F. V. Filson, *Origins of the Gospels* (1938), pp. 157 ff.

the things about the Lord Jesus, with all boldness, none
forbidding him"—ἀκωλύτως, "unhindered"—the last
word of the book and its climax. Not direct "Paulinism,"
then, but the leaven of Paul's teaching influencing the
common faith of the earliest church in the West, and
hence affecting the tradition as it came to Mark some
years later—that is what we may reasonably look for in
Mark's Gospel. And this is what we find, as many
scholars now maintain—especially, perhaps, in the doctrine of the Cross.[4] As Bishop Rawlinson finely says,
echoing Johannes Weiss, "Jesus is, for St. Mark, the Messiah, not *in spite of* His sufferings—as the earliest believers of all may for a time have been disposed to express it—but precisely *because of* His sufferings."[5] So
also may be the doctrine of the disciples' failure to understand Jesus' Way of the Cross, and the blindness of
the Jews who rejected him and put him to death. Yet
we must not overlook the old tradition here too: "Now
brethren, I know that you did it in ignorance, and so
did your rulers."[6] So Peter is represented as preaching
in Solomon's Portico at Jerusalem soon after the Resurrection!

We must not press too strongly, then, the possibility
of Pauline influence, and what Mark does *not* do in the
way of conforming the tradition to Paul's theological
outlook is probably more significant than an occasional

[4] E.g., Mark 10:45.
[5] *Commentary*, p. lii.
[6] Acts 3:17.

word or turn of expression found also in the letters of
Paul. "Mystery,"[7] "covenant," "blood of the covenant"[8]
—the words sound Pauline; but further study shows that
they are not used in the precise sense Paul assumed, but
reflect the common thought and language of the Gentile
church, perhaps influenced by Paul, but not slavishly
devoted to him and possibly not even comprehending
him very clearly. Even the ransom saying[9] is probably
more un-Pauline than Pauline in its real connotations.
True enough it represents a circle of ideas one will find
in Paul; but Paul scarcely did more than touch the idea
and pass on—he had other and richer and more suggestive figures[10] for explaining Christ's death than that
of a ransom paid to death, or to Satan, or even to God—
it is not said to whom the price is paid. The other great
doctrines of Paul—in addition to the significance of
Christ's death, which after all he himself owed to the
early community[11]—are not even echoed in the Gospel
of Mark. Hence we must conclude with Professors
Branscomb, Lohmeyer, Werner, Bishop Rawlinson, and
other recent writers, that Mark's point of view is that
which was "in general characteristic of the Gentile-
Christian Church of the first century," but that it was
not, "in the narrower and more distinctive sense of the
words, a 'Pauline' Gospel."[12]

[7] Mark 4:11.
[8] Mark 14:24.
[9] Mark 10:45.
[10] See Adolf Deissmann, *Paul*, esp. chap. vii.
[11] I Cor. 15:3; 11:24.
[12] Rawlinson, *Commentary*, p. xlv.

> concerning his Son,
> who was born of the seed of David [as far as his
>   human nature went],
> but who was marked out as the Son of God with
>   power [by the holy Spirit]
> through resurrection from the dead—
>   Jesus Christ our Lord." [18]

This creedlike passage sets forth the primitive faith, which was taken for granted and then further built upon by Paul, and shared by him—so he implies—with all Christians everywhere: Jesus *became* Son of God, Messiah, by the power of the Spirit at his resurrection from the dead. But Mark goes beyond this: Jesus was already Son of God *before* his death and resurrection, in fact from the day of his baptism, when the heavenly Voice had proclaimed,

> "You are my Son, my Beloved!
> You are my Chosen!" [19]

The proclamation had been repeated at the Transfiguration, addressed now not to Jesus himself but to the three intimate disciples,

> "This is my Son, my Beloved.
> Listen to him." [20]

Some scholars think the transfiguration story was originally an account of one of the resurrection appear-

[18] Rom. 1:2-4.
[19] Mark 1:11 (Goodspeed).
[20] Mark 9:7 (Goodspeed).

ances—the first one, to Peter in Galilee after his flight from Jerusalem and return to Galilee.[21] Whether this be so or not, it is certainly for Mark, and for the other evangelists, an *anticipation* of "the glory of his resurrection." In fact the conclusion of the preceding section in Mark suggests this, since it points forward to this scene with the words, "I tell you, some of you who stand here will certainly live to see the reign of God come in its might." [22]

The way in which Mark interprets the earthly life of Jesus is messianic; Jesus became Messiah not at his resurrection but at his baptism. The later evangelists press the origin back to a still earlier point. He was "born King of the Jews," [23] or he was announced even before his birth to be "holy, and the Son of God." [24] John goes farther still, and indeed the farthest distance possible:[25] Jesus was the Incarnate Word, who had been with God from "the beginning" and now at last had become flesh and dwelt upon earth.[26] Step by step, the growing doctrine or theology of the church pressed the *origin* of Jesus' heavenly Messiahship, of his divine nature, back to the very confines of time and place, and then beyond. It was Mark who began this process of trans-

[21] See Morton S. Enslin, "The Date of Peter's Confession," in *Quantulacumque* (1937), pp. 117-22; also S. V. McCasland, "Peter's Vision of the Risen Christ," *Journal of Biblical Literature*, 47:41-59.
[22] Mark 9:1 (Goodspeed).
[23] Matt. 2:2.
[24] Luke 1:35.
[25] Though the later creeds do go even farther in exalting the Son's relation to the Father, since Arianism could accept John 1—interpreting it by Prov. 8.
[26] John 1:14.

valuation, as far as we can make out at this distance, by insisting that Jesus became Messiah at his baptism—though perhaps the evangelic tradition had already received this interpretation in the Roman community, or even, earlier still, in Palestine or in the early Gentile church.[27]

The probability seems to be that it was Mark who inaugurated the process[28]—one of untold moment for all later Christian faith, devotion, and doctrine! Yet it was a simple step to take. If Jesus was now the risen, glorified Lord, soon to return as Judge of all mankind, he must have known what his destiny was to be, even while he walked upon the earth and healed and taught, and when he died he must have foreseen his heavenly office; moreover, if he foresaw it all, how could he fail to act the part? Must he not already have been Messiah, and not merely Messiah-designate, Messiah-elect, while he lived upon earth? Not only was his Messiahship *after* the

[27] See the "hymn" in Phil. 2:6-11, and note Paul's doctrine of Christ's pre-existence. If the "hymn" is earlier than Paul, and hence quoted by him, it may even have been Roman in origin.

[28] Although Paul, for example, assumes that Christ was pre-existent, that he "came" or "was sent" (e.g. Gal. 4:4), and that the title "Messiah" or "Christ," that is, Son of God, was rightfully his during his earthly life—though for Paul the word "Christ" is less a title than a personal name—still Paul thinks of his earthly life as chiefly the scene of his suffering, death, and resurrection, not of his messianic career. For Paul, Jesus' messianic career still begins with the Resurrection—so primitive is the real basis of Paul's thought. He never once intimates that Jesus wrought miracles or "mighty works," or that foregleams of his messianic glory were apparent at his baptism or transfiguration, let alone his birth. See Martin Brückner, *Die Entstehung der Paulinischen Christologie* (1903); also Henry Beach Carré, *Paul's Doctrine of Redemption* (1914). How Paul's faith—or Mark's—was related to the *Kyrios* faith of early Gentile Christianity, for example at Antioch, we do not know. *As far as we know,* it was Mark who first applied the idea of conscious Messiahship to Jesus' earthly life.

Resurrection the greatest disproof of the charges against him, the most powerful vindication of his claims, and the most complete victory over his enemies; his Messiahship *before* the Resurrection shows that he must have accepted defeat and death voluntarily, as the will of God and as the means to the realization of God's purposes. There was something divine, then, rather than anything ignominious, about such a death! It followed naturally, as in the lines of the Philippian hymn:

> He *chose* renunciation,
> obedient to death,
> to the death upon the cross.[29]

Prophetic scripture had foretold it: Jesus knew the Scriptures, and he had willed to accept all that was in store for him.[30] So death had not come upon him unawares; he had foreseen it, perhaps from the beginning, and he had told his disciples repeatedly that he must die—in fact, at three different times he had foretold his death in detail.[31] He had been no victim of the blind hatred and jealousy of the Jerusalem authorities; instead he had marched as a victor to the fray, conscious of his strength and certain of eventual triumph.

Of course this interpretation runs counter to some phases of the old tradition. Mark himself pictures the dismay of his followers as they went toward Jerusalem;[32]

[29] Phil. 2:8.
[30] Mark 9:12; cf. John 19:28.
[31] The three passion announcements, Mark 8:31; 9:31; 10:33-34; see also 12:8; 14:8, 21, 27, 41.
[32] Mark 10:32.

if Professor Turner was right, there is pictured too the strain and tension that filled Jesus' own mind as he advanced at the head of his band of disciples. There is also the story of the agony in the garden,[33] perhaps a secondary element in the passion narrative but so old a tradition that an echo of it is found even outside the Gospels, in the Epistle to Hebrews.[34] But in principle is was a historical interpretation; to say the very least, Jesus could not have gone up to Jerusalem, the very stronghold of his enemies, unaware of the dangers he should encounter there.

It is significant that Mark's interpretation of Jesus' earthly Messiahship—that is, of his Messiahship realized even during his earthly ministry—takes the form it does. As we have seen, the interpretation is completely bound up with the doctrine of the "Son of Man." Even though the title "Son of God" is used in the account of the Baptism, presumably the origin of Jesus' Messianic consciousness—as many modern scholars interpret the passage—nevertheless the whole idea of his acceptance of death is formulated in terms of the heavenly Man who has power and authority upon earth,[35] who fulfills what is written of him, who dies and rises again, and is to come in glory as the supreme advocate or judge.[36] And

[33] Mark 14:32-42.
[34] Heb. 5:7-8. It is noteworthy that John omits the incident, though even he has echoes of it—not the "Jesus wept" of 11:35 but the "Now is my soul troubled" of 12:27.
[35] Mark 2:10, 28.
[36] Mark 8:38; 13:26 f., etc.

it is closely related to the conception of his followers' duty of witnessing and, if necessary, of dying for him and his gospel which we find set forth in the central section, "the Way of the Cross." As Bishop Rawlinson again quotes from Johannes Weiss, "He only can understand the secret of the Cross who has disposed himself towards service, humility, renunciation, suffering, and martyrdom."[37] The words might almost come from the *Theologia Germanica* or *The Imitation of Christ*, but they are surely true of the Gospel of Mark. For Mark's interpretation of the life of Jesus as the career of the heavenly Son of Man, walking about Galilee incognito, dying and rising again, is the theology of a martyr church; and like all vital theology it is in closest relation to the daily life of those who thought it and believed it. Jesus had not intended to be the Jewish Messiah of popular hopes.[38] Here again the old tradition, at one stage of its development, ran counter to his theory; for Jesus had accepted the shouts of acclamation at his triumphal entry into Jerusalem.[39] In fact, Mark appears to think that Jesus himself planned the demonstration.[40] And there are other suggestions of earthly, that is, nationalistic Jewish, Messiahship to be found in the old tradition—more fully elaborated in the other Gospels, especially, as we have seen, in Luke. But what does that prove? Only that

[37] *Commentary*, p. lii; cf. Weiss, *History of Primitive Christianity*, II, 694. See also *The Growth of the Gospels*, pp. 154 ff.; D. W. Riddle, *The Gospels, Their Origin and Growth* (1939), pp. 140 ff.
[38] See *The Gospel of the Kingdom*, p. 154.
[39] Mark 11:9-10.
[40] Mark 11:1-7.

Mark did not go through his Gospel and erase everything that conflicted with the interpretation set forth
in the central section, and especially in the passion announcements. Are all theologians consistent? And let us
remember, Mark was not a theologian, nor even trying
to be one!

The evidence for Jesus' Messiahship during his earthly
career is further strengthened by the explicit cries of the
demons, who "knew him," [41] and by the confession of
Peter[42]—which now moves back from the first resurrection appearance[43] to become the first affirmation of
faith in Jesus as Messiah while upon earth. But the interpretation faces certain difficulties. Why was it, if the
disciples believed in Jesus' Messiahship, and had been
repeatedly forewarned of his impending fate, that they
all forsook him and fled at the time of his arrest? [44] And
if Judas knew of Jesus' claim to be Messiah, why was this
testimony not produced against Jesus at his examination
before the high priest? Mark answers these objections,
and solves the problem, with his theory of the messianic
secret. Jesus had silenced the demons when they acknowledged his divine superiority and called him "the
Holy One of God." [45] He had forbidden his disciples to
make known his Messiahship to anyone.[46] The Trans-

[41] Mark 1:34.
[42] Mark 8:29.
[43] I Cor. 15:5; Luke 24:34; etc.
[44] Mark 14:50.
[45] Mark 1:24.
[46] Mark 8:30.

figuration was to be kept a secret until after the Resurrection.[47] And when he went through Galilee on his way to Judea, he did not wish anyone to know it.[48]

Ever since the publication in 1903 of Wilhelm Wrede's famous book on this subject, *The Messianic Secret in the Gospels,* scholars have been compelled to take seriously the thesis it set forth, namely, that the whole conception of the secret Messiahship is an intrusion into the tradition, either read into it by Mark or at a late pre-Marcan stage in the development of the tradition, and not really consonant with the story of Jesus as it was handed down in the earliest Christian circles. The very notion that it was a secret to be kept until after the Resurrection seems to betray it as a later insertion—like the interpretation of Jesus' words about the temple found in John 2:21-22. We cannot at this point deal fully with the theory.[49] But enough has been said to indicate that in principle the thesis must be accepted. Yet it would not be true to limit Mark's contribution—or interpretation—to his theory of the messianic secret.[50] It is subsidiary to his whole interpretation of the life of Jesus as already Messiah while upon earth, and long before his resurrection. And his theory of the secret, like his theory of the parables as purposely meant to mystify those who heard them,[51] and his theory of a divine judgment upon the

---

[47] Mark 9:9.

[48] Mark 9:30.

[49] See my "Note on Christology," *Frontiers of Christian Thinking* (1935).

[50] See Martin Werner, *Der Einfluss paulinischer Theologie im Markusevangelium* (1923), discussed below in chap. ix.

[51] Mark 4:11.

Jews causing them to be blind to Jesus' true calling and mission (perhaps a Pauline idea,[52] but more probably pre-Pauline[53]) and likewise also his theory of a supernatural restraint upon the disciples[54] so that they could not keep their eyes open (a Hellenistic concept, with many parallels in ancient literature!)—all these theories are subsidiary to his main thesis, and are thrown up in order to forestall objections to it. If Jesus was already Messiah during his earthly career, why was he not recognized as Messiah? The answer is, he *was* recognized, even by the demons, who had supernatural insight, and by his disciples, through faith; and yet the disciples were forbidden to declare it, and the demons were silenced; and if the Jews as a whole did not recognize him, it was because their eyes too were "holden," and because they were already bringing upon themselves a judgment for their sins. Here was a mystery, a divine mystery, God's secret purpose: since the Son of Man *had* to die,[55] as in the denouement of some ancient tragedy the forces at work were now furthered, now hindered, until God's ends were achieved. "Thus God's purpose prevailed," as Homer might have put it: Διὸς δ' ἐτελείετο βουλή.[56] So even Euripides might have celebrated the divine mystery and its unfolding:

> Great treasure halls hath Zeus in heaven,
> From whence to man strange dooms be given,

[52] Cf. Rom. 9–11, esp. 11:25.
[53] Cf. Acts 3:17.
[54] Mark 14:40; cf. 9:6.
[55] Mark 8:31; 14:21.
[56] *Iliad* A. 5.

> Past hope or fear.
> And the end men looked for cometh not,
> And a path is there where no man thought:
> So hath it fallen here.[57]

That is how Mark ponders and wrestles with and finally solves the problem: Christ had to die—it was the divine decree—but Christ voluntarily accepted his death, as "for many"; and the characters in the tragedy all express, the events in the story all serve, this one overmastering purpose.

The question will now be asked, What does this type of literary criticism do to the historicity of the Gospel? In answer, let me say that it seems to set the original tradition before us more clearly than ever in its pure and pristine simplicity and power. And it recognizes a principle which all New Testament research steadily and inescapably forces upon us, namely, that all history is interpretation. No history is ever produced or preserved in a vacuum. What we have in the New Testament is no barren transcript of stenographic records, but a series of rich, human, inspired interpretations. In the second place, the New Testament is a book of *faith*—of a faith still living and real, whose formulations are partly historical, partly superhistorical, partly visible and open, partly hid in the depths of personal religious experience. And it is certainly possible to share this faith without repeating the identical language in which it was first formu-

---

[57] *Medea*, final chorus, tr. Gilbert Murray.

lated. That lesson is involved in the history of all the creeds and their interpretation, in the history of our hymns and liturgies, of all our sacred books and their interpretation. We too know Christ as Master and Savior and Lord, though we may no longer use some of the terms which the early Christians used, or though we may use them in a somewhat different sense, inasmuch as the ideas originally conveyed by them are no longer familiar and natural. If, for example, we no longer expect Christ to return upon the clouds of heaven to hold the Last Judgment, as the heavenly Son of Man of the old Aramaic-speaking communities in Palestine, we do not honor or reverence or even worship him any the less. And the reason for this is simple: Jesus was *not less* than the Jewish Messiah, or than the apocalyptic "Son of Man" seen in visions and dreams by his worshipers;[58] he *was*— and *is*—in fact *far more*.[59] What the early Christian believers and writers, for example Mark, tried to do was apply to him the highest conceivable categories, human and divine; but in the end these all proved inadequate, as the later church soon discovered; for Jesus *means* more, *was* more, and *is* more than any of these categories could convey.

It is of the very first importance to recognize that the study of New Testament theology involves more than an understanding of the terms and concepts used by the earliest Christians, both in the Palestinian milieu and

[58] Rev. 1:13; Acts 7:56; etc.
[59] See the quotation from T. R. Glover in *The Gospel of the Kingdom*, p. 139.

also in the great world outside Palestine, the field of the growing Gentile mission. True, the concepts, and the terms used to express them, are of great importance, especially for the later history of doctrine; and we are not likely to minimize them if we view New Testament theology as Book One or perhaps Chapter One in the History of Christian Doctrine. Nor are we likely to minimize their importance, in view of our difficulty in comprehending them! But there is far more to New Testament theology, and specifically to the theology of Mark, than this; for we must take into account the *motives* that lay behind the choice and use of the concepts. Chief among them all was the religious motive of attributing to Christ a character adequate to account for what men discovered in him through their own personal experience. The new life in Christ, the consequent transformation of all their hopes and expectations, the sense of fresh power to achieve the hitherto impossible, the vital awareness of the change which had been effected in their relations with God, the confidence of sin forgiven and of restoration to divine favor, the "joy in the holy Spirit," and confident looking forward to great events still to come, and soon, as the result of Christ's exaltation at God's right hand and of his promised coming as Redeemer and Judge—all this lies behind the choice and the use of technical terms or concepts borrowed, first of all, from current Jewish messianism. The doctrines of the New Testament of course require a theological interpretation, at the proper time, and before that a historical interpretation, explaining their relation to one another and to the beliefs held commonly by Jews and by Gentiles in the first century; but even prior to the historical interpretation must come the psychological. By that I do not mean an explanation which does away with the doctrines, but one that shows how they are related to the actual experience of men, to the new stream of religious vitality which flowed into the world through the apostolic community of those who first followed Jesus of Nazareth and "hoped that it was he who should redeem Israel."

There is considerable diversity in the theological outlook, conceptions, and terminology of the New Testament writers; as Canon Streeter pointed out, there are at least seven distinct theologies or patterns of theological thinking in the New Testament. But these patterns are not in chronological order, in the New Testament as it stands, nor can they be set in strict chronological order by any process of reconstruction. They were not successive stages in development; they overlap; some began early and continued late, while others were of briefer duration; some began simultaneously, and only a few survived. What we see taking place is, in this respect, what normally takes place in every course of development—biological, social, and intellectual.[60] It is the normal expression of change, everywhere in the world—whether it is always progress, or improvement, is of course another question. But there is also unity as well as variety in the theology of the New Testament. And this

[60] The evolution of natural species affords an interesting illustration of the process.

unity finds its center, not in an authoritative body of opinions, beliefs, or principles, like the *dogmata* of the ancient philosophical schools, nor in an authoritative creed or confession, as in the later church. The unity of the New Testament is the unity of life itself—that life which flowed from the risen, exalted Christ through the Spirit, and held the Christians together as one body, the Body of Christ, as Paul called it, nourished and vitalized from its common Head, to continue the figure.[61] In a word, the unity of the New Testament theology is a religious unity, derived from its fundamental and original *motivation,* not from the language or the ideas commonly used to set forth its convictions, inferences, and beliefs.

The factors of chief importance in the development of this theology were: (*a*) the Old Testament—and Judaism—(*b*) the tradition of religious thought in the Hellenistic world, (*c*) the earliest Christian experience of Christ and conviction about his person, mission, and nature—this soon became the tradition of the faith or the "true doctrine"—and (*d*) the living, continuous, ongoing experience of Christ—only in theory to be distinguished from the preceding—in worship, in preaching, in teaching, in open proclamation and confession, as the manifestation of the present Spiritual Christ within his church. None of these factors can be overlooked, even though the last is the most important and most decisive. In a sense, the development of New Testament doctrine was a "dialectical" process—not only in the

[61] Eph. 4:16.

sense often maintained, that each writer, or each apostle, contributed something to the current dialogue or discourse of Christians about Christ, each in agreement with every other. There was tension, disagreement, debate—as in the famous controversy over the Jewish Law. There was also tension between positive affirmations on the same side, as between John's conception of the miracles or of the Messiahship of Jesus, for example, and Paul's conception—or Mark's. I am using the term "dialectic" in its ancient and etymological sense, and it seems appropriate to describe the process by this word; for instead of an aprioristic, deductive method of procedure, the process was one of answering questions and objections *as they arose,* not in anticipation, and not as the unfolding, *more geometrico,* of a system implicit within a body of axioms or first principles which one needed only accept and then all the rest followed logically to the final Q.E.D. There are systems of theology like that—probably every theology developed as a system is like that—but the New Testament theology is not one of them. Some questions were never raised, and therefore were never answered, in the New Testament; some areas of religious thought were never entered—for example, cosmology, where the traditional Jewish doctrine was tacitly assumed, though there may be traces of Hellenistic or older pagan concepts in one or two passages.

The problem, then, is to get back of all these "dialectical" tendencies and developments in the thinking of the early church to the one which antedates them all. This must be done if we are to locate Mark's point of emergence in the process, and to assess its influence and importance. The earliest type of Christian doctrine in the New Testament is without doubt that reflected in the sources underlying Acts 1–12—whatever the date of the writing of Luke-Acts. The conception of Christ, his mission, office, person, and nature, reflected in these chapters is the one required to explain the later developments of Christology—and it scarcely needs mentioning that the earliest Christian theology was essentially a *Christology;* this was the new, specific, distinctive Christian teaching. But is even this conception the very earliest? May it not be an advance upon some still earlier stage? I should say it is the earliest of which we have any trace, and further that it is hard to see how any simpler or more primitive conception could have resulted in a new departure in religious doctrine, with the total result that not only the New Testament but all early Christian theology makes evident. If the earliest conception of Jesus had been something *less* than that reflected in Acts 1–12, Christianity would perhaps never have arisen as a religion distinct from the Jewish. As Johannes Weiss described it in his famous Book I of *The History of Primitive Christianity,* this doctrine centered in the belief that Jesus rose from the dead as the glorified, heavenly Messiah. This doctrine recognized that his death was "for our sins" as Paul also states, in summing up the traditional doctrine[62]—but there is no doctrine of the Atonement, as yet. The belief in Christ's resurrection, that is, his exaltation, is based, not upon any report of the open

[62] I Cor. 15:3.

tomb—which came later—but upon the visions of the earliest witnesses; the technical term for their experience is the very one (ὤφθη) used in the Old Testament and elsewhere to tell of heavenly appearances, "epiphanies," and visions. (Though to call them "visions" is to emphasize unduly the subjective element in the experience, and to raise a whole series of modern questions. The earliest tradition says only, "He *appeared* to Cephas . . . ." and to others. There was absolutely no question whatsoever of the objective reality of the one who appeared thus in "vision." [63]) It was not even certain when, precisely, the first appearance took place, whether "on the third day" or, more probably, "after three days"—the tradition varies, as Weiss points out. The idea of the Ascension after a long interval, say forty days, is a very late conception, not reflected anywhere in the earliest tradition. The earliest view—reflected even in John 20: 17—is either that Jesus ascended at once, or that his resurrection *was* his ascension and exaltation.[64] Those who first saw him risen from the dead saw him in glory—Paul draws no distinction between his own vision of the glorified Christ and the form in which he had appeared earlier to others.

It was this conviction, which lay at the heart of the oldest Christian tradition, that Mark took for granted

[63] I should like to repeat the note which I inserted in Weiss's *History of Primitive Christianity*, I, 28: "If we are to conceive of a spiritual 'body,' it must nevertheless be completely 'spiritual.' Objectivity and spirituality are not opposed, save in relation to the ordinary range of our organs of sense. 'Objective' is used here in the sense of external to our *minds*, not our bodies."

[64] Luke 24:50-51 is a later modification of this view.

when he advanced the further step of assuming, and endeavoring to demonstrate, that Jesus was *already* Messiah, already the "Son of Man," during his earthly life, and before his death and resurrection. Not only, as we have seen, did the disciples suspect it—though forbidden to speak of it until later—but the demons, with supernatural insight, recognized him; and at the Baptism and the Transfiguration there were visible foregleams of his coming glorification. Now this type of christological advance was followed by the later Synoptists—though not without survivals of the older view found in some of their other sources. It was also followed by John,[65] who carefully lists the seven great "signs" by which Jesus manifested his divine "glory" during his earthly ministry— though for some reason John has not one word about the exorcism of demons. It was also, obviously, followed by the later theology of the church—all the way to Pope Leo's *Tome* and the Creed of Chalcedon. But it was not followed by all writers of the New Testament. Paul—who of course antedates Mark—takes his departure from an earlier type of doctrine, according to which Jesus was no doubt the Christ during his earthly life, but secretly; his "glory" he laid aside, temporarily, when he became man, and he resumed it when raised from the dead "by the glory of God the Father";[66] not even the demons recognized him in his true nature, else they would never have

---

[65] Whether or not he knew the Gospel of Mark. See P. Gardiner-Smith, *St. John and the Synoptic Gospels* (1938), a very convincing argument for "John's" complete independence of the Synoptics.

[66] Rom. 6:4.

put to death the Lord of glory;[67] his crucifixion was not
their victory but their defeat. Nor does Paul suggest anywhere that Jesus had wrought miracles, least of all exorcisms of demons; nor does he refer to him as the "Son
of Man." A similar view to that of Paul and of the primitive community is set forth in the creedlike passage of
First Peter.

> Christ . . . . suffered for sins once,
>   the righteous for the unrighteous,
> that he might bring us to God;
>   being put to death *in the flesh,*
>   but made alive *in the spirit.*[68]

Now Paul's theology must be studied as a *Jewish* theology *modified* by the conception of Jesus as the Risen
Messiah; that is, it was a Jewish theology—of the high
Pharisaic type, in some respects; in others, quite un-
Pharisaic, and making much use of apocalyptic conceptions, as Brückner and others have shown—and to this
Jewish theology was added the new, distinctive, trans-
forming conviction that the Messiah was none other than
the lowly Jesus, dead, raised to glory, and soon to come
again. This is what gave Paul's theology its distinctive-
ness—and the heart and core of it was derived from the
primitive community, not perhaps at Jerusalem but more
probably at one of the new outposts of Hellenistic Christianity, in Damascus or in Antioch.[69] Its distinction from

[67] I Cor. 2:8.
[68] I Pet. 3:18.
[69] This is one of the main presuppositions of Wilhelm Bousset's *Kyrios*

Mark's theology is not its origin, but its point of departure—perhaps from an earlier level than Mark's—and its transcendental or metaphysical development, which in the end left that of Mark far behind, though chronologically Mark is some years later than Paul.

At the same time it must be recognized, as we have already observed, that Mark's theology likewise went back to the primitive tradition for its basic structure. The underlying tradition in the Gospel of Mark, and its view of Jesus, is fundamentally Palestinian—this all historical critics now recognize. It also, then, is a Jewish theology, modified by the conception of Jesus as the "Son of Man"; but it is not the same type of Judaism, that is, of Christian Judaism, that Paul presupposes. It seems to reflect, not the full Hellenistic conception of Jesus as "Lord," nor the Judean conception of him as the "Messiah, the King of Israel," but the Galilean view of him as the "Son of Man," a conception which, as Lohmeyer maintains, was probably current in the north, where the Enoch, Noah, and Daniel sagas had their greatest currency and perhaps their origin.[70] One of the most important steps in the development of primitive Christian doctrine, and by far the most important for the tradition embodied in Mark and the Synoptics, took place when Jesus was identified with this celestial figure of apocalyptic expectation. It

---

Christos (3rd ed., 1926). There have been many criticisms of the details of Bousset's argument; the main thesis seems to me to be established. However, I should want to modify the statement of it in some respects; see my "Form Criticism and the Christian Faith," *Journal of Bible and Religion*, 7(1939):9-17; and a final "Note," *ibid.*, 7:177-80.

[70] See chap. vi above, "Jerusalem or Galilee?"

may have been a second step, following the first which
identified Jesus with the Messiah—a view held more
firmly in the south—or it may indeed have been the very
first step, direct and immediate, from the appearance
of the risen Jesus to the inference that he was now the
anticipated heavenly figure of Daniel's vision, as cur-
rently interpreted. It may, in fact, as many believe, go
back to Jesus' own self-identification, though this seems
more than doubtful, or to Jesus' own words about the
coming heavenly "Man," with whom his followers now
identified him. Whatever its origin—and I myself agree
with Wellhausen and others in attributing the identification to the primitive Christian community, as their least
inadequate and only possible term for one who was thus
both human and divine and yet not God (which would
have been unthinkable in their realm of ideas)—whatever its origin, this first great step in the advance of
Christology was of endless significance for the later development of Christian doctrine, and it was of paramount importance for the Gospel of Mark. It at once
provided the author with a clue to his quest: the hidden,
secret "Son of Man" was the Messiah living incognito
—or practically incognito—during his earthly life, and
yet in truth already the divine being whom all Christian
faith acknowledged as the head of his community since
the Resurrection. But it also set him his problem: How
could Christ *remain* unknown? Above all, how could
he have been put to death? The former question he answers with his theory of the messianic secret; the second
brings us to the Marcan passion narrative.

VIII

MARK'S PASSION NARRATIVE

WE HAVE SAID THAT THE PASSION NARRATIVE IS NOW
recognized to be the oldest continuous narrative in the
Gospels. It no doubt received its consecutive form at an
early date. How else could the story be told, except as
one continuous, consecutive whole? It is noteworthy, too,
that although Matthew and Luke rearrange the order of
other parts of Mark, they adhere quite consistently to
the Marcan order in these two chapters, 14–15. Even
John, writing last of all, generally adheres to it, though
whether or not he knew it in its present Marcan form
may be debated;[1] and though he does not scruple to
rewrite the whole account of the ministry, he keeps the
passion narrative more or less in the order in which
Mark gives it. From these facts it seems only just to infer
that the Marcan passion narrative was already, when
Mark wrote, in fairly stable form, and that it continued
to be told and retold in practically this form—possibly at
the Christian services of worship[2] and quite apart from
the written Gospels, indeed before they were compiled.
One part of it, the account of the Last Supper, was

[1] No doubt he adheres to it not because it is Mark's but because it is
the traditional passion narrative.

[2] Cf. Gal. 3:1. See Georg Bertram, *Die Leidensgeschichte Jesu und der
Christuskult* (1922).

175

probably so used,[3] and came in time to form the very heart of the Eucharistic liturgy, conspicuously and distinctly so in the Western church.

The question now arises, What was the original extent and contents of this passion narrative? Did it contain an account of the Resurrection? Were any of the incidents it now contains added to the narrative by Mark? In answer, let us go over the narrative in detail, as it is reconstructed by various modern scholars, more or less in agreement—notably by Martin Dibelius, Rudolf Bultmann, Hans Lietzmann, and others.[4]

The plot against Jesus—14:1-2

[Jesus at Bethany—3-9; this was once an independent pericope, as we may infer from Luke and John—cf. Luke 7:36-38; John 12:1-8]

The Treachery of Judas—10-11 (continues verses 1-2)

[The Preparation for the Passover—12-16. The Marcan character of this section is apparent from its parallel to 11:1-7. The time reference in vs. 12 is wrong, and conflicts with vss. 1-2 and with the Gospel of John. It has even been suspected that this is a Hellenistic story of an early Christian looking for a church service! Note that a man is carrying the jar of water, not a woman as it would be in Palestine.]

[3] Cf. I Cor. 11:23-25.
[4] See Dibelius, *The Message of Jesus Christ* (1939), pp. 30-34, 144-47; Bultmann, *Die Geschichte der synoptischen Tradition* (2nd ed., 1931), pp. 282-308; also Klostermann, 3rd ed. of his commentary in the *Handbuch*, p. 139 n.; Lietzmann, *Der Prozess Jesu* (1931); R. H. Lightfoot, *History and Interpretation in the Gospels* (1934), chap. v; A. T. Olmstead, *Jesus in the Light of History* (1942), chaps. xi, xii; Maurice Goguel, *The Life of Jesus*, chaps. xv-xx; Joseph Klausner, *Jesus of Nazareth* (1925), Bks. VI, VII. In the following table, and in the reconstruction, I have placed within square brackets the verses and passages that may be thought to be secondary— even in the pre-Marcan passion narrative.

The Last Supper—17-25. [Vss. 18b-20 may be an elaboration of the theme found in Ps. 41:10, yet even the Johannine tradition represents Judas as present at the Supper, chap 13. Vs. 21 is a Son of Man saying, indeed a double one, and probably secondary—even if late pre-Marcan.]

The prediction of the disciples' desertion—26-31. It looks forward to the flight in vs. 50, and to Peter's denials. [Vs. 28 breaks the connection, and is probably a gloss—related to the one in 16:7. Its early date is suggested by the passive form of the verb, "raised up"—contrast the passion announcements, with their active form, "rise."]

[The agony in Gethsemane—32-42. This scene, which *ex hypothesi* the disciples could scarcely have reported (vss. 37, 40, 41), is really a dramatization of the central petition of the Lord's Prayer, as the temptation narrative (in its Q form) is a dramatization in another direction, with another emphasis. Note another Son of Man saying in vs. 41.]

The arrest—43-53a, 54. [Vs. 53b is clearly editorial, and improbable; it prepares for the "all" in vs. 64. Vs. 54 belongs with the later account of Peter's denials, which it introduces. Probably that is where it stood originally, that is, before vss. 53b, 55-65 were inserted into the story.]

[The examination before the high priest—55-65. This section has been most adversely criticized. It contradicts the traditional rules of Jewish legal procedure at fourteen distinct points! And though it is sometimes argued that the rules set forth in the Mishnah (tractate Sanhedrin) are either purely theoretical or have been projected backward from the second century, this is not likely. The rules were traditional; and since the Jewish Sanhedrin ceased to exist as a civil court after A.D. 70—tradition says it lost its authority to inflict capital penalties forty years earlier—the whole point of the tradition was its preservation of earlier usage, possibly with a view to a future restoration. This was the point, similarly, of the preservation of the temple measurements in tractate Middoth, long after the actual temple had been destroyed. The scene portrayed in these verses is often thought to reflect the trial before Pilate—especially vs. 60— from an anti-Jewish point of view and with the purpose of placing the responsibility for the death of Jesus upon the Jewish authorities. Note also that it includes another Son of Man saying (vs. 62), and assumes that Jesus here avowed his identity not only with the Christ (vs. 61), further defined in non-Jewish terms as "the Son of the Blessed One," but also with the coming "Son of Man"—who, it is further assumed, is also identical with the Christ. This is the climax of the whole series of Son of Man sayings in the Gospel of Mark.]

[Peter's denials—66-72; introduced, as already noted, by vs. 54.]

Jesus before Pilate—15:1-15. Note that the account of the trial entirely ignores the findings of 14:55-65, and properly: the claim to Messiahship was not only not blasphemy, but did not justify the charge that Jesus claimed to be "King of the Jews." Nothing was made of the disciples' knowledge—which Mark assumed—of Jesus' claim, though Judas was in contact with the Jewish (?) authorities, nor of the blundering charge that Jesus had threatened to destroy the temple.

[The mockery and scourging—16-20. This is probable enough, in view of Roman practice, but the narrative fits in badly after vs. 15. John locates the account of the mockery during the trial, 19:1-2. There are other difficulties with the story, noted in the commentaries.]

The crucifixion—21-39. [Some details are probably secondary, for example vs. 23, which comes from the Old Testament (Ps. 69:21); so may be vs. 24, which would be suggested by Ps. 22:18. Vs. 25 may be original, though see John 19:14, which has "the sixth hour," not the "third." (Vs. 28, an Old Testament quotation, is omitted by most modern editors.) Vss. 29b-32a (certainly 31-32a) seem to be motivated by the same anti-Jewish tendency that inspired the account of the "trial" before the "Sanhedrin." Vs. 38 seems to be purely symbolistic in purpose. On the other hand, vss. 34-37 are too lifelike, too non-Hellenistic, and set too many problems for Christian explanation to be anything but original.]

[The watching women—40-41. This really introduces the narrative of the empty tomb, 16:1-8, and is probably no part of the primitive passion narrative. The burial, vss. 42-47, interrupts this narrative (after which, as Turner thought, 16:1a repeats from 15:40 and 47), and is accordingly secondary, though it is needed as the setting for 16:1-8. The story concludes, not with the resurrection narrative—Mark has no resurrection narrative, and his story of the empty tomb is independent of what precedes—Mark's passion narrative concludes with the testimony of the centurion: "This man was a Son of God." [5]]

Following this brief analysis, let us read consecutively the reconstructed narrative, reading it as we would the old pre-Marcan passion narrative if we could recover it in some ancient manuscript. It is the story of the death of Jesus as it was told and retold among the Palestinian

---

[5] It is clear that the third passion announcement (Mark 10:32-34) presupposes the Marcan passion narrative in its present form (see Klostermann, Commentary, 2nd ed., on 10:33, p. 119). That is, it includes steps, or incidents, which we have omitted as secondary. The steps in the procedure are: (1) the Son of Man is to be delivered to the high priests and scribes ("the elders" of 8:31 is omitted; 9:31 has "men," though the original text may have read "Gentiles"), (2) condemned to death by the Sanhedrin, (3) handed over to the heathen, (4) abused ("they will ridicule him and spit on him and flog him"—ἐμπαίζειν, ἐμπτύειν, μαστιγοῦν, as in the passion narrative), and (5) killed; (6) "after three days" he will "rise again" (the earliest tradition always said "be raised," not "rise"). The parallel announcement in 8:31 has only steps 2, 5, 6; that in 9:31 has only 1 (or 3?), 5, 6. It seems clear from a comparison of these passages with the passion narrative that (a), as we have argued (see The Growth of the Gospels, pp. 104-8, 136), the Gospel "grew backwards from the passion narrative," and that (b) the three passion announcements are indubitably by Mark himself, and secondary, that is, not part of the early tradition.

Jewish Christians, perhaps circulating first in Aramaic and then translated into Greek—though when, we do not know—and afterwards brought to Rome and circulated there, perhaps long before Mark made it the basis of his account of the crucifixion and death of the Son of God.

It was two days before the Passover. And the high priests and the scribes were seeking a way to seize him by stealth and put him to death; for they said, "Not during the feast, lest there be a public riot." Then Judas Iscariot, who was one of the Twelve, went to the high priests to betray Jesus to them. When they heard it, they were glad and promised to give him money. So he was waiting for an opportunity to hand him over to them.

[On the first day of the festival,] at evening, Jesus came with the Twelve. [As they reclined and were eating, Jesus said, "Of a truth I tell you, one of you will betray me, even 'one who is eating with me.'" They were distressed at this and said to him one after another, "Can it be I?" But he said to them, "It is one of the Twelve, who is dipping his bread with me in the same bowl."] While they were eating, Jesus took a loaf, and when he had said the blessing he broke it and gave it to them and said, "This is my body." And he took a cup, and when he had given thanks he gave it to them, and they all drank from it. And he said to them, "This is my blood of the Covenant [which is poured out for many]. I tell you truly, I will never (again) drink of the fruit of the vine until that day when I drink it new in the Kingdom of God."

When they had sung a hymn they went out to the Mount of Olives. And Jesus said to them, "You will all fall away, for it is written,

> *'I will strike the shepherd,*
> *And the sheep will be scattered.'"*

But Peter said to him, "Even if all are to fall away, yet I will not."
And Jesus said to him, "Truly I tell you, today—this very night,
before cockcrow—you will deny me three times." But he pro-
tested vehemently, "Even if I must die with you, I will by no
means deny you." So likewise said they all.

While he was still speaking, Judas came (who was one of the
Twelve), and with him a crowd (armed) with swords and clubs
[whom the chief priests and scribes and elders had sent]. Now
the betrayer had agreed with them upon a signal, saying, "The
one I kiss, that is he; seize him, and lead him away securely."
So when he arrived he [at once] went up to Jesus and said to
him, "My master," and kissed him. Then they laid hands on
Jesus and took him prisoner. And one of those standing by drew
a sword and struck the servant of the high priest and cut off
his ear.

Then Jesus spoke to them and said, "Have you come out as
against a robber, (armed) with swords and clubs to capture me?
Day by day I was with you, teaching in the temple, and you
did not arrest me. [But (this has come to pass) in order that
the scriptures might be fulfilled!]" Then they all forsook him
and fled. And a certain young man followed them, with nothing
but a linen cloth about him; and they seized him, but he left
the linen cloth and ran away naked. So they led Jesus before the
high priest.

[And Peter followed him at a distance, until he was inside
the courtyard of the high priest's house. Here he was sitting with
the guards and warming himself at the fire. While he was below
in the courtyard one of the maids of the high priest came, and
seeing Peter warming himself she looked at him and said, "You
too were with the Nazarene, Jesus!" But he denied it, saying,
"I do not know nor understand. What is it you are saying?" But
he went out into the gateway. Here the maid saw him and again
began saying to those who were standing there, "This is one
of them!" But he again denied it. Once more, a little later, those
standing by said to Peter, "There is no doubt you are one of

*them—you are a Galilean!" Then he began to curse and swear,
saying, "I do not know this man you are talking about!" And
at once the cock crew, and Peter recalled the words Jesus had
said to him, "Before cockcrow you will deny me three times."
And he broke down and cried.*]

As soon as it was morning, the chief priests held a consulta-
tion with the elders and scribes [and the whole Sanhedrin] and
bound Jesus and led him away and delivered him to Pilate. [And
Pilate asked him, "Are you 'the King of the Jews'?" Jesus answered, "You have said so" (or, "That is for you to say!" or, "Do
you say so?").] And the chief priests accused him of many
things. (But he answered nothing.) So Pilate [again] asked him,
"Have you no answer to make? See how many charges they
bring against you!" But Jesus made no further reply, so that
Pilate was surprised.

Now at festivals he used to release to them a prisoner, anyone
they asked for. There was one named Bar-Abbas, who lay bound
with those who were guilty of insurrection and in the insurrection had committed murder. The crowd came up and began to
ask him to do for them as he usually did. Then Pilate answered
and said, "Do you want me to release to you 'the King of the
Jews'?" (For he knew that it was out of jealousy the chief
priests had delivered him up.) But the high priests stirred up the
crowd to ask to have Bar-Abbas released to them instead. So
Pilate spoke to them again and said, "What then do you want me
to do with the one you call 'the King of the Jews'?" They cried
out [again], "Crucify him!" But Pilate said to them, "What
crime has he committed?" At that they shouted all the more,
"Crucify him!" So Pilate, wishing to satisfy the mob, released
to them Bar-Abbas, and ordered Jesus to be flogged and crucified.

So they led him out to crucify him. (On the way) they compelled a man passing by, Simon the Cyrenian, who was coming
in from the country—he was the father of Alexander and Rufus—
to carry his cross. And they took him to the place called Gol-
gothá (which means, the Place of a Skull). [And they offered

him a drink of wine with myrrh in it, but he would not take it.]
And they crucified him. The inscription stating his crime read,
"The King of the Jews." With him they crucified two robbers,
one at his right hand and one at his left. And the passers-by
reviled him . . . . and the two who were crucified with him
upbraided him.

When the sixth hour had come, darkness came over the whole
land until the ninth hour. At the ninth hour Jesus cried out with
a loud voice, "Elôi, Elôi, lamá sabachtháni?" (which means,
"My God, my God, why hast thou forsaken me?") Some of the
bystanders, when they heard it, said, "Listen, he is calling for
Elijah!" One of them ran and soaked a sponge in vinegar and
put it on a stick and offered him a drink, and said, "Wait and
see if Elijah will come and take him down!" Then Jesus uttered
a loud cry and breathed his last. When the centurion who was
standing opposite him saw that he had died, he said, "Surely
this man was a Son of God."

As we now read this consecutive narrative, in the form
in which I have ventured to reconstruct it, freed from
the secondary passages, we find, I believe, that this simple
story contains all that might be thought to be derived
from the earliest Christian tradition upon the subject.
Of course it was amplified from other sources, by Mark
himself and also by the later evangelists—it was still being amplified in the second and third centuries by the
writers of the apocryphal Gospels,[6] as it is still further
amplified by modern imaginative writers, not to mention
most of us preachers of the gospel, church school teachers, and others! We are not now considering the source

[6] See the Gospel of Nicodemus and the Gospel of Peter—most con-
veniently accessible in M. R. James, *The Apocryphal New Testament* (1924),
pp. 90 ff.

or the value of the "secondary" elements, but only of the passion narrative in its pristine form.

The main, unforgettable impression which we gain from the story in its earliest recoverable form is not that of human treachery and vindictiveness, or of the sufferings endured by the martyr-hero, as in the Maccabean tales and in many Christian martyrologies, but an impression of the calm certainty with which Jesus goes to his death. He does not argue, or even parry the thrusts of a debate, as in the Gospel of John. The colorful touches which Luke added to it are not here—Luke was an artist in words, and his narrative paints a scene; even Antipas reappears. But the primitive story, embedded in Mark, is one of stark simplicity. "Pilate asked him, 'And so you are the King of the Jews?' He replied, 'You say'" —σὺ λέγεις—which may mean simply "Yes" (so Matthew surely understood the words), or may be an interrogation, as Hort suggested ("Would you say so?" or, "Do you say it?"), or may even be an imperative ("You answer! That is for you to say!"), though this last suggestion is perhaps too subtle for this simple narrative. "And the priests brought all manner of charges against him. Then Pilate asked him again, 'Won't you answer? You hear what they are saying against you!' But Jesus made no further reply, so that Pilate knew not what to think of him." There is no studied drama about this scene. It is a Galilean peasant preacher and healer, caught in the net spread by the fanatical temple priesthood of Jerusalem, on trial for his life before the Roman governor. And he makes no reply, no defense.[7] The prophet of Nazareth is a stranger to courts and Roman procurators, and to the machinations of a powerful priestly clique. He is bound, with his hands behind him. But even were he unbound and free, he would not attempt either escape or defense. Already his silence is crying out, as the Good Friday hymn describes the scene. All his life he has trusted in God, and accepted the course of events as the manifest will of God for him. If it is God's will, then he must drink the cup. If it is God's will that he must die—and events point clearly that way—then he will still trust in God, knowing that God has a plan and purpose which his death must serve, and that if he trusts God utterly and to the very end, God will use him, living and dying, to bring his Kingdom to pass. Thus he dies a martyr—but not a martyr to a *cause,* like the Maccabees, or the early Christians. This "martyrology" is different—Jesus dies because he cannot free himself from God, because his will has been utterly and without reserve made over to God, and he does not ask to see his way or to know the meaning of each successive step.[8] The meaning would be clear enough when the battle was over, the victory won.

The very simplicity and directness of the story carries the sense of mystery. Underlying this simple scene is the

[7] It may be thought that this feature is derived from Isa. 53:7. On the other hand, it may equally be true that Jesus' silence brought this verse to mind.

[8] A point I have tried to bring out in an article, "The Beginning of Jesus' Ministry," *Journal of Biblical Literature,* 52:189-202; also in my *Life and Times of Jesus* (1921).

profoundest mystery of all our life in this world. Why must any man suffer? Why, above all, must Christ suffer? Why, in a world under God's sovereign control, must the best of men suffer the worst of fates? The early Christians, who told and retold this story, saw what it meant, saw, that is, some way into the dark abyss of mystery; and they saw by the light of Jesus' resurrection and exaltation. God did not, God could not abandon him in death [9]—in spite of the mysterious last cry that fell from his lips. Death could not hold him in restraint[10]—not such a one as he, surely. God had willed and foreseen it all—and God had used it all, for his purposes of redemption, so that sin might be done away, so that its power might be broken, and so that actual sins of men might be blotted out. But all this, the explanation, came later; what we have in the primitive Passion Narrative is the stark recital of facts, with only a minimum of the current interpretation—the story of Jesus' death as it was recited in the early Christian communities for almost forty years before Mark took pen in hand to write out the full story of Jesus as he had heard it and as he understood it.[11]

The task of interpretation is with us still. We have not fathomed even yet the full depths of the meaning of

[9] Acts 2:27.

[10] Acts 2:24.

[11] Of course the interpretation is introduced into the narrative, as was perfectly natural in ancient popular religious writing as well as in tradition. We should probably add it as an explanation, and then take great credit to ourselves for adding such an illuminating bit of wisdom! But then we lack the objectivity as well as the naïveté of those who handed down or wrote down ancient religious traditions.

Jesus' suffering and death, though the main lines are
clear. And we shall never understand fully, no doubt,
unless we too are called to share his baptism and drink
his cup. But the Christian martyrs in the Roman arena,
in Mark's day, knew what the death of Jesus meant.
They drank his cup—to its very dregs. And they likewise knew "the power of his resurrection." "They were
put to death with exquisite cruelty," says Tacitus, "and
to their sufferings Nero added mockery and derision.
Some were covered with the skins of wild beasts, and
left to be devoured by dogs; others were nailed to the
cross; numbers were burnt alive; and many, covered
with inflammable matter, were lighted up, when the day
declined, to serve as torches during the night." [12] These
were the men and women who handed down the story
of Jesus' death—the old Roman passion narrative underlying Mark's account in chapters 14 and 15. What it
meant to them is probably something we shall never
guess, unless we too stand someday in the same desperate
place of utter need, and cry out for sympathy and compassion to One who himself faced all the blind, venomous
hatred, the implacable, vindictive fury of brute, senseless
power, and pray, with them and with the martyr Stephen, "Lord Jesus, receive my spirit."

[12] *Annals* 15.44, tr. Murphy.

IX

WAS MARK A PAULINE GOSPEL?

IT IS NOW QUITE GENERALLY HELD THAT THE GOSPEL OF Mark reflects the influence of the teaching of Paul, though not, perhaps, in a direct and unmodified form. This influence is seen especially in such phrases as "the gospel of God," [1] in the ransom saying,[2] and in the words at the Last Supper, "This is my blood of the Covenant, which is shed for many." [3] On the other hand, the latest commentary in English, by Professor Branscomb, insists that these supposed examples of "Paulinism" really reflect the common Gentile Christianity of the time rather than the explicit or distinctive teaching of Paul. At once the question arises: What, then, was Paul's relation to Gentile Christianity? What elements in it did he take for granted; what elements—if any—did he contribute to it? It has too often been assumed that Paul alone was responsible for Gentile Christianity, and that all of early Gentile Christianity therefore bore the impress of his thought. But it seems clear that a very important stage of early non-Jewish Christianity had been reached before Paul began his missionary career, and that he himself

[1] Mark 1:14. See my note above, p. 153, on the textual reading here, and also my article, "Studies in the Text of St. Mark," *Anglican Theological Review,* 20:103 ff.

[2] Mark 10:45.

[3] Mark 14:24.

was dependent in no small degree upon this earlier development. That he owed a debt to "those who were in Christ [that is, Christians] before me," as he says, though not to the *Jerusalem* apostles,[4] seems certain—he himself appears to take it for granted his readers will know this. But to what degree, and upon what specific points? These are questions that require an answer—and the problem of the supposed "Paulinism" of Mark is thus part of a still larger problem, involving the whole development of New Testament theology.

The most thorough recent examination of the hypothesis of Pauline influence upon Mark is the book by Martin Werner of the Swiss University of Berne, *The Influence of Pauline Theology in the Gospel of Mark: A Study in New Testament Theology,* which appeared in 1923 as the first *Beiheft* to the *Zeitschrift für die neutestamentliche Wissenschaft.* It begins with a review of previous treatments of the problem, from Volkmar and Holsten to Holtzmann and Harnack, and with a discussion of the proper method of dealing with the subject. Earlier writers had recognized that Volkmar went too far in his attempted demonstration of Mark's dependence upon Paul—he found evidence of such dependence on almost every page of the Gospel—but his view was such a welcome relief from the one-sided Tübingen theory, according to which Mark was a "neutral" in the great apostolic controversy over Jewish Christianity, that the main thesis of Volkmar was accepted without careful scrutiny of his supporting arguments. As to method, the older view

⁴ Gal. 1–2.

was rooted in the traditional ecclesiastical theory of
Mark's derivation from Matthew—which modern Synoptic study completely reverses—and it took for granted
a conception of "Paulinism" which made the Apostle to
the Gentiles responsible for everything in primitive Christianity which could not be squared with a crass, reac-
tionary Christian Judaism; it completely ignored the development of a Gentile type—or types—of Christianity
apart from and even prior to the work of Paul. Moreover, the allegorical or "symbolical" interpretation of the
Gospel, which Volkmar, Holsten, and Schulze had
pressed to its utmost limits, still survived—at least in the
interpretation of certain crucial passages. For example,
the cursing of the figtree was thought to be a "symbolical" judgment upon unfruitful Israel; the Transfiguration symbolized the superior glory of Christ in contrast
to that of Moses;[5] the strange exorcist of Mark 9:38 represented a party in the early church, and the question,
"Who is greatest?" referred to the Jewish Christians
versus the Gentiles; the leaven of the Pharisees was the
theory of salvation by works (still attributed to Peter!);
the healing of the blind man was the release of the disciples from "Jewish blindness"; names like Jaïrus and
Bartimaeus contained subtle allegorical meanings; the
Gerasene demoniac symbolized idolatrous heathenism;
the rending of the temple veil meant the end of Judaism; the darkness at the Crucifixion symbolized the
darkness of men's minds apart from Christ; the healing
of the deaf mute was the symbol of conversion—either

[5] II Cor. 3:7.

of Jews or Gentiles, it was not certain which! And so on. Werner examines each of these passages in detail and concludes that in none of them is the allegorical method of interpretation necessary, while in most it is positively excluded. Mark is a factual writer, not a symbolist or allegorist, and the allegorical principle does violence to his simple, direct manner of presentation; often it does violence to his actual text. The demonstration is complete, and we need only add that if anyone is still inclined to look for allegory in the Gospel of Mark, let him work carefully through the brief twenty-two pages in Werner's book where he refutes the theory in detail.

With the allegorical principle once set aside, much of the support for the supposed Paulinism of Mark disappears. As in most examples of allegorical or symbolical interpretation, the interpreter's views are first subtly read into the text and then adroitly extracted by a pretended exegesis. But what is this "Paulinism," which is so subtly read in? It is extraordinary how widely interpreters differ. Even Harnack, in his *Luke the Physician,* could write: "Whoever confessed Christ as Lord (*Kyrios*), and renounced both the good things and the burdens of this life, and looked upon the Old Testament as God's revelation, and looked forward to the resurrection, and proclaimed this to the Greeks without requiring them to be circumcized and to observe the ceremonial law—such a person was a Paulinist." [6] Not everyone who holds the Gospel of Mark to be "Pauline" would accept this definition of Paulinism! And it certainly seems overly

[6] P. 101; Eng. tr., p. 142.

simple—one can hardly distinguish this from the early Gentile Christianity reflected in the sources presumably underlying the first half of Acts; while the great cardinal doctrines of Paul, his distinctive and characteristic doctrines of salvation (or "justification") by faith, the new mystical life "in Christ," the Christian's freedom from the Law (not only the ceremonial law), the guidance of the Spirit, the future of the Jewish people, Christ's death "to sin," the relation of flesh and spirit, the atonement upon the cross—none of these distinctive and characteristic doctrines of Paul are included. What is required is not an examination of Mark in the light of common Gentile Christianity, which Paul shared and presupposed, but a point-blank comparison of every possible contact between the theology of Mark and that which was specifically and uniquely Paul's own. The result will be a better-focused view of both theologies—though Paul's is the more explicit of the two, and Mark's has to be inferred and read between the lines. Neither author was writing a systematic treatise in theology, but Paul is assuredly more of a theologian than Mark.

Werner begins his investigation with Christology—for the doctrine of God is not explicit in either Paul or Mark, but must be inferred from the concrete expression of the divine relations to the world, to mankind, to sin and salvation.[7] Paul of course assumes that Christ was the incarnation of a divine being; therefore his existence embraces three stages, one prior to his incarnation, one

[7] Werner is quoting H. J. Holtzmann on p. 32.

during his earthly-historical life, one following his resurrection and exaltation. It is a question if Mark shared this view, and distinguished these three stages. It is a further question how far Mark and Paul were in agreement in viewing the earthly-historical life of Jesus under the category of Messiahship or of a messianic career. Mark uses the term "Christ" only rarely, and where he does so it still bears its primitive significance as a title: Jesus is the "Messiah" of Jewish expectation, though the Jewish etymology and primary meaning, the "Anointed," is not stressed. On the other hand, for Paul "Christ" has become a personal name. This is probably not distinctive of Paul—he got it from the primitive church—though his own characteristic inversion "Christ Jesus" occurred (in the original text of Paul's letters) probably as often as, or perhaps even oftener than, the familiar order "Jesus Christ." It is clear that Mark's use of the term owes nothing to Paul; both Paul and Mark derive their usage from the common Christianity of the time, Paul often going beyond this to invert the order for emphasis; but of this characteristic Pauline advance not a trace is to be found in Mark.

When we turn to the title "Son of David," we are struck at once by the fact that Mark represents Jesus as repudiating the Davidic descent of the Messiah, as if it were a scribal interpretation[8] and not a matter of inspired prophecy; while Paul insists upon the Davidic descent[9] as a matter not of historical evidence but of exegesis,

[8] Mark 12:35-37.
[9] Rom. 1:3.

though limiting it to the earthly life of Christ (κατὰ σάρκα) in contrast to his divine Sonship (κατὰ πνεῦμα) which was demonstrated by the Resurrection. It is almost as if Mark and Paul were dealing with the same problem, the importance of Davidic descent for the Christian Messiah; Paul solves it by recognizing Jesus as Son of David only "according to the flesh," Mark by denying the necessity of such descent. Mark of course distinguishes the stages of Jesus' preresurrection and post-resurrection Messiahship, but there is no trace in Mark of the Pauline terminology "according to the flesh" and "according to the Spirit"—not to mention the question whether or not Mark thought of Christ as pre-existent (probably not). It appears to be quite impossible that Mark can have been influenced by Paul at this point.

Even more remarkable is the contrast between Mark and Paul when we turn to the title "Son of Man." For Mark this is the self-designation used by Jesus himself, and used only by Jesus, not by others. It occurs fourteen times in the Gospel, and is unquestionably understood by Mark to refer to Jesus' heavenly office or nature—"a supernatural being who ranks between God and the angels." [10] Mark assumes that his readers will recognize the reference to Jesus, and will find its meaning in "the scriptures." [11] But back of Mark is certainly a process of exegesis, which *combined* sayings in the Old Testament that could be understood to refer to the coming of the Son of Man with other sayings that could be interpreted

[10] P. 42.
[11] Mark 9:12; 14:21.

to prophesy the sufferings, death, and resurrection of someone—presumably now also the Messiah or the Son of Man. What is distinctive and most striking about this exegesis—"the one unheard-of novelty"—is the conception of the Son of Man living upon earth *prior* to his coming in glory: he not only will come, sometime in the future, on the clouds of heaven; he has already come, has suffered, has died, has risen again! Even the passages[12] which used to be interpreted of "Christ's human nature" or "man in general" are now recognized to belong with the others referring to "the Son of Man upon earth" prior to his death and glorification.

Now one might expect that this pattern of interpretation would have been retained by Paul, if historical—that is, if set forth by Jesus himself or found in the earliest tradition of his sayings or expounded in the early church —or one might even think it possible that Mark derived from Paul some hint of this system of exegesis of the Old Testament and of interpretation of the career of Jesus as a heavenly being appearing upon earth prior to his exaltation and his dying (as a heavenly being) upon the cross, though unrecognized in his true nature until the Resurrection. But the astonishing fact is that Paul never uses the term "Son of Man"! As against Johannes Weiss's exegesis of I Corinthians 15:45-47, Werner insists that Paul's "man who is from heaven" is simply exegesis of the first two chapters of Genesis, and has nothing to do with Daniel 7; the very order is reversed—the earthly man comes first, the heavenly is the second. (This

[12] Mark 2:10, 28.

cannot possibly refer to the two stages in Christ's existence: Christ is not ψυχικός; and the two "men" are contrasted, Adam and Christ.) What Paul is controverting is the idea that there were two steps in the creation of man, first the Primal Man, the heavenly, spiritual Urmensch, then the mortal copy of this immortal being, the first representative of the human species—a widespread Hellenistic conception which had left traces of its influence even upon Judaism. On the other hand, Mark's use of the term "Son of Man" owes nothing to Paul—since Paul does not use it—but is centered in the early Christian interpretation of the Son of Man vision of Daniel 7. That both Mark and Paul think of Christ as a supernatural being does not argue the dependence of one upon the other—the whole development of Gentile Christianity, Pauline and non-Pauline, took that for granted.

It is the title "Son of God," as Werner maintains, that most clearly expresses Mark's Christology. It occurs in the title of the Gospel, and again at the end of the passion narrative.[18] From 8:38 it is evident that the Son of God and the Son of Man are identical: "When he [the Son of Man] comes in the glory of his Father." When Jesus became Son of God, Mark does not say; but the moment of his baptism, when the Spirit came upon him—or to him, literally "into"—was probably the moment when he was so chosen and dedicated. At once follow the words of divine approval, "Thou art my beloved Son: in thee I

[18] Mark 15:39: "Truly this man was the Son of God"—so Werner translates.

am well pleased"—here Jesus is first "set forth as Son of God," though not yet "with power";[14] that came later, at the Resurrection. It is not at all probable that Mark thought of Christ as pre-existent; the title "Son of God" is only one more messianic title, and does not connote a metaphysical, hypostatic union with the Father—13:32 and 10:18 rule out that idea.

What, then, becomes of the theory that "Mark's Christology is quite as high as that of Paul"? For Mark, Jesus of Nazareth became Son of God at his baptism, through the endowment of the divine Spirit; for Paul, on the other hand, the Son of God was a divine being who existed with God before the creation of the world, who became the intermediary cause or agent in the creation and remained the sustaining principle of the universe. In due time, this being became man; then after fulfilling his earthly life he died, rose again, and was exalted by God to a place in heaven even higher than that which he had enjoyed at the beginning.[15] His specific messianic office he will fulfill at the Parousia. It is hardly necessary to go into a detailed comparison of the two Christologies; in their main outlines they are wholly incompatible. As Werner puts it,

For Mark, a man becomes Messiah. For Paul, the Messiah becomes (temporarily) a man. For Mark, the Messiahship is sketched out in the picture of a human life; for Paul, the human life is an episode in the history of a heavenly, messianic being. To put it in a formula, which of course may be pressed too far:

[14] Rom. 1:4.
[15] Phil. 2:9.

The miracle, for Mark, is the deification of Jesus; for Paul it is the incarnation. That is to say, Mark's Christology is at its basis entirely different from Paul's.[16]

It might be argued that Paul's Christology is a further development of Mark's; but that is impossible, chronologically. What we have in Paul is a further, and very distinctive, development of the primitive Christology, partly on the basis of pre-Christian Jewish and even syncretistic—that is, partly pagan—speculations[17] which Paul evidently indulged in before he became a Christian, partly on the basis of the ongoing life and thought of the early Gentile church, which Paul shared.

Furthermore, the whole conception of the earthly life of Jesus is different in Mark and in Paul. Mark is endeavoring to show, among other things, that Jesus was Messiah "even during his earthly life"—as Johannes Weiss put it. Therefore the gift of the Spirit at the beginning of his messianic career; therefore the resulting "mighty works" of healing, exorcism, and miracle; therefore the cries of the demons, with their supernatural insight, upon recognizing him; therefore the divine at-

[16] Pp. 49-50.

[17] Paul's contact with the pagan world of his time is recognized in most modern studies; indeed, it is sometimes exaggerated. Fundamentally, of course, he was a Jew, but he was not a Palestinian scribal Jew. Instead, he was a Jew of the Diaspora, and his type of Judaism was already in contact with speculations originating outside Judaism. See Weiss, *History of Primitive Christianity*, Bk. III, "Paul the Christian and Theologian"; Brückner, *Die Entstehung der paulinischen Christologie* (1903); Wilfred L. Knox, *St. Paul and the Church of Jerusalem* (1925) and *St. Paul and the Church of the Gentiles* (1939); W. Morgan, *The Religion and Theology of Paul* (1917); Bousset, *Kyrios Christos* (3rd ed., 1926), chaps. iii, iv; A. D. Nock, "Early Gentile Christianity and its Hellenistic Background," *Essays on the Trinity and the Incarnation*, ed. A. E. J. Rawlinson (1928), also his *St. Paul* (1939).

testations at the Baptism and Transfiguration. For Paul, on the contrary, the endowment of the Spirit is renounced by the heavenly Messiah at his incarnation, and resumed again at his resurrection; as for miracles, "wonders and signs" of his supernatural office, nature, or power—they are totally lacking! [18] Paul's fundamental conception of the *kenôsis,* and of the hiding of the divine glory during Jesus' earthly life, is flatly contradicted by Mark's story of the Transfiguration. Thus, as Paul Wernle put it, "The Christology of Mark conflicts with that of Paul at almost every point."

The same is true of the conception of the death of Christ.[19] Both Paul and Mark view it as effecting salvation, the removal of sin or guilt. But for Paul it is the only act of Christ in his earthly life that had messianic significance. Christ came, or was sent, in order to die.[20] This is not Mark's view. He thinks of Christ's mission "to destroy the works of the devil"—almost as in the later Johannine epistle—and represents the Son of Man as "having power upon earth to forgive sins," [21] that is, during his earthly life, and not depending upon the efficacy of his death. The purpose of Christ's death, according to Mark, is "to give his life a ransom for many";[22] his blood is the "blood of the covenant which is shed for

[18] Note that Paul mentions none of Jesus' miracles, though his raising of the dead would have provided a very strong argument in 1 Cor. 15, for example.

[19] Pp. 60 ff.

[20] Rom. 8:3; Gal. 4:4.

[21] Mark 2:10.

[22] Mark 10:45.

many";[23] yet Mark does not elaborate the principle or
explain how it was that "the many" were to benefit by
Christ's death. That death, the death of the Son of Man,
was necessary, for it was revealed in scripture, and was
therefore in accordance with the will of God.[24] But this
goes no further than the doctrine as Paul received it
from the primitive church. As he writes to the Corinthians, "Among the very first things I delivered to you
what I myself had received, namely that Christ died for
our sins in accordance with the scriptures."[25] In other
words, the teaching that the death of Christ was (a) for
sin and (b) in accordance with the scriptures was derived
by both Mark and Paul from the primitive church; the
doctrine of the Atonement is *not* Paul's unique and distinctive contribution to Christian thought, for it is really
pre-Pauline; further, it is not at all the central, cardinal
doctrine in "Paulinism," but a subsidiary one;[26] finally,
the conception of the way in which Christ's death becomes effective, as Paul conceived it, is peculiar to Paul
and finds no trace in Mark or indeed elsewhere in the
New Testament[27]—Paul thinks of it as a conquest of the
demonic powers in the very hour of their greatest aggression and apparent triumph.[28] We can scarcely hesitate to agree with Werner, Wernle, and Feine: "The

[23] Mark 14:24.
[24] Mark 8:31; etc. Also Mark stresses Jesus' voluntary acceptance of the
divine decrees.
[25] I Cor. 15:3. See also I Thess. 1:10; Gal. 3:13; 4:5.
[26] Indeed, it is a component one—it forms part of the doctrine of the
new creation in Christ.
[27] Save in passages demonstrably dependent on Paul.
[28] See again Henry Beach Carré, *Paul's Doctrine of Redemption*.

Marcan saying about the ransom for many can best be understood by a complete disregard of all Pauline ideas on the subject." [29] So understood, the saying takes on a new meaning—and may indeed be authentic. "Mark's interpretation of the death of Jesus not only reflects the tradition of the primitive community directly and without dependence upon Paul, but even reflects it in a pre-Pauline form." [30] Instead of Mark's being influenced by Paul, it is the primitive, pre-Pauline view—which Mark still retains—that is the indispensable presupposition of Paul's own thought; Paul advances upon Mark, not Mark upon Paul! For Paul takes the primitive idea of the death "for many" and interprets it to mean "for Christians," indeed first of all applying it to himself.[31]

So also with the view of Christ's resurrection.[32] For Mark, Jesus' resurrection involved the empty tomb; his resurrection body was still his natural body, transmuted, transfigured, glorified. But for Paul the doctrine of Christ's resurrection is not in the least dependent upon the empty tomb. In fact, the resuscitation and glorification of Jesus' physical body was an impossible conception, for it would still be σάρξ, "flesh," not πνεῦμα, "spirit"; and the whole force of his argument in I Corinthians 15 involves the *substitution* of a glorious spiritual body for the earthly, "fleshly" body in the Resurrection. "God giveth it a body"—and the same applies to

[29] P. 65, quoting Wernle, *Synoptische Frage*, p. 200.
[30] Pp. 70-71.
[31] Gal. 2:20; see also Weiss, *History of Primitive Christianity*, I, 116-17 = *Urchristentum*, p. 84.
[32] Pp. 72 ff.

Christ. Mark of course does not share Paul's abhorrence
of "the flesh," that is, σάρξ, and so he can think of the
transfiguration of Christ's earthly body—as on the Mount
of Transfiguration, probably viewed as an anticipation of
the Resurrection—without the least question of the continuity of Christ's physical body.

On every point of Christology, accordingly, the supposed influence of Paul upon Mark turns out to be, by
Werner's demonstration, merely evidence for the dependence of Mark upon the common Gentile Christianity of
his time, in fact in its pre-Pauline or non-Pauline form;
and this in spite of the agreements—which are natural,
considering Paul's dependence likewise upon "those who
were in Christ before him." The distinctive, unique, positively Pauline development of these doctrines is simply
not to be found anywhere in the Gospel of Mark.

If this statement can be made regarding their Christology, it is not likely that other doctrines will upset the
relationship—for Christology is of fundamental importance to both Paul and Mark, and to all of primitive
Christianity. Nevertheless Werner proceeds to examine
other doctrines and teachings: the Law, the gospel, faith,
sin, flesh and spirit, sacramental teaching, eschatology,
the view taken of the primitive apostles, the attitude toward the Jewish people, also that toward the heathen;
and he concludes with an examination of the vocabu-
laries of the two writers. On every point the distinctively
Pauline teaching is found to be absent from Mark, while
their agreements nowhere go beyond the common basis

of non-Pauline Gentile Christianity. The final chapter, on the diction of Mark and Paul, substantiates what has been the reader's growing conviction all along, namely that the hypothesis of Pauline influence upon the Gospel of Mark is a perfect mare's nest of absurdities, of which exegesis of the New Testament and historical research into Christian origins had better be completely rid at once.

Now if Werner's thesis is true, and if we accept his demonstration as final, certain positive inferences are bound to follow, and not merely the negative one already described—important as that is.

1. For one thing, early Gentile Christianity, and probably also early Jewish Christianity, was much farther advanced in the christological and soteriological areas than has been admitted by most writers.

2. Paul's conversion, or at least the beginning of his missionary career, can hardly be dated as early as the majority of critics are inclined to place it. Time must be allowed for the growth of doctrine in the Gentile mission field. Thus one more item of evidence supports the view which some of us already hold upon other grounds, namely that Paul's conversion belongs nearer A.D. 40 than 30—perhaps in 37 or 38.[33]

3. Paul's own distinctive contributions to Christian thought are to be sharply distinguished from what he received by tradition; and it will be found, when these are segregated, that they point to several sources: (a) his

[33] See John Knox, " 'Fourteen Years Later': A Note on the Pauline Chronology," *Journal of Religion*, 16:341-49; "The Pauline Chronology," *Journal of Biblical Literature*, 58:15-29.

own personal experience, that of an intense spiritual nature with a keen imagination and a desperately sensitive conscience; (*b*) a peculiar exegesis of the Old Testament, partly rabbinic, partly early Christian, but more probably derived from his own reading and pondering of the Greek version of the Jewish scriptures; (*c*) a set of cosmological and anthropological views that owed not a little to the vast mélange of Hellenism and Orientalism flooding the world where he grew up, and providing him with the unique setting for still other ideas, of sin, Satan, death, of the sinful and therefore mortal nature of man—as "flesh"—of the "spiritual" forces arrayed against God and his Messiah and all the faithful, of the victory to be won by the Messiah when he should at last appear—all these ideas were shaped to the mold of certain half-Jewish, half-pagan ideas which Paul seems to have derived from the world about him. The Diaspora Judaism that Paul knew in Cilicia must have been very different from the Judaism of Palestine, and even from the Diaspora Judaism of Philo in Alexandria!

First-century Judaism, in the Diaspora and even in Palestine before the crisis of A.D. 66-70, was a much more diversified religious phenomenon than that of the era of retrenchment and conservatism which followed, especially after the second fall of Jerusalem in 135. Philo was forgotten, by the Jews—only the Christian church preserved his writings. The Septuagint was discarded as too free a rendering of the Old Testament, and other, even painfully literal, translations took its place—it too was abandoned to the Christians, and one rabbi even

proposed to commemorate it by an annual day of fasting. Along with the Septuagint went the Apocrypha—the
additional books in the Greek canon—and the apocalyptic writings, perhaps already interpolated, certainly
interpreted, by the Christians in the interest of their
own peculiar doctrines. The schools established at Jamnia
and Tiberias were to study only scripture and the Oral
Tradition. A more rigorous system of exegesis was to be
inculcated, following explicit rules. And at the same time
the world-wide mission of Diaspora Judaism came to an
end.[34] It was like the Counter Reformation in the Roman
Church of the sixteenth century, with its Council of
Trent, determined henceforth to leave no more openings
for Protestant "reformations."

But the era before the late sixties of the first century
was much freer and much more varied in outlook, much
more hospitable to foreign influences and combinations
of ideas—like medieval scholasticism, before Trent. This
goes a long way to account for the type of Judaism Paul
knew and rejected—an inexplicable enigma to all modern Jews, however "liberal." It was certainly not the
"normative" Judaism that arose in Palestine after the
year 135; and it was probably not even the central, orthodox, middle-of-the-road Judaism of the scribes and
Pharisees of Palestine in the first half of the first century. It was perhaps already in contact with speculations regarding the divine purpose in the creation of the

[34] See T. R. Glover, *The World of the New Testament* (1931), p. 135,
and refs. to Bentwich, *Hellenism*, pp. 287 ff., 301; G. F. Moore, *Judaism*,
I, 83-109.

world, the angelic powers, the figures of Adam, Death, Satan or Antichrist, the Heavenly Man, the coming salvation, the relation of spirit and flesh, soul and body—speculations which were at least tinged, no doubt, with Gnosticism. "Gnosticism" is of course a later word; in the first century it was only, as Wendland defined it, the religion or theology of syncretism, well adapted to the mélange of cults which characterized the eastern provinces under the early empire. Hans Böhlig, in his *Geisteskultur von Tarsus* (1913), stressed the possibility of contacts with Mithraism; but there were other possibilities—as W. L. Knox recognizes in his *St. Paul and the Church of the Gentiles* (1939). For more than two hundred years there had been Jewish settlements in Cilicia; and the Aramaic inscriptions in the neighborhood—not necessarily Jewish, but surely accessible to Jews—reflect a decided strain of syncretism.[35]

I cannot at this point enter into the discussion of types of Diaspora Judaism affected by contact with paganism; I wish only to record my conviction (1) that Paul's Judaism was not of the orthodox Palestinian type, which later became normal, and normative; and (2) that early Gentile Christianity, both before Paul and also outside the area of his influence, was far more substantial than the Book of Acts and the surviving Pauline letters have led many to assume. It is this type of Christian teaching, "common Gentile Christianity," rather than Paulinism, that lies behind the Gospel of Mark.

[35] E.g. those given in Lidzbarski, *Ephemeris für semitische Epigraphik*, I. 1, pp. 59-74.

X

WAS MARK ANTI-SEMITIC?

IT IS ONE OF THE STRANGEST AND ALSO ONE OF THE MOST abhorrent and diabolical paradoxes of Western civilization that the people among whom Christianity arose, and to whose religion it owed the most historically, have been for nineteen centuries the object of undying animosity. Moreover, at no time during all the so-called Christian centuries has this hatred risen to such a height as at the present day in central, eastern, and southern Europe. That this is a Western trait—that is, European and, alas, to some extent American—is evident. In no other quarter of the globe is this hatred felt, save in parts of northern Africa, where it is a recently imported prejudice, and in Palestine, where modern Zionism has complicated the relations between Arabs and Jews. Across the remaining vast stretches of the other continents, the Jewish minorities live at peace with their neighbors and in mutual respect. There is at present no open antagonism toward Jews in Great Britain. Here in this country it has recently broken out in certain quarters, with a few ignorant and noisy advocates and an illiterate and credulous following; but, please God, we shall stifle the hateful monster before it grows to threatening proportions, to plague, destroy, or disgrace us.

One wonders how anti-Semitism ever got started. It certainly existed in the Greco-Roman world before the rise of Christianity. But Christianity as certainly added fuel to the fire, instead of putting it out. One wonders how this could ever come to pass; for, equally certainly, the gospel of Jesus, that is, the gospel which he taught, does not countenance hatred—of his own or of any people. The New Testament also reflects, of course, a variety of views later than Jesus. And though Paul was willing to be anathema—accursed by God—for his brethren's sake,[1] there were other voices. Matthew interpolates into the passion narrative the tragic scene in which Pilate first endeavors to set Jesus free, then dramatically washes his hands of the whole affair, "and all the people . . . . said, His blood be on us, and on our children." [2] This is of course a later touch, legendary and polemical, like the story of the sealed tomb.[3] It reflects the growing antagonism between church and synagogue during the era that succeeded the Fall of Jerusalem in A.D. 70—it may even be second-century in origin. In the Gospel of John this antagonism is still more bitter: Jesus is accused of being a Samaritan, and possessed by a devil, and in retort he calls the Jews "liars" [4] and "sons of the devil." [5] All critics now recognize that this is not the historical Jesus speaking, but the dramatic figure whom John has set in his place—the mysterious, half-mythical, half-

[1] Rom. 9:3.
[2] Matt. 27:25.
[3] Matt. 27:62-66; 28:11-15.
[4] John 8:55.
[5] John 8:44.

Gnostic protagonist of light and truth who attacks the darkness of this world and dies at the hands of his own people, but in doing so "overcomes the world." The antagonism is not between Jesus and "the Jews," but between church and synagogue in the early second century; the Johannine controversies clearly reflect this later situation. That this critical, historical point of view has not yet penetrated certain areas where the Bible is still taken "just as it is" surely goes a long way to explain the renewed outbreaks against Judaism and the Jews in our time—even in our own country.

But anti-Semitism goes back of the later Gospels. There are traces of it even in Mark—or at least so Mark may be understood. Professor H. A. L. Fisher has observed, in his brilliant new *History of Europe,* that although Christianity was originally Jewish, and hence the two sects were apt to be confused by the Romans, after Paul

Christian and Jew sprang apart. As time went on, the story of the Crucifixion, told with exquisite simplicity and pathos, and becoming widely known wherever Christians met together, deepened the gulf, and the crime of a handful of priests and elders in Jerusalem was visited by the Christian churches upon the whole Jewish race. It is thus that St. Mark, the earliest evangelist, appears to many Jews as being, although without malice, the first of the line of anti-Semitic authors.[6]

How did this anti-Semitism arise? Was Mark the author of it, "although without malice"? Or did it char-

[6] Vol. I, p. 6.

acterize the tradition that Mark received? It is not found
in Paul, as we have just noted. Certainly it is not found
in the Q cycle, or in L, or even in what are probably the
most basic, noneditorial parts of M. Luke has none of it,
either in the Gospel or in Acts. Nor is it found in the
Apocalypse, which even takes over and incorporates older
Jewish material—though "Sodom" and perhaps even
"Babylon" are probably disguises for Jerusalem,[7] and
the phrase "those who say they are Jews but are not"[8]
comes as a surprise to the readers—as the fact probably
came to the author. Nor is it found in the Epistle to Hebrews—though that is scarcely the book's original title,
supposing it originally bore any title. Nor anywhere else
in the New Testament—nowhere do we find the bitter
antagonism which is reflected in John,[9] and to some
extent in the late additional material in Matthew.

Now it must be recognized that the New Testament
is a collection of *Greek* writings. As Professor Goodspeed
has insisted, it is the literature of early Greek—that is,
Gentile—Christianity.[10] What preceded it we do not
know, and can reconstruct only by inference and hypothesis. That oral tradition was in circulation long before
the Gospels were written is obvious, and it circulated in
Greek before these Greek books were written. That it
had circulated in Aramaic before being translated into
Greek is most probable—as we have seen, the evidence

---

[7] See Philip Carrington, *The Meaning of the Revelation* (1931), pp. 247,
266, etc.

[8] Rev. 2:9.

[9] See *The Growth of the Gospels*, p. 218.

[10] *Introduction to the New Testament*, pp. xii-xiii.

of the actual contents of the Gospels points strongly that way. It is held by some that there were Aramaic writings, probably Gospels;[11] but most of us doubt this, though admitting the Aramaic origin of many of the separate pericopes of oral tradition. From this general hypothesis, plus the fact that no other Gospels have survived—if ever there were any others—than those in Greek, it follows that the accounts of the life and teaching, the death and resurrection of Jesus are only those traditions that were preserved, *in Greek,* by the Greek, or Gentile, church, and for its own purposes. These purposes were not biographical, but served only the ends of edification, instruction, controversy, and worship. And it also follows that the influences or "tendencies" at work in the Gospels, and in their underlying Greek tradition, were possibly not the same as those which had operated upon the underlying Aramaic tradition before it was translated into Greek. This is the main point of tradition, or form, criticism—the attempt to trace the history of the gospel tradition, and to recover its earliest form, that in which it circulated long before Gospels were written, if possible long before the tradition ever got translated and circulated in Greek.

In the case of Mark, it seems likely that the original tradition of the trial and crucifixion of Jesus was not anti-Semitic in coloring; if anything, it was, like the traditions in Acts 1–12, critical of the authorities in Jerusalem, the "rulers"—including Roman as well as Jewish—the "high priests and scribes and elders," but not of the

[11] See chap. v above.

Jewish people, and not of the Jewish authorities alone. How could it be otherwise?—those who handed on the tradition were themselves Jews. It has often been pointed out, for example by Wellhausen, that the account of the "trial" before the Sanhedrin is modeled upon that before Pilate;[12] that no disciples were present, and hence they could only infer what the proceedings had been; that the inference had to be based upon the charge which the Jewish leaders preferred against Jesus when he was arraigned before Pilate; that it assumes, wrongly, that the claim to Messiahship would be understood as equivalent to blasphemy, and that it had at the same time to be corrected and defined by the addition of the claim to be the "Son of Man," [13] in order to give it meaning in the light of the Galilean tradition of Jesus' ministry and also in that of current Christology; that the charge before Pilate is taken by Luke in an entirely different sense, probably upon the basis of other tradition, Jesus being charged with being an insurrectionist who interfered with the collection of tribute;[14] and that, finally, the account of the examination of Jesus by the high priest as given by John is far more probable: "The high priest therefore asked Jesus about his disciples and about his teaching" [15]—there is not a word here about Messiahship or the advent in glory of the Son of Man. And it should

[12] See chap. viii above; also George A. Barton, "The Trial of Jesus Before the Sanhedrin," *Journal of Biblical Literature*, 41:205-11; A. T. Olmstead, *Jesus in the Light of History* (1942).
[13] Mark 14:62.
[14] Luke 23:2.
[15] John 18:19.

be added that this criticism of the account of the trial before "the high priests, the elders, and the scribes" [16] has nothing to do with the question of anti-Semitism, but arose upon purely historical grounds. The probability, as we have already noted, is that the earliest tradition of the passion narrative gave no details of this "trial," but that Mark—or the Greek tradition prior to Mark— has added it in order to fill out the story.

Why was it added in this particular form? Was Mark himself anti-Semitic, or anti-Jewish? Was the Roman community, which cherished the tradition, anti-Jewish? It may be so—for it is clear that Mark had an inadequate knowledge of Judaism and equally of the Old Testament. It used to be supposed that the earliest Christian community in Rome was largely Jewish, but recent research finds the evidence pointing the other way.[17] This we might have assumed from the conclusion of Acts: Paul meets with the Jewish elders, states his case, gets nowhere, and they go their separate ways. We might also have inferred this from Paul's Epistle to the Romans, addressed to the Christians in the capital some years

[16] Mark 14:53.

[17] See Hermann Vogelstein, Rome ("Jewish Community Series"; Philadelphia, 1940); E. Schürer, Geschichte des jüdischen Volkes (4th ed., 1909), III, 57 ff.; Jean Juster, Les Juifs dans l'empire romain (1914), I, 180, esp. valuable for refs.; Hans Lietzmann, Geschichte der alten Kirche, I (1932), 109, etc.; also his Petrus und Paulus in Rom (1927); C. H. Dodd, The Epistle to the Romans, "Moffatt Commentary" (1932); George A. Barton, "The Interpretation of the Epistle to the Romans," Anglican Theological Review 21:81 ff.; R. M. Hawkins, "Romans, a Reinterpretation," Journal of Biblical Literature, 60:129-40, esp. pp. 132-33; George La Piana, "Foreign Groups in Rome During the First Centuries of the Empire," in Harvard Theological Review, 20:4 (Oct., 1927), esp. chaps. vi, vii.

before his arrival there. And we might have gathered it from the earliest names of Christian believers that have come down to us—in Romans 16 [18] and elsewhere. The Epistle to Hebrews may be a Roman book, as many hold; but it is not Jewish—its Judaism is only that of the Septuagint, as read by Greek-speaking Christians. If, as seems likely, the early Christian church in Rome was a Gentile church, then we may surmise that some of those Christians brought their anti-Semitism with them when they entered it; there was plenty of such prejudice in the pagan world about them, not least in Rome itself, as the Latin authors of the Silver Age make clear. The vast, tragic pity of it all is that the gospel of Jesus did not at once neutralize this prejudice, on the part of Christians, and exorcise the demon which was destined to work such havoc throughout the Christian centuries to this day. But, it is all too clear, the earliest Gospel was more interested in the deeds of Jesus than in his teaching, and even represented his teaching as an esoteric mystery[19] which "those outside" were not even expected to understand—were indeed prevented from understanding! This fatal defect in Mark's representation of the tradition was corrected in a measure by the later Gospels of Luke and Matthew; but the harm had been done, and we Christians have not yet succeeded in undoing it. Such a book as the recent one by Professor Zeitlin, *Who Crucified Jesus?* ought never to have needed to be written, save as an interesting piece of historical research. Of

[18] See Dodd's new commentary.
[19] Mark 4:11.

course the Jews did not crucify Jesus—that was no Jewish mode of capital punishment! Our Lord was crucified by a weak and vacillating Roman governor, alarmed over his threatened authority, cowed by a mob, egged on by a handful of Sadducean "quislings," as Zeitlin calls them, and no doubt concerned for his official record at Rome.

As far as the later history is concerned, the relations between Jews and Christians in the East remained friendly for at least five centuries—probably down to the Mohammedan conquest. The breach between church and synagogue was effected in the West, in the area of Gentile Christianity and, I cannot but agree with R. T. Herford, chiefly as the result of the complete disregard of the Pharisaic *Halakah* by Paul and others. Of course the separation was inevitable—but it need not have been so violent, nor have brought such tragic consequences in its train. Jewish persecution of Christians may have had something to do with it, or Jewish ostracism,[20] with the result that Christians could no longer find shelter under the general toleration which, since the days of Herod and his munificent benefactions outside Palestine and his services to the early empire, had been enjoyed by Jews generally. Christians were forced into the open, where they now faced the mob with its clubs and the praetor with his sword. That is about the situation at the time Luke-Acts was written, and it gives the point to its apologetic

[20] But see Ernest C. Colwell, "Popular Reactions Against Christianity in the Roman Empire," *Environmental Factors in Christian History*, ed. J. T. McNeill, M. Spinka, H. R. Willoughby (1939), pp. 53-71.

argument: Christians are not Jews, but neither are they revolutionists; in fact, they are truer Jews, religiously, than those who claim to be Jews by race.

The separation was inevitable—like the growth of the acorn into an oak that sunders the rock—and it was eventually in some ways a blessing, no doubt. But it brought a curse as well as a blessing, not only for Judaism but for Christianity. If only the Jews had accepted Jesus!—not as Messiah, which many present-day scholars think he never claimed to be; not as the Son of Man destined to come on the clouds, for that also may be a "claim" made on his behalf by his followers, who identified him with the one described in the visions of Daniel and Enoch; but as "the teacher of the way of God in truth," the revealer of God, the Redeemer and Savior of his people, the one chosen by God to be the divine agent in the full realization of the Kingdom of God upon earth! That is where the heart of Christianity has always beat soundest, not in the realm of apocalyptic eschatology or messianism; and that is where the mission of Jesus to Israel should have found its richest fulfillment.

And if only Christians had always been able to see their Lord through Jewish eyes—the tender, affectionate, proud eyes of his own people! If they could only have realized that his gospel was "glad tidings for the poor," not a "mystery" like those of the pagan cults, to be kept safely out of reach of the uninitiate; that his mission was first to Israel and then through Israel to all mankind; that his gospel meant a new way of life for men to live, not a set of ideas to be accepted or rejected; that his scriptures were more than a series of obscure prefigurings of events in his own life, that in fact they set forth the basic ethics which he reiterated, renewed, and completed; that his way of life was utterly and forever incompatible with imperialism, exploitation, the exclusive and corrupting pursuit of wealth and power, racial antagonism and prejudice, and all the mass of trickery and lies that lead to aggression and conquest, and shackle the human race in the bonds of death. Instead, men in the West forgot that Jesus was a Jewish teacher, and they made him out to be a medieval baron, a prince, a magnate, a warrior, an emperor, a pope. We too thought we had accepted him on our own terms—but he escaped us. For all the while he insisted upon a revelation which we ignored, but which was the foundation of his ethics as it was of those of Pharisaic Judaism: "Thou shalt love the Lord thy God with all thy heart and mind and soul, ... and thy neighbor as thyself." We forgot the Old Testament, or misinterpreted it, substituting an elaborate typology for its plain meaning and its searching ethical requirements.

How much the gospel has suffered by being severed from the Old Testament and from Judaism, both of which it presupposes, is clear from the interpretation of the Sermon on the Mount during the past forty years.[21] It has been understood to teach an "interim ethic"—the

[21] Two of the most important recent books on the Sermon on the Mount are by Hans Windisch, *Der Sinn der Bergpredigt* (2nd ed., 1937), a magnificent book that ought also to be in English, and Martin Dibelius, *The Sermon on the Mount* (1940). On the latter, I may refer to my article, *Anglican Theological Review*, 25:131-44.

foolish theory would have been condemned at once if men had noticed the similar teachings in the old Jewish literature, which certainly taught no interim ethic! Or it has been thought purposely to present a demand which was impossible, in order, forsooth, to declare the divine judgment upon human failings, and proclaim the need for divine grace—rather than for human effort. This even more perverse theory could not be maintained for a moment if its authors either knew familiarly or took seriously the ancient Jewish religious teaching. It is as gross a caricature in the case of the Sermon on the Mount as it would be in that of the Testaments of the Twelve Patriarchs or of Second Enoch. And without the Old Testament the ethics of the New are only a fragment.[22]

An example of the importance of the Old Testament for a proper understanding of the New may be seen in Matthew 5:48: "Be ye therefore perfect, as your heavenly Father is perfect." For many generations, indeed for centuries, this verse has been, for theological exegetes, the scene of violent contention. On the one side were those who held that it involved the duty either of self-perfection or of such a complete response to divine grace that the result was a perfected, finished Christian personality. For the ascetics, this meant a realization of the goal of personal holiness, the full manifestation of the divine likeness in man, who is made in God's image—the Fall, as the Schoolmen held, had obliterated the

---

[22] On the presupposition by the New Testament of the Old Testament ethics, see "The Church's Present Task," *Religion in Life,* 8:339 ff., esp. pp. 346-49.

"likeness," not the "image." [23] For others it meant the attainment of an ideal of Christlikeness, namely the state of being like Christ, who is like God and is God. Christ is the pattern man, the Perfect Man, and we are to grow in his likeness, as Paul said, "unto the perfect man." [24] On the opposite side were those who held that all this ethical and devotional idealism—"perfectionism," as they labeled it—runs counter to the facts of human nature and history, and that we cannot, in simple truth, know anything about such a goal. "Such knowledge is too wonderful for me," as the psalmist admitted. The whole idea or ideal of a perfect human being is non-biblical, and smacks of pagan ethics, with its ideal of the wise man or sage or philosopher. Hence the command must signify only a flashing glimpse of "the heroic for earth too hard," designed to convince our impotent human nature of its inability ever to achieve such an end, and also to force upon us the acknowledgment that we are saved either by the eternal election of God, whose inscrutable will controls his whole creation, or by the sheer work of grace—in either case by no merit or effort of ours. It is unnecessary to enter into the details of this long debate, which began before Augustine and has continued to the present day. Kierkegaard's proposal may be noted, however; he proposed to translate the verb as a future indicative, not an imperative: "So you will be perfect, as your heavenly Father is perfect." I shall come

---

[23] See Thomas Aquinas, *Summa Theol.*, I, qu. 93, esp. art. 9; also F. J. Hall, *Creation and Man* (1912), p. 189.

[24] Col. 1:28; cf. Eph. 4:13.

back to this translation in a moment; it has much to be said for it.

Now if we ignore, for the time being, all the later theological interpretation of this saying, and set it against its true and only proper background of Judaism and the Old Testament, it will appear at once that the words are an echo of Deuteronomy 18:13.[25] This sends us back to the passage in the "Book of the Law" (*sepher ha torah*) which, presumably, was found in the temple in 622 B.C.; but it sends us first to the Septuagint, the Bible of the early church: τέλειος ἔσῃ ἐναντίον κυρίου τοῦ θεοῦ σου. Surely the Matthean verse echoes that, with its ἔσεσθε οὖν ὑμεῖς τέλειοι! The difference is chiefly that "ye" is plural, while the Old Testament command is addressed, in the singular, to the individual Israelite. Now the word τέλειος ("perfect") in the Septuagint looks in the direction of the philosophical ideal of the "perfect" man;[26] this was perfectly natural—Greek words bore Greek connotations, and in this case a set of implied ideas which may or may not have been present in the Hebrew original. But let us turn to the Hebrew: "Thou shalt be perfect (*tamim*) with the Lord thy God." [27] But the verse in Deuteronomy must be read in its context, 18:9-14. It is a simple, direct, summary command to have nothing to do with divination, necromancy, sorcery—all the super-

---

[25] The new edition of Huck's *Synopsis* prints it as such, with the Greek words for "Ye shall be perfect" in italic type.

[26] As in Wisd. 9:6; Sirach 44:17.

[27] Incidentally the Septuagint may reflect at this point a different reading from the present massoretic Hebrew—possibly *lip'nei*, "before," "in the presence of," rather than the simple *'im*, "with." Codex A does read ἔναντι!

stitious voodoo of the heathen who lived in Canaan before the Israelites moved in. Not that anyone would
abandon the worship of Yahweh for such black arts; but
men always like to play safe, and superstitious men—as
we learn from Isaiah—would readily add to their main
religious worship the practices which the passage con-
demns. (I know a woman who invariably consults a
physician when she is ill, but also, for good measure,
telephones the neighboring Christian Science practi-
tioner; of late she has even added a third consultant, a
popular "numerologist." Her "psychology" is no doubt
the same as that of people in eighth or seventh century
Israel!) Now after denouncing such practices, the Deut-
eronomists added, "You must be *tamim* with Yahweh
your God"; and that means, surely, you must be honest
with him, upright and sincere, having wholeness and
integrity, not double-dealing, not trusting him to his
face and then, behind his back, resorting to "the wizards
that chirp and that mutter"; for Yahweh is a jealous
God, and will not overlook such perfidy—he knows all
about it, and will not tolerate it.

Tamim, that is the grand Old Testament word that
lies behind our text. It was the word that described
Job's fidelity and virtue—there was a man "perfect and
upright (*tam w'yashar*) before the Lord." That was the
virtue the psalmists praised over and again, a virtue in
man, and an attribute of God himself—that is, of God as
revealed in his ways, his works, his law.

It seems clear, then, that four stages of biblical interpretation or reinterpretation—"progressive interpretation,"

as Professor Bewer calls it[28]—led up to our text: first,
(1) the old Hebrew admonition to be "honest" and "upright," as a member of the sacred covenant, in all one's
dealings with Yahweh, who is himself "faithful"[29] to
all who put their trust in him: then, (2) the Greek
rendering of the idea, reflecting both the deepened meaning *tamim* had come to have for pious Jews in the third
century—see their Psalter!—and also (3) the wealth of
association the Greek word τέλειος had come to have
for religious minds, Jewish and other, in the Greek-
speaking world outside Palestine; finally, (4) the use
made of the text by our Lord, and recorded in the
sublime passage of the Sermon on the Mount. Hence one
need hardly turn to the philosophers to inquire the meaning—it is plain on the face of it. "Love your enemies,
and pray for those who persecute you, so that you may be
sons of your Father in heaven. . . . . Then you will be
like God"—or, "So you must be like God." The choice
between Kierkegaard's rendering and the usual imperative is probably to be settled in favor of the latter—see
the parallel in Luke: "Be merciful"—though the whole
premise and presupposition of that imperative is the
assurance that in so doing you *will* be like God, your
heavenly Father.

If only we take the Old Testament background in
earnest, we shall get rid of all the later philosophical
notions that have been read into the crystal-clear saying
of Jesus, for example the notion that as God is "perfect"

---

[28] See his article with this title, *Anglican Theological Review*, 24:89-100.
[29] Deut. 7:9.

in his order, so man must be "perfect" in his; or even that man's perfection must somehow equal the perfection of God, and realize its final end as God realizes his final end! Such Aristotelian, Stoic, or Scholastic ideas have simply no relevance whatsoever in this connection. Neither the Old Testament, nor first century Judaism— except for Philo and a few other Phil-Hellenes—nor Jesus himself, nor the early Christians who handed down the gospel tradition—least of all those responsible for M—had the slightest contact with the philosophical ethics of the contemporary Greek schools. I am afraid that I must cast my vote, likewise, to reject Professor Torrey's conjecture that the word here was the Aramaic *g'mar,* which he translates, "Be all-including (in your good will)." The clue which the Old Testament allusion has given us fits the context in the Sermon on the Mount far too perfectly, is much too natural, and would too readily be understood by those whose chief if not sole literature was the Old Testament, for us to abandon it for Dr. Torrey's brilliant suggestion. It is to be noted that he does not carry over the idea into Matthew 19:21, where he retains the traditional rendering, "If you will be perfect."

Now this is only one illustration among many that might be selected. The whole of the teaching of Jesus, as recorded in the Gospels, and likewise that of Paul and of the rest of the New Testament, presupposes a background of intense, informed, earnest, and consecrated Judaism. If the serious New Testament student is to avoid pitfalls in exegesis, he must have the Septuagint constantly at his side or, better, in his memory—it was the Bible of the early church, of Greek-speaking Gentile Christianity. And the Septuagint he must check constantly with the Hebrew, not only for its translation, whether free or literal, of the original, and for variations from the current text of both the Greek and the Hebrew Old Testament, but also, and above all, for the light it sheds upon the gospel tradition; for the Hebrew Old Testament, whether with or without the oral Aramaic Targum, was the Bible of Jesus and of his earliest followers. It is not enough to use even the best of modern versions; they are important—but the cross-shadings, allusions, the echoes and innuendoes of the original can simply never be reproduced in any other language. And, I would add, the serious New Testament student must steep his mind in Judaism, especially of the period from the Maccabees, or better from Ezra, to the end of the Tannaite age, say to the end of the second century of our era. By "Judaism" I mean what the late Professor G. F. Moore called "normative Judaism," [30] the religion of the Torah and the Psalter, of the Liturgy and the early Midrash, of the Oral Tradition and of the great homiletical, exegetical, and ethical tradition of the ancient synagogue. It is not enough to know simply the Apocrypha and Pseudepigrapha. Some of these works do cast a flood of light upon the actual religious life and

---

[30] See his *Judaism in the First Centuries of the Christian Era . . . . the Age of the Tannaim* (3 vols.; 1927-30); also his earlier articles, "The Rise of Normative Judaism," *Harvard Theological Review,* 17:307-73; 18:1-38. 38.

thought of ancient Judaism, for example Tobit and
Judith—especially chapter 8 of Judith, one of the noblest
utterances of Jewish religion the world has ever heard.
"Popular" novels like these found people where they
lived, and expressed the common religious thought and
aspiration of their times; but they are not the whole
of ancient Judaism, by a long way. As for the apocalypses,
they were self-confessedly the literature of esoteric groups;
and, though valuable once the student knows enough
about Judaism as a whole to evaluate them properly—
especially the noble ethical doctrine some of them contain—still they are not to be taken as representative of
the central convictions of Judaism generally. For first-
century Judaism, far from being a religion moribund
or bankrupt, was the purest religion the world had ever
known; and Christianity, which built upon its foundation, would have been impossible without it. Its rich
and wholesome piety penetrated every nook and corner of
the Jew's daily life; from his cradle to his grave it
shielded and supported him, his inspiration in youth,
his strength in maturity, his comfort in old age.

Now I do not mean that all of Judaism, in the first
century or at any time, has risen to its highest possible
level. What religion ever rises to its full height, as seen
in the lives and in the thought of all its followers? But
I am sure that, taken at their best, Judaism and Christianity are not two religions but one. And if it be argued
that this is to ignore the doctrine of the Incarnation,
which is central for Christian dogma, I would reply that
the essential element in this doctrine might also have

been accepted long ago—not in its Greek formulation,
but in one more natural to Semitic thought—by
Christian Jews had it not become the watchword of
partisans and persecutors. At the same time, let us add,
the doctrine of the Incarnation might have been stated
in terms less rigid, less mechanical, less materialistic if
it had retained closer contact with history and revelation, both of which were the heritage of Judaism. Tell
me not of the *Tome* of Leo! The true approach to the
doctrine of the Incarnation is in the old tradition: "The
Kingdom of God is at hand, repent!"; "If I by the finger
of God cast out demons, then is the Kingdom of God
come upon you"; "The Lord hath anointed me to preach
. . . . to the poor"; "Many will come from the east and
the west and sit down . . . . in the Kingdom of Heav-
en"; "Think not that I came to destroy the Law and
the prophets: I come not to destroy, but to fulfill"; "I
was not sent but unto the lost sheep of the house of
Israel"; "Who is my mother? and who are my brethren?
. . . . Whosover shall do the will of my Father who is
in heaven, he is my brother, and sister, and mother."

Of course not all Jews were able to receive the message or to accept the Messenger. There was in truth "a
hardening in part that had happened unto Israel."[31]
Mark shares that view; it is the explanation of the "re-
jection" of Jesus by his own people, at least in Jerusalem,
and he seems to wonder if the disciples themselves were
not afflicted with it. It was a ready-enough explanation,

[31] Rom. 11:25.

in those days. Josephus advances a similar view, in accounting for the blindness of both leaders and people as they plunged into war with Rome.[32] But if we consider the possibilities latent in Jesus' proclamation of the gospel, as John Hutton has done in his book, *The Proposal of Jesus* (1921), it will be evident that the sanest and safest way out of the impasse in which Judaism found itself in the first century would have been to accept the way of Jesus, renounce Zealotism and the appeal to arms, abandon the dream of world empire and even that of political independence, and become simply a religion, a church, instead of endeavoring to become a free, autonomous political state. Political freedom was out of the question anyway; the nation—as Josephus repeatedly insists—could never hope to contend successfully with Rome.[33] And Jesus foresaw all this with prophetic clarity of vision, and proclaimed it as vigorously and vividly as did the ancient seers who announced the impending fall of Jerusalem—"Jerusalem shall become heaps, and the hill of Zion as a plowed field." But unlike them, his message did not center in a future restoration of the old conditions—after some period, long or short, say "seventy years." Instead, he viewed the catastrophe as final: after the divine judgment the New Age would dawn, and "many will come from the east and the west and sit down . . . . in the Kingdom of God." But there was still time. It was no fixed, inevitable fate that hung over the

---

[32] *War* 5. 8. 2; 6. 5. 3; etc.

[33] Especially in the great speech which he places on the lips of King Agrippa in *War* 2. 14. 4–16. 4 = §§345-401.

nation. God's decree was conditional, and the nation's doom might be averted by repentance: "Except ye repent, ye shall all likewise perish." [34] This too is a fundamental Jewish doctrine—which even Josephus reflects, for all his wavering loyalty: "For there stands about us that fortune which, by its very nature, is *mutable*." [35] If the nation will repent and return to the Lord, there is the promise of salvation, even now, at this late hour; but if they will not repent, then the Judgment will overtake them—though a remnant, the true Israel, will survive.

Though this element in the common prophetic faith is not stressed in the gospel tradition, it is clearly taken for granted in Jesus' teaching, and it is also a presupposition of the earliest Christian preaching. It suggests the answer to the question, What would have happened if the whole Jewish people had accepted Jesus and his message? For one thing, he would not have died on a cross at Jerusalem; and his doctrine of the Kingdom of God would no doubt have been embodied in a group, a church, of which he would have continued as the visible head; and Judaism would have been transformed and exalted into the most spiritual religion the world has ever seen, more Jewish, in the true sense, than the Judaism that survived, more consonant with the purest religion of the Old Testament Law, Prophets, and Wisdom; and the Jewish nation would have escaped the horrors of the two catastrophes in A.D. 70 and 135, with their age-long

---

[34] See Luke 13:1-5.
[35] *War* 4. 1. 6. The words are attributed to Vespasian, but the idea obviously has Josephus' approval.

entail of suffering and exile to this day. This is "the history that might have been"; and we can add to it the advantages Christianity would have enjoyed had the chosen people of God's earlier revelation responded and maintained the leadership which was rightfully theirs— a far purer form of Christianity would have resulted than the synthesis with a superficially converted paganism that grew up in the West during the Dark Ages.

Of course this is not to exonerate those who first introduced the virus of anti-Semitism into the thought of Christians in the West—among the very first, alas, being those who handed down the Marcan tradition, perhaps in Rome itself. There is much more to what we call "the Jewish problem" than merely anti-Semitism. But if only we could get rid of the latter, the former might be nearer a solution; the remaining problems, such as the clannishness of the Jews, their resistance to absorption, their segregation, their preference for urban life and their detachment from the soil, their tendency to crowd into three or four professions, such as medicine, law, music, and finance—all these problems are conditioned and immensely aggravated by anti-Semitism. And it is surely time that we Christians recognize frankly that our own scriptures have been affected by this malicious spirit; that although there are books in the New Testament from which it is absent, there are also one or two—chiefly the Gospel of John—in which it is present in an extreme and aggravated form; that the controlling, dominant spirit of the gospel itself, that is, the teaching of Jesus, has been disregarded and misrepresented in such writings; and that we must no longer let it be assumed that the spirit of Christ is compatible with religious persecution, theological prejudice, or racial hatred. If we yield to these, there is no hope of universal peace, nor is there any hope of the triumph of the spirit of Christ over the diabolical evils in our world. We may exonerate Mark—clearly he wrote "without malice"; but we cannot exonerate ourselves if we share in perpetuating the mis-representations and prejudices upon which this hideous monster of anti-Semitism continues to thrive.

XI

MARK AND THE SOCIAL GOSPEL

THE GOSPEL OF MARK IS THE SACRED TRADITIONAL BOOK—
that is, the book setting forth the sacred tradition—of a
religious movement or sect. In its origin, this tradition
arose inside the religious thought-world of contemporary
Judaism, to which it belonged and which it consistently
presupposed. However, some time before the Marcan
Gospel was compiled, the new sect had been cut loose—
or had cut itself loose—from Judaism, and was now
launched upon the broad seas of the Hellenistic world
with its many competing cults and religions. It still remained a sect—or, if we prefer, a religious movement—
but with no implications of nationality, race, people, or
soil. It was now a "universal" religion in process of development. Thus the Gospel of Mark, though deriving its
tradition from Palestine, was the sacred book of tradition
of the early Gentile church. It still presupposed the Old
Testament—not however, as the sacred Law of God
binding upon one particular nation, but as the scripture
of an independent religious movement by which it was
now reinterpreted. In large measure the Jewish element
in it was explained away and its primitive flavor neutralized, for it was now no longer a Hebrew book, but a
Greek thesaurus of most ancient oracles. The Gospel of

Mark also presupposed the conditions of life in Palestine in Jesus' day: but the book could be understood by readers with only the scantiest and sketchiest knowledge of things Palestinian. Indeed, the author himself is not wholly familiar with Palestinian geography or history. He lets "Herod," that is, Herod Antipas, remain a "king," as in the popular tale he takes over.[1] He has Jesus return to Galilee from Tyre and Sidon by way of Decapolis;[2] and it is not likely that he himself knew any more about the location of such places as "Dalmanutha"[3] or "Bethphage and Bethany"[4] than the average modern Bible reader knows, or that he knew who the "Herodians" were,[5] or what the argument about korban involved.[6] Enough that these names were found in the tradition; all he did was pass them on. For this we must ever be grateful; if Mark had edited his material more severely, he would only have cut away these old roots and presented us with a dry stock instead of a living tradition.

Thus Mark retains tradition, but it is a tradition that has already been torn loose from its native soil. The process has not gone so far as it has in the Fourth Gospel; but it is already in process. Mark is interested in theology—a very elementary theology, but a real one—rather than in history; that is to say, a theological idea is more important to him than the actual course of

[1] Mark 6:14.
[2] Mark 7:31.
[3] Mark 8:10; but see p. 100 above.
[4] Mark 11:1; but see p. 117 above.
[5] Mark 3:6; etc.
[6] Mark 7:11-12; see p. 118 above.

events in the life of Jesus. The sufferings, the death and resurrection of the divine Son of Man are the pattern to which the tradition is conformed, rather than a "biographical" outline of Jesus' career. Not that there ever was a purely historical account of Jesus' life, traditional or other; the only reason for remembering the events of that life, from the outset of the Christian movement, was the "theological" meaning they held.[7] But the process and the emphasis, which may be seen more fully in the Gospel of John, are quite clear in Mark. The author is not a theologian, certainly not a systematic theological thinker; but he is profoundly interested in an idea, or in a group of ideas, which can be described only as "theological." And it is no private theology; it is the theology, very primitive and very simple, of a group, the early Gentile Christian church. This group, as we saw, was a sect uprooted from its native soil and transplanted to the larger world of Hellenistic popular religion, and growing steadily, now, into a purely nonnationalistic, universal religion. The seeds of that universalism were doubtless present from the first, that is, in the teaching of Jesus; but only in the wider Gentile world was the church now beginning to realize the potentialities of that germ of life.

We can see this all the clearer if we contrast with it the tradition found for example in Q and M, the purely Palestinian and Syrian tradition underlying the Sermon on the Mount. Here the figures of speech, the examples selected, and the persons addressed all belong to the

[7] See my "The Christ of the Gospels," *Religion in Life*, 10:430-41.

villages of Galilee—the savorless salt thrown into the street, the one lamp that lights the whole household, the village blasphemer with his string of profanity and terms of abuse, the temple pilgrim offering his one gift, the village judge and the jailer, the local ruffian swift to strike, the king's man or garrison officer who compels the peasant to carry his baggage or to yield up his own cloak, the sinner's field wet with the same rain that falls on his righteous neighbor's, the local tax collector, the birds of the air and the lilies of the field, the child asking to be fed, the fruitful trees and the unfruitful, the wise and foolish house-builders. Nothing here about kings and councils, armies and tribute, civil or criminal law, the administration of government, the rights of the people, the duties of statesmen or rulers, the merits of various constitutions! Aristotle would have been much puzzled by these chapters, and so will we also be, unless we recognize that here is no formal treatise upon ethics, not even an examination of its major problems, but only the exposition of a religious principle—even more systematically formulated, as it stands in Matthew, than in Jesus' actual teaching—the principle found in the ancient law: "You therefore shall be perfect," as your heavenly Father is perfect.[8]

If we now inquire about Mark's "sociology" or his

---

[8] Matt. 5:48; cf. Deut. 18:13; Lev. 19:2. I have presented a similar point of view in "Ethics and Eschatology in the Teaching of Jesus," Journal of Religion, 20:359-70. This problem is one that is fundamental to the whole presentation of the gospel at the present day. We have already seen some of its bearings in the preceding chapter, and also the historical exegesis of Matt. 5:48.

"social ethics," we shall be checked at once. *Hoc genus non est!* Instead of the Sermon's provision for cases at law, for the exercise of charity, for civic virtue, presupposing if at the same time reinterpreting the requirements of the ancient national code; instead of the Old Testament Law with its provisions for the inheritance of property, for various kinds of civic and social duties, albeit of a primitive order, which the Sermon presupposes,[9] Mark has the ethical outlook of the sect. The rich, that is, the propertied, can be saved either not at all, or only with great difficulty.[10] Renunciation is the rule for all,[11] and the compensations are as simply and absolutely set forth as is the requirement: the good things of this life, such as they are, the blessings of family and of property, will be shared by all within the community, "now in this present time: houses, and brethren, and sisters, and mothers, and children, and lands, *with persecutions;* and in the world to come eternal life." The Christian religion, in all its long history, has never been able to absorb or assimilate that text. It has been the irritating grain of sand in the oyster, around which the Catholic ages deposited the priceless pearl of supernatural, otherworldly piety; but for the modern church it has remained an impossible ideal of asceticism, an ideal whose very first precondition of fulfillment is lacking, namely, the eschatological outlook upon the world, the belief in the impending Judgment and the Age to Come. What

[9] Matt. 5:17-20.
[10] Mark 10:23-27.
[11] Mark 8:34-37; 10:21, 28-31.

Mark did, apparently, was select out from the body of Jesus' sayings those which emphasized the prospect of suffering and persecution in the "last days," and the requirement of abnegation and renunciation on the part of his followers. These sayings, or most of them, were certainly authentically Jesus' own, though some may have been produced by imitation or further emphasis in the course of handing down the tradition.

We find genuine parallels to them in the other traditions—Q, L, and M. But Mark simply left out the sayings which offset and balanced these in the primitive tradition. He was writing, not for a group within a group, the Palestinian church living on under the shadow of the Jewish synagogue and a part, though a somewhat segregated part, of Jewish society, observing its own peculiar *Halakah;* Mark was writing for a martyr church in the world's metropolis, under the darkening shadow of a tyrant's throne and in the midst of a corrupt society of which the church could not possibly form a part. To take Mark's presentation of Jesus' teaching as normative, or final—as on the older "Marcan hypothesis"—is simply out of the question, and sets before the Christian religion, as we have seen, a problem which nineteen centuries have now demonstrated to be insoluble. Never has this been clearer than now: if the church were consistent, we hear, it would not concern itself with worldly goods, or political affairs, or the rights and wrongs of classes, groups, nations; and—this we are not told, or not by the same persons!—it would play at once and completely into the hands of tyrants, international gangsters, and murderers. But the church is not consistent—that is, not with this one-sided presentation of Jesus' message—and it recognizes the importance of such "worldly" matters as education, hygiene, social justice, wages, freedom, and the common welfare. But the problem, I repeat, is there simply because the conditions under which the earliest Gospel was written excluded all consideration of these issues and questions.

But we must go still further back, in our study of the origin of this problem of the application of the gospel. Was Jesus himself as completely unconcerned with "social" problems and questions as the Marcan tradition—and with it a large element in the rest of the tradition—presupposes? Surely the answer must be Yes! For the conditions under which he lived were not wholly unlike those in which his Roman followers found themselves forty years later.

Palestine in the first century was a country in a state of transition.[12] It lay between East and West, North and

---

[12] See the *Gospel of the Kingdom*, esp. chap. v. I may also refer to my earlier book, *The Economic Background of the Gospels* (1926). That pioneer work should be supplemented—not to say supplanted—by a study of the great modern researches of M. Rostovtzeff, *The Social and Economic History of the Roman Empire* (1926; new ed., 1940), and his magnificent three-volume work, *The Social and Economic History of the Hellenistic World* (1940). Another important work is F. M. Heichelheim, "Roman Syria," *An Economic Survey of Ancient Rome*, ed. Tenney Frank (1938), IV, 121-257. See also the chapters on economic history in the *Cambridge Ancient History*, esp. in the last 6 volumes, and Joachim Jeremias, *Jerusalem zur Zeit Jesu* (1923-29). The chapter in Joseph Klausner, *Jesus of Nazareth* (1925), dealing with economic conditions (pp. 174-92) is important. It is unfortunate that Charles Guignebert's *The Jewish World in the Time of Jesus* (tr. 1939) pays practically no attention to economic conditions. On the other hand, W. O. E. Oesterley, *A History of Israel*, vol. II (1932) pays

South, as the land bridge connecting Asia and Africa. Much of it lay "between the desert and the sown." For centuries it had fronted eastward toward that desert, a thoroughly Oriental country. Now for the space of a few centuries it turned ever so slightly toward the West, toward Europe, Rome, and Occidental civilization, though it never completely faced westward and soon went back to its original orientation.

> The East bow'd low before the blast,
> In patient, deep disdain.
> She let the legions thunder past,
> And plunged in thought again.[13]

The Maccabean War, begun in 168 B.C., had ended twenty-five years later in the freedom of the nation under Simon. During the next eighty years, from 143 to 63 B.C., the later Maccabean kings considerably extended the borders of Palestine, so that when Pompey arrived at Jerusalem in the year 63 he did not attach Palestine to the province of Syria forthwith, but contented himself with arranging the internal affairs of the kingdom in accordance with Roman policies. When Herod became king in the year 40, he was a *rex socius,* or allied king; but it was perfectly clear that Roman policy was henceforth to dominate Syria and Palestine. Following the banish-

---

considerable attention to them; see chaps. xii, xxi, etc. H. H. Rowley's chapter in *Record and Revelation* (1938) is a welcome exception to the common neglect of the economic background on the part of Old Testament students. In this respect the volume marks a decided advance upon its predecessor, *The People and the Book* (1925).

[13] Matthew Arnold, "Obermann Once More."

ment of Herod's son Archelaus in A.D. 6, a succession
of Roman procurators were sent out to govern Judea
and Samaria. It is true, Galilee and Perea were still
under another of Herod's sons, the Tetrarch Antipas,
while the region up in the northeast of Palestine was
ruled by his brother Philip. But there was not the slightest
prospect in the world of a restoration of the Jewish
monarchy.[14] By this time, the handwriting on the wall
was clear for all to read. The divided nation was steadily
slipping piecemeal under the mailed hand of Rome.

It was likewise a period of economic as well as political
transition. Although according to the latest researches,
the general level of prosperity was increasing throughout
the Roman empire during the first century, and although
Palestine might have been expected to share this increase
along with a larger volume of trade, both import and
export, and although this prosperity was apparently accompanied by a widespread increase in population,
nevertheless Palestine was still geared to the past. Its
economic outlook was more or less patriarchal and
archaic—in a word, "old-oriental." There was no great
gulf fixed between the rich and the poor, at least nothing
comparable to our modern extremes of wealth and poverty. But at the same time the power and rule of the
king—when there was one—was almost unlimited. It

[14] There was even less hope of a restoration of the priestly theocracy
either in an independent priestly state or under such loose supervision as
the nation had enjoyed in the days of the Persians. Josephus notes,
however, that this plea was made repeatedly at every crisis in the political
history of the period after the Maccabees. See *Ant.* 14. 4. 5; 13. 1-2; 15. 9;
17. 11. 2; etc.

was no longer as in the good old days when a king could go out to water the asses in the evening or visit his shepherds and see how the sheepshearing was progressing; the Herods had other ideas. Herod the Great had laid about every possible economic burden upon his people. Many of his vast undertakings were economically nonproductive, like the temple and palace which he built at Jerusalem, the fortified cities farther north, and his vast gifts to foreign cities. Though no doubt they earned the good will of the ruling classes in such cities as had large Jewish settlements and thus served to stem the rising tide of anti-Semitism, at least for a time, Herod's benefactions were as economically nonproductive as was the tribute he had paid to Cleopatra, to Antony, and to Caesar.

In other words, Palestine was already in the throes of steadily declining prosperity. The fertility of the soil, the very productivity of the land was declining. Palestine represented a countercurrent or, we should say, an eddy in the flowing stream of imperial economic progress. There is remarkable testimony to the truth of this observation in the fact that the two periods which apparently marked the peak of Roman imperial economic achievement, namely the reign of Vespasian and later that of Trajan, saw Palestine ravaged and repressed and Jerusalem a heap of ruins. It is one of the saddest tragedies in all history. While the rest of the world prospered, the Jewish revolt of A.D. 66-70 ended only in the utter and complete defeat of the Jews; and the unrest that broke out again under Trajan[15] led the way to the second revolt under his successor Hadrian in the years 132-35, when for a second time in two generations Jerusalem was totally destroyed.

These are factors that must be taken into account in all our study of the New Testament and the rise of Christianity. Over the whole era was written the legend of change.

> Time goes, you say? Ah no!
> Alas, Time stays, *we* go.[16]

The ethos of this period in Palestine is very different from that of the world outside, and it is vastly different from the ethos of the early Maccabean period and even the early Herodian. We must acknowledge that our historical sources are not wholly adequate; but, such as they are, this fact of change and decline is unmistakably written all over them. Our chief source, at least for the sequence of events, is Josephus, supplemented of course by Philo, the New Testament, the Jewish traditions, and bits of contemporaneous literature.[17] But Josephus remains our chief—and almost our only—source for the history of Palestine in the period from the Maccabees to the fall of Jerusalem in A.D. 70. It is the fashion nowadays to

---

[15] It is a question just how extensive was the revolt under Trajan; I accept Schürer's view—*Geschichte* (4th ed.), I, 661 ff.—"Palestine does not appear to have been involved to any great extent in the revolt. . . . . It hardly amounted to a real war."

[16] Austin Dobson, "The Paradox of Time."

[17] See, e.g., Théodore Reinach, *Textes d'auteurs grecs et romains relatifs au Judaïsme* (1895).

emphasize the failings and limitations of Josephus as a
historian, without adding a due recognition of his merits—as formerly it was the fashion to criticize Tacitus
as "morose," "severe," "pessimistic," and "biased." Of
course Josephus is not a very good historian. There are
serious gaps in his history, and there are many things
he ought to have told us, if his history was to be as clear
to us as it probably was to his own generation. If only,
for example, instead of giving us in long detail the in-
trigues of Herod's family, he had described in equal
detail the religious, social, and economic conditions of
his country, or even the buildings of Herod! But Josephus'
purpose is apologetic (in the *Antiquities*) and laudatory
(in the *War,* where he describes the prowess of the Jews
in fighting Rome). His histories, both of them, are histories of growing tyranny. The tyrants occupy the center
of the stage. There are few other figures than the mon-
archs and their satellites—but that only reflects the character of the age—Roman history, Mediterranean history
generally, in that century, was a history of Führers and
Duces, strutting about imperiously and wreaking their
destructions upon the earth. It is not a very good history,
but it is probably as good a history as we can expect,
not only because it is the best of its kind, and practically
the only survival of its kind[18]—that is, a Jewish history

[18] Several other authors, according to Josephus, had undertaken to write
accounts of the revolt—see the opening paragraphs of his preface to *The
Jewish War*. His only surviving rival is Tacitus, but unfortunately there are
large lacunae, which we would give almost anything to recover. One of
these dealt with the end of the Jewish War and the Fall of Jerusalem. See
The Gospel of the Kingdom, p. 198, n. 7.

down to A.D. 70—but also because it is the only kind
of history we have a right to expect from such an age
of turmoil and destruction. Let it be acknowledged then
that Josephus is not a first-class historian; but the failure
to recognize the validity of his facts, especially in that
part of his work which lay largely within his own experience and recollection, and the truth of his interpretations, as far as they go—he is never exhaustive—is
surely responsible for the neglect of his writings by too
many interpreters of the New Testament at the present
time, and for the rise of theories which leave not only
Josephus but likewise the New Testament out of the
reckoning.[19] To be no more than fair, it must be acknowledged that his *Jewish War* is one of the most
gripping, dramatic histories ever written. Superficial,
apologetic, and not lacking in considerable personal bias
or prejudice, no doubt, but nevertheless a deeply moving
tragic narrative, it is really a prose tragedy of gigantic,
epical proportions. Our grandfathers, who read Josephus
along with the Bible, and were the first to buy the multi-
tudinous cheap reprints of Whiston which may still be
obtained at second or third hand, had a juster impression
of the background of the times of Jesus and the apostles.
One wishes that present-day Bible students would take

[19] Henry St. John Thackeray, *Josephus, The Man and the Historian*
(1929), has done a great deal in our generation to revive interest in Josephus
and to show his value for historical study of the Bible. F. J. Foakes-
Jackson's *Josephus and the Jews* (1930) is another volume that deserves
mention. Above all, recent study of Josephus in the English-speaking world
owes most to Thackeray's text and translation in the Loeb Library (1926 ff.),
now being continued after Thackeray's lamented death by Professor Ralph
Marcus of the University of Chicago.

Josephus more seriously—and also that writers who discuss the relations of Judaism and Christianity, or "the
Jewish question" as a social-historical problem, would
read and reread that profoundly tragic history until its
full meaning sinks deeply into their minds. For there
was the turning point of all Jewish history—not a point,
really, but a vast curve, through whose arc the whole
course and direction of Jewish history swung into a new
line. Judaism has never recovered from that era; it has
never been the same since the fall of Jerusalem that it
was before.

Bousset has pointed out the gradual transformation of
Judaism, during the period between the Old and New
Testaments, from a national cultus to a religion of individual piety—a religion of *observance* rather than of
theology, on the one hand, or of deep personal feeling,
on the other.[20] This process was of course vastly accelerated after the fall of the temple, but it had already been
under way for several generations. Palestine was accordingly undergoing religious change as well as political
and economic.

The old nationalistic religion of Israel was steadily
being replaced by a type which undertook to retain all

[20] Despite some criticism in detail, Bousset's *Die Religion des Judentums*
remains one of the great works of modern scholarship. In the first edition,
it must be admitted, it did make too much of the apocalyptic literature.
This disproportion was corrected in the second edition (1906) and even more
thoroughly in the posthumous edition prepared by Hugo Gressmann (1926).
Another important work that deserves to be better known in this country
is that of J. Bonsirven, *Le Judaisme palestinien au temps de Jésus-Christ*
(2 vols., 1934, 1935).

the gains of the old—the prophets and the Law—but to intensify and individualize those gains. This was in line with tendencies already observable before and during the Exile—as President Julian Morgenstern insists, "Jeremiah, not Ezra, was the real father of Judaism." By the first century, it is clear, Judaism was a fully-developed system of piety, that is, of pious observance—not a system of theology, nor a code of law, merely, but a system of piety. This is a point of view difficult for present-day Christians to grasp, in estimating that ancient religion, but one that is of vital importance; without it we are sure to misjudge first-century Judaism. Perhaps Roman Catholics might be expected to understand this more readily than Protestants, since Catholicism is likewise a system of piety; but at the same time Roman Catholicism has also a rigid system of theology and a rigid canon law, while Judaism was almost totally lacking in theology, at least beyond the main and fundamental tenets of monotheism, revelation, the spirituality and the sovereignty of God, and the divine election of Israel.[21] Judaism had also a canon law; but it was still in process of evolution, in the first century, and many questions were still open, were still *sub judice,* and the full and final elaboration of the *Halakah* was only in process. Many questions of observance, ceremonial and other, and even rules of morals, were still hotly debated, and the process did not reach even a relative finality until Rabbi Judah

[21] See the works of Bousset, Moore, and Bonsirven mentioned above; also Louis Finkelstein, "The Role of Dogma in Judaism," *The Thomist,* Jan., 1943, pp. 103-10.

and the written Mishnah at the end of the second century of our era.

As a religion of observance, a system of piety founded upon Torah (divine revelation), interpreted by the prophets and expounded by the scribes, first-century Judaism is best studied in its liturgy and prayers, its Psalter, its homiletic tradition, preserved in the later Midrash, its popular writings, and even its tales, parables, collections of aphorisms and wise sayings, and not solely in the later codified *Halakah*. The books of Judith, Tobit, Wisdom, Sirach, First and Second Maccabees, above all the Psalms in their final revision, and the great prayers of the Synagogue, the primitive Kaddish and the ancient Palestinian recension of the Shemoneh Esreh, echoing in almost every line the thought of the Psalter and the Second Isaiah—it is here that we feel the vital pulse-beat of genuine Judaism. It was anything but a decadent religion, moribund, steeped in formalism, hypocrisy, and artificiality! It was in fact the most vital, most inspiring religion in the whole world at that time; and if we are tempted to contrast it with Christianity, say with the religion of the gospel or with Christianity as it ought to be, let us add that Judaism is likewise to be judged by what it aimed to be, not by what it empirically was; and also, that Christianity owes a vast debt to Judaism— in fact, as we have already observed, the best in Judaism and the best in Christianity are not two religions but one, historically and essentially. What happened to Judaism later, in the Talmudic era, and what happened later to Christianity, in the conciliar and imperial periods, lie equally outside our range of consideration at this point. Other times brought other conditions, other needs! Even so, empirical, actual Judaism, in the first century, like empirical, actual Christianity in the apostolic age, was something far too sublime and inspiring, far too creative, to be lumped into a formula, and then discarded! But it was a religion in *transition*—that is the point I am trying to make just now. And this transition was taking place under the pressure of other changes, already noted—political, economic, and social. Hence the background of Jesus' "social" teaching was this complicated, shifting religious-economic-political situation of first-century Palestine—the background not only of the question about the tribute money, but also of his teaching on non-resistance, oaths, offerings, Sabbath observance, vows, divorce, and other matters of which we read in the Gospels.

Now there is a true sense in which Jesus' teaching was not "social" at all; but this negative statement is only relatively true—for all Hebrew-Jewish religious teaching was socially conditioned. It was not only messianism that was "social" in outlook since back of the visions and rhapsodies of the apocalyptists and seers lay social dreams and urges, wants and aspirations.[22] Back of the prophets' visions of the future lay a social conception of religion, or, much more, a social conception of God's relation to the world and of the world's relation to God. Back of

---

[22] See "The Economic Significance of Messianism," *Anglican Theological Review*, 6:196 ff.; 7:281 ff.; and "Economic Messianism and the Teaching of Jesus," *ibid.*, 12:443 ff.

the Torah likewise lay that concept. The very foundation of Judaism itself, the Second Commonwealth, the work of the pioneers—Haggai, Zechariah, Zerubbabel, Nehemiah, Ezra—was idealistic and utopian enough, and rested upon a firmly fixed "social" ideology, namely a holy nation devoted to the worship and obedience of the one, true, holy God. Since Jesus' teaching was closely related to the Jewish religious tradition and made use of its concepts, since he took for granted the fundamental conception of all Jewish religion, the eventual triumph of the will of God, and since his teaching is vitally concerned with the object of all prophetic hopes and predictions—in a word, since Jesus was Jewish—his religion was essentially "social." It could not be otherwise with a religion centered in a sacred covenant between God and a whole people and expressed in a sacred Law which set forth the will and the purpose of God for this people as a whole. It is true, Jesus revised this conception, and broke down its ultranationalistic limitation; but in the very fact of his revision of it, he presupposed it.

It grows clearer every year, as we study the Gospels, that Jesus took for granted the religion of the Old Testament with its "ethics"—which was quite inseparable from the religion—and that he was not setting up a new religion or ethics in place of the old but deepening, spiritualizing, renewing, "fulfilling" the old. This is the main point of the great array of parallels to Jesus' teaching adduced from the ancient Jewish tradition and literature, for example in Strack and Billerbeck's *Commentary on the New Testament from Talmud and Midrash*. It is only when his ethics is separated from the ethical teaching of Judaism—which he deepened and spiritualized—and is then given a purely apocalyptic setting, that it can be described as "interim ethics." What he presupposed was (a) the truth of the ancient revelation, (b) the final arrival of that stage in the accomplishment of the divine will which the prophets had predicted as coming to pass in "the latter days," and (c) the validity of his own insight into and declaration of the divine purpose and commandment. This is "eschatological," of course; but so is all prophetic religion, in Judaism as throughout the Old Testament generally—it is a teleologically orientated religion, and looks steadily forward to the eventual triumph of good, of the will of God, and the establishment of God's reign over all the world. Jesus' teaching is "eschatological" in outlook, but it is not necessarily "apocalyptic"; that is, it did not take for granted the visions, dreams, chronological calculations and symbols, the vast array of angelic and other supernatural figures, or the mechanical and deterministic schemes of history which were characteristic of the apocalyptists. This apocalyptic element is certainly present in the Gospels, and it was present in the gospel tradition; but it probably came in at a point early in the history of the tradition, and it grew stronger in some circles as time passed, reaching its climax in the Gospel of Matthew—only to be all but completely rejected in John!

When we come back now to the question with which we began, Was Jesus himself as completely unconcerned with "social" problems as Mark represents? we must answer, Yes—and No! For his ethics has no concern with the secular relations of men, but only with men as members, or potential members, of the Kingdom of God. Problems that arise only upon a secular basis of thinking, whether legislative or merely prudential—like the division of property[23]—have no interest for him. "Seek first the Kingdom of God and his justice, and all these things shall be added unto you!"[24]

It is from this point of view that we must approach such a question as that of the tribute money: "Render unto Caesar the things that are Caesar's, and unto God the things that are God's."[25] Not that there are two worlds, the secular and the sacred, each autonomous and each sovereign within its own boundaries—that mistaken exegesis lay at the heart of the mediaeval dichotomy of church and state. Instead, it is clear from Jesus' teaching as a whole, as it is from the Bible as a whole, that he took for granted the principle that all sovereignty belongs to God. Since that is so, render to Caesar, as you must, what belongs to him—it is not much! But this neither dispenses you nor prevents you from offering to God what belongs to him; indeed, Caesar's dominion is temporary, while the dominion of God is eternal. Surely it is something like this that Jesus meant, judging from the rest of his teaching. It is not mere "clever evasion" on his part; nor is it mere quibbling about the propriety

[23] Luke 12:13-14.
[24] Matt. 6:33.
[25] Mark 12:17.

of handling a heathen coin with its profile of the emperor or its pagan inscription—as has recently been suggested.[26]

Our answer must be Yes—and No! Jesus' teaching was not "social," in our modern sense of sociological utopianism; but it was something vastly profounder, a religious ethic which involved a social as well as a personal application, but within the framework of the beloved society of the Kingdom of God; and in its relations to the pagan world outside it was determined wholly from within that beloved society—as the rest of the New Testament and most of the other early Christian literature takes for granted. Members of the Kingdom are still members of the Kingdom when they buy and sell, eat and drink, walk the streets of pagan towns, or—God forbid!—appear before pagan tribunals. There was no dichotomy in morals, so that one might be compelled to do as a citizen or a tradesman what he was forbidden to do as a disciple of Christ. There lay the area of tension—and there too shone out the heroism of early Christian ethics. It is reflected in the Gospel of Mark, brief and one-sided as is its selection of Jesus' teachings appropriate to its own special situation, that of a church facing martyrdom; but it is also reflected in Matthew, with its presupposition of a more settled community life, though at the same time facing a steady threat of persecution; and it is reflected clearly in Paul and in the letters he wrote to those who, like himself, were "in jeopardy every hour" for the faith that was in them. It was a social gospel they

[26] Herbert Loewe, *"Render unto Caesar"* (1940).

proclaimed, yes—but only as the gospel of the coming
Reign of God over all the earth, and as the new *Halakah,*
the description of "life in accordance with the sayings of
the Lord" who was God's final Messenger to his elect.
It was no message of social reform, no blueprint for a
perfect human society, save in the ultimate sense that the
Kingdom of God is to take the place of all earthly so-
cieties, when "the kingdom of the world becomes the
Kingdom of our Lord and of his Christ."

XII

EPILOGUE

THE CONSEQUENCES OF MARK'S EMBODIMENT AND EDITING of the evangelic tradition in his brief apologia for Jesus' Messiahship were far-reaching. It is not quite accurate to say that he took the gospel of Jesus—that is, the message which Jesus himself had preached and taught—and made it over into the gospel about Jesus; for that is what the Christian message had been all along, from the very beginning of the Christian movement, ever since the assembling of the disciples after the Resurrection and their first proclamation of the good news about Jesus. But Mark, or those who formulated the message in the terms which we read in his Gospel, undertook to give it an interpretation in accordance with which Jesus had already been Messiah, and had been recognized and confessed as Messiah, even during his earthly life, before the Resurrection when—according to the primitive traditional belief—he "became" or "was manifested" as such. What Mark undertakes to do is to prove that Jesus did not need to wait until the Resurrection in order "to manifest his glory," as the later Johannine Gospel uses the phrase. He was already Messiah as he went about Galilee; for he had been proclaimed the Son of God at his Baptism; the demons had recognized him

253

as divine; the disciples had confessed him to be the
Messiah, their conviction voiced by their spokesman,
Peter; at the Transfiguration the chosen three "beheld
his glory," to use again the more explicit Johannine
idiom, ordinarily hidden but now momentarily revealed;
finally even the centurion in charge of the crucifixion
had confessed him "a Son of God." Though Jesus had
not, it is true, announced himself to Israel as the Messiah,
and had forbidden the demons to make him known—
"since they knew him"—and had even commanded his
disciples to be silent about their recognition of his Messiahship, nevertheless, at the last, in the high priest's
court, he had admitted unequivocally that he was the one
who should sit at the right hand of the divine Power
(God) and come with the clouds of heaven.[1] As we have
seen, this theory of the messianic secret, or rather of
Jesus' secret Messiahship, was Mark's answer to the question which his fundamental thesis, that Jesus was already
Messiah during his earthly ministry, at once suggested:
Why then was he not recognized, why was he put to
death? It is almost as if Mark had undertaken to answer
the questions Paul had put, in his letter to the Roman
Christians—Mark's own church—"Did they not hear?
. . . . Did Israel not know?"[2] Had they known and understood, they would never have put to death the Lord
of glory. It was surely in ignorance that the Jews and
their rulers had put him to death, as the old tradition

[1] Mark 14:62.
[2] Rom. 10:16-21.

affirmed.[3] But this ignorance was in part at least the result of a mysterious blindness that had come upon them as a judgment for their sins, their initial unresponsiveness mounting eventually to active hatred and a "blind" fury of malice by which they attributed everything he said or did to the inspiration of Beelzebul, the chief of devils. Even the disciples had not wholly escaped its toxic effects: their eyes had been "holden," they had "slumbered" during the crucial hour of their Lord's career in Gethsemane, and at his arrest they had "all left him, and fled"; Peter, their leader and spokesman, had even denied that he so much as knew his Master. This is part of Mark's answer. The other part was that Jesus had commanded them to be silent about even the little they had guessed or discovered of his secret: Peter's confession and the vision in the mount. "And he charged them that they should tell no man about him." [4] "He commanded them that they should tell no man what they had seen, save when the Son of Man should have risen from the dead." [5] This is not the full formulation of the answer as the author of the Fourth Gospel was someday to give it,[6] namely that the disciples did not really understand either Jesus' words or their own experience with him until after the Resurrection; but the idea is implicit in Mark, and the explanation is already moving in the "Johannine" direction—John only makes more explicit what Mark's theory has already presupposed.

[3] Acts 3:17.
[4] Mark 8:30.
[5] Mark 9:9.
[6] Cf. John 2:22; 12:16; 14:26; 2:17.

But it was not only the theory of the messianic secret which was of such grave consequence, which did such violence to the older tradition, and which had to be explained and corrected by the later evangelists—and explained away by John. It was the basic thesis of Mark, to which the theory of the secret was an interpretative corollary, which was of the gravest consequence not only for the later New Testament writings but also for the whole development of Christian doctrine and devotion, and has been so to this day. For it shifted the whole center of gravity in the gospel; it placed in the forefront of consideration, as the real subject of the gospel, the person of Jesus rather than the Kingdom of God.[7] Stated bluntly, Mark substituted a theological idea of the person of Jesus for the Kingdom of God, and interpreted "the gospel of the Kingdom" to mean the message—or indeed the "mystery" [8]—of Jesus' Messiahship. Perhaps this was not surprising in a Roman Gospel, in a "defense and confirmation of the gospel" meant for Greco-Roman readers, whether converted Christians or still pagans, in a Hellenistic, Western, non-Jewish, non-Oriental apologia for the Christian faith. Whereas the East was interested in Wisdom, the divine Law, and the Kingship of God, the less abstractly minded, more concretely thinking and believing West—it will be said—demanded the adoration of a person, of a divine-human being, a Son of God, as the center of its religious loyalties. So it had already been

[7] For Jews, perhaps even for many early Jewish Christians, the central figure in the Kingdom was certainly not the Messiah, but God himself. See *The Gospel of the Kingdom* (1940).

[8] Mark 4:11.

for Paul, and perhaps for the gospel tradition even before Mark wrote—though there are passages in Mark's Gospel that run counter to this view—for example, "Why callest thou me good?" [9] Paul presupposes it in the very language he takes over from earlier Hellenistic Christianity, for which Christ was already Κύριος, "Lord," that is, the head of a cult. Indeed, the change in emphasis may go back farther still, and Mark's representation may be viewed more as a result than as a cause of this tendency; the initial movement in this direction was perhaps the result of the resurrection and glorification of Jesus, and the consequent centrality which he possessed for the salvation of his followers. And so it has been ever since: the *person* of Jesus, which is really the final mystery, and not to be approached until all other considerations have been weighed—his teaching, his ethics, the new way of life which he opened up to men, his revelation of the character and the purpose of God—the person of Jesus rather than his teaching or his revelation has been placed in the forefront of Christian consideration, and logicians trained in Western metaphysics and law have gone at the problem in a way unthinkable for the world in which Jesus lived, in a way unthinkable for Jesus himself.

It is the person, not the personality, of Jesus which is the center of interest. Mark, like other ancient writers generally, has no interest in "personality," which is a very modern conception. And it is the "person" of Jesus *as a theological idea,* not as a historical person, the subject of biography, which he thus sets at the center of Christian

[9] Mark 10:18.

thought. Perhaps the only way open, historically speaking, if the church was to bring home to men the paramount and final importance of Jesus' revelation, was to emphasize the theological idea of his person; only so could this revelation be made clear and authoritative to the Greco-Roman world. Thus the gospel was concentrated in the person of Jesus; the hope of the Kingdom receded and became eventually only another name for "heaven," the other world, the state of bliss beyond death, or, as in Thomas Aquinas, a term for the divine theodicy in general—though in truth this interpretation really emphasized a fundamental element in the whole biblical conception, in Jesus' teaching as elsewhere—and thus an intellectual concept of the person of Jesus tended to become central for Christian doctrine, theology, and devotion, rather than the person of God, his sovereignty and his redemptive will, his wisdom and his love.

One result of the process—which certainly Mark would not have encouraged, though his work started the development in that direction—is the sentimental, saccharine, sickly-sweet Jesuolatry that has mistaken strong emotion for an evidence of religion, has softened the ethical fiber and beclouded the whole theological sky of certain areas of Christianity. This worship of Jesus has tended to crowd out the sturdier, less exuberant faith in the living God, whose mercies are over all his works but whose judgments are in all the earth. In consequence, God the Father became once more the veiled deity, the dark Fate or Destiny standing behind the throne of Zeus—as conceived by many generations of earlier Mediterranean religion. In much the same way the worship of the Virgin later supplanted that of the Son, in some quarters. We may not quarrel with the fact; but the whole development, beginning with a concentration upon the idea of Jesus' own person as of central importance for religious faith, certainly represents a shift in emphasis from Jesus' own teaching. The reality of the Spiritual Christ is of course recognized throughout apostolic Christianity. This was no creation of the Gospel of Mark—indeed, Mark steps back from it, in the act of trying to prove that Jesus was secretly the divine Son of Man during his life upon earth. For Mark's "theological idea" was not so much the *present* reality of the divine person, the exalted Lord of his community, nor yet was it the glorious and unique *historical* person, Jesus of Nazareth, but the mysterious, half-divine, apocalyptic "Son of Man" who had lived incognito upon earth, died, and risen again.

No doubt the church has been right in acknowledging the deity of Christ and the Incarnation as the fullest measure of the divine revelation of which human nature is capable; though it should be pointed out that the church as a rule undertook to stand fast and to hold the ground of the traditional, historical faith, enshrined in the New Testament, and—as the histories of dogma make clear—only took over metaphysical definitions which had already been hammered out on the anvils of logical and exegetical disputation. Often these definitions were fashioned in the shops of the heretics themselves—weapons sometimes as dangerous to those who fashioned or wielded them as they were to their opponents! But even so, the church has still retained, through all the long centuries of its history, a lingering conviction that Jesus was primarily a Teacher; and it has steadily acted upon this haunting assurance in preferring the Gospel of Matthew, above the others, in its liturgy. For the Gospel of Matthew "corrected" the Gospel of Mark, in the process of editing and revising it, by incorporating the teaching of Jesus, and by representing him as the Revealer of the Kingdom, the expounder of the New Law—the Messiah, indeed, but a Messiah who appeared first of all as the Teacher of Israel. In some passages he appears as the Second Moses, *the* Prophet par excellence, the ideal Scribe and teacher of religion.[10] Luke also incorporated Jesus' teaching; but Luke's conception of the Messiah is still in large measure the Marcan "Son of God," the King Messiah of the popular hope combined with the secret "Son of Man" of Mark's interpretation.[11] Only Luke's careful literary art obscures the fact that he has combined the two ideas, though he retains more of the former than of the latter—a fact illuminated and explained by the hypothesis of Proto-Luke.[12]

Among these portraits of Christ, the Gospel of John assumes the Marcan thesis—or its equivalent—as proved, but ignores its corollary, the secret Messiahship; or rather, the secret is not the result of Jesus' purpose, but is due

[10] Cf. Matt. 23:2-10; etc.

[11] Although he does not really grasp Mark's theory of the hidden Son of Man. See chap. vi above.

[12] Proto-Luke is the combination of Q and L; into this combination the author later inserted the Gospel of Mark in seven sections. See *The Growth of the Gospels*, pp. 157-75.

to the blindness and hatred of "the Jews." Jesus is not so much the strange, unknown "Son of Man"—"Who is this Son of Man?" is a question "the Jews" ask[13]—as he is the "Messiah," the "King of Israel";[14] on the contrary, from the very outset, far from concealing his identity he proclaims it boldly and unequivocally, and backs up his self-proclamation with a series of great "signs" or epiphanies, manifestations of his "glory." The unreality of this procedure, from the historical point of view, is obvious at once—history and interpretation have not been simply interwoven; another figure is required! They have been stirred together in a mortar, and the two elements have completely neutralized each other in a compound which is neither history nor interpretation, but mystical rhapsody and poetry of devotion, not so much a theology as a half-Gnostic Christian theosophy—history turned inside out in order to reveal its inner meaning, but ceasing to be history in the process.[15]

And yet how precious this book has been, and still is, to countless numbers of Christian believers, saints and martyrs and ordinary people! It sums up, as no other book has ever done, the total impression of Christ upon men: he is the Light of the World, the Lamb of God, the Resurrection and the Life. You cannot start with Jesus, if you take him seriously, without inevitably taking him into consideration in all your deepest thought about God and about the whole problem of human life and destiny.

[13] John 12:34.
[14] John 1:41, 49.
[15] See *The Growth of the Gospels*, chap. viii, "Hellenistic Mysticism and the Fourth Gospel."

In the end, all our thought of God and the world, and of ourselves as well, has to be brought into relation to him, to be judged by the light of his revelation of the Father. No book in all the world makes this clearer than the Gospel of John. And it is no accident that John has been the favorite Gospel of countless Christians, rather than Mark; or that, indeed, Mark has always been the least popular of the four, with its mysterious, forbidding, really unapproachable "Son of Man" conception in place of the Jesus of Galilee.

It is a long way from the gospel of Jesus in Galilee to the Gospel of John in the Hellenistic setting of early second century Christianity, at war on all fronts with an unbelieving world and not least with "the Jews," who are now viewed as implacable and inveterate foes.[16] Somewhere about midway in this course of development we find the Gospel of Mark. What it took for granted in the way of earlier tradition and interpretation, and what it undertook to do in the way of further interpretation, combined to make it for all later Christian doctrine and devotion one of the most important—in some respects one of the most fateful—books ever written. For it *began* the process which eventually read back into the lifetime of Jesus the later doctrines, institutions, sacraments, and even to some extent the canon law of the church—notably in Catholicism, but also in large measure in the older, historic Protestantism.[17] How different the story would have been if, under the influence of Paul, the founding

[16] See Ernest C. Colwell, *John Defends the Gospel* (1936).
[17] See Friedrich Heiler, *Der Katholizismus* (1923), p. 17.

of the church, its organization and institutions, and the origin of its faith had been attributed to the exalted Christ, guiding his church through the Spirit!

What is the meaning of this earliest Gospel for our time? In its own time, and first of all, it set forth the message of salvation to men and women who lived in a world not unlike our own; indeed the "world," that is, human society, has not changed very much in nineteen centuries, and the message of salvation is as greatly needed now as then, or ever. Man is in reality, many persons now tell us, a biological species, with a superficial adaptation to those artificial conditions of life which we call civilization; but under his skin, and beneath the thin top level of his inquiring, aggressive, clever mind, he is still what he has always been—an acquisitive, competitive, power-seeking, warring beast, with which the divine Spirit must still "strive," even as at the beginning of human history.[18] The tyrannies and destructions of our day are really the same in kind as those that made human life either a shambles or a prison house, or both, in the days of Nero when this earliest Gospel was written. Its author looked forward to the end of such a society; like the Jewish apocalyptists, like the author of the passage in Genesis,[19] he could see no future for mankind but only the impending cataclysm. Out of the ruins, once more, God would raise up those who should truly serve and obey him; and this divine Rule was to be inaugur-

[18] Gen. 6:3.
[19] Gen. 6:5-7.

ated—so Mark and his fellow Christians believed—when the Son of Man, who was identical with Jesus crucified, raised from the dead, and exalted to heaven, should return on the clouds to hold the Last Judgment, when he should come "in power" with the angels of God to reign with his elect over a renewed earth. And back of the earliest written Gospel, which partly presupposes this view, partly expresses it, lies the tradition of the primitive Christian communities. That tradition likewise enshrined a hope of salvation. It was an eschatological gospel—an assured hope of things to come.

Moreover, back of this primitive tradition was the life and the teaching of One who had himself lived man's life, under the conditions of growing political oppression and injustice and of the threatened extinction of Jewish faith and worship and of the whole Jewish way of life. Again, the conditions were not unlike those of today, certainly over large areas of our world. But Jesus' teaching was a message of hope and of assured salvation: it was no screaming apocalypse, savagely threatening the divine vengeance upon all oppressors and apostates; instead it was the description, in words, and the demonstration, by example, of a way of life which men might lead even under the impossible conditions of the present.[20] On the other hand, it was no optimistic view of progressive human betterment, grounded in a naïve confidence in the better nature of men; it was centered wholly and decisively in the nature of God and in his just and loving purpose. Jesus looked into the future and saw the

[20] See Lily Dougall and Cyril W. Emmet, *The Lord of Thought* (1922).

rising tension of his day culminating in the destruction and desolation of the people and the land he loved; like the prophets of old, he foresaw the doom of judgment meted out, not on the heathen only but upon his own nation, its leaders, its people, its temple. But, he insisted, that dire destiny might even now be averted by repentance, by a complete return to God, by setting the Reign of God above all other considerations and goals of effort.[21] And he proclaimed a way of life in accordance with the will of God which, if Israel followed it, would make possible not only immediate salvation for the individual here and now, under the present conditions of tyranny and oppression, but also his survival in the future— whether in this world or beyond death—and perhaps, by the mercy of God, it would result in the survival of the nation, though not as a political entity but as a religious group.

Jesus' "program," if we may call it that, was never tried on a wide scale, as it was intended to be tried; that is, the gospel was the divine message to all Israel, but all Israel did not hearken, and only a few responded.[22] Nor has it ever been tried, on the full scale, by any other people or by any single generation since that time. And yet if we are ever to have a world fit to live in—to say the very least—the gospel of Jesus must be given a fair trial! Perhaps the time has come, as the world now faces a new era, to put Jesus' gospel into deeds, not words, and thus to let God bring to pass his Reign over the world.

[21] Matt. 6:33.
[22] Rom. 10:16; John 1:11-13.

The results might astonish even the most ardent believers; and we might begin, say in this very year, not an era but an age—an age which will endure, if it turns out to be an age of justice and peace, for not merely a thousand years but forever. This cannot be done by human effort alone; but God requires our co-operation if it is to be done at all, for he does not coerce men or compel them to be saved! Nor will the result be the final Kingdom of God, but only its beginning, its outward manifestation, its "dawning point."

It is this hope of the Kingdom, as valid and relevant today as ever, with which the Gospel of Mark confronts our generation. True, that Gospel somewhat obscured the message, by substituting a theological idea—the person of Christ, conceived as the secret, mysterious "Son of Man"—for the primary and central element in Jesus' own teaching, with consequences that ran on for five or six centuries in the christological controversies and survive to this day. It represented a major step in what Harnack called "the Hellenizing of the Gospel," and we need to read between its lines, to read back from it to Jesus himself and his life and teaching. Nevertheless, without this idea we might possibly never have had such books as the Gospels, and in consequence the Christian religion might not have continued to bear within itself the means of its own correction, revitalization, and renewal. We must be grateful to Mark for what he did—rather than blame him for what he failed to do, or for the inadequate performance of what we wish he had undertaken.

At the same time it seems clearer than ever before that only religion, actual faith and practice, genuine obedience and response to the gospel of God's Reign over the world, will ever save us or the society we live in. Theology will not do it—clearly, nineteen centuries of theology have not done it, however important and however inevitable theology must ever be. Nothing short of the complete renovation and remotivation of human life will suffice— only a genuinely ethical faith, only "faith working through love." More attentively than ever before, therefore, we must wait for "fresh light to break forth from the Word of God"; and, having seen, we must *act!*

INDEX

References covered by the chapter titles and primary topics treated throughout the book are not included in the index.